MODERN HISTORY OF PUNJAB

CONCEPTS IN COMMUNICATION
INFORMATICS & LIBRARIANSHIP
(CICIL)

For a list of titles in this series,
see pp. 310-12 at the end of the book.

ABOUT THE AUTHORS

J.C. AGGARWAL (*b.* 1928), a retired Deputy Director of Education/Executive Director of Delhi Bureau of Textbooks, Delhi Administration has a varied experience in the field of education. He has singly/jointly authored about 130 books on Education, Social Sciences and Current Problems. In collaboration with S.P. Agrawal, he has written *Documentation Encyclopaedia of UNESCO and Education* (in two Parts); *Women's Education in India*; *National Policy on Education: Agenda for India 2001*; *Indian Writings on Education, 1979 to 1986*; and *Vocational Education in India*.

His other recent publications include: *Yearbook of Indian Education, 1991: World Overview; Ramamurti Report 1990, on National Policy on Education in India*; and *Survey of Educational Documents in the World Since 1983*, etc.

S.P. AGRAWAL (*b.* 1929) was Director, National Social Science Documentation Centre, ICSSR, and Member Secretary, Indian Association of Social Science Institutions. He was also the Vice-Chairman of the Asia and Pacific Information Network in Social Sciences (APINESS). In 1988 he was awarded the degree of Doctor of Philosophy in Education (Honoris Causa) by International University Foundation. Presently, he is Member, Round Table on Research in Reading, IFLA, and Member, International Committee for Social Science Information and Documentation. He is also Member of Board of Studies of National Archives of India and Hindi Advisory Committee, Ministry of Coal, Government of India. Born and brought up in the cradle of our freedom movement which he joined at the tender age of twelve he gained an insight into political problems and Developed a sense of responsibilities which bore fruits as an information scientist committed to Gandhiji's philosophy and action-plan in the field and its social concept. He has written extensively on various aspects of education, Indian Polity and library and information science.

Concepts in Communication
Informatics & Librarianship-37

General Editor : **S.P. Agrawal**

MODERN HISTORY OF PUNJAB

A look back into ancient peaceful Punjab focusing confrontation and failures leading to present Punjab problem, and a peep ahead

Relevant Select Documents

J.C. AGGARWAL
Former Executive Director
Delhi Bureau of Textbooks, Delhi Administration

S.P. AGRAWAL
Former Director
National Social Science Documentation Centre, ICSSR, New Delhi

CONCEPT PUBLISHING COMPANY, NEW DELHI 110059

ISBN 81-7022-431-4

First Published 1992

Published and Printed by
Ashok Kumar Mittal
Concept Publishing Company
A/15-16, Commercial Block, Mohan Garden
NEW DELHI 110059 (India)

Lasertypeset by
Microtech Advance Printing Systems (Pvt.) Ltd.
H-13, Bali Nagar,
NEW DELHI 110015

PREFACE

Absolute objectivity in historical facts and happenings is rather a myth.

An attempt has been made here to present documents including letters, reports of various Committees and Commissions, and statements on the complicated Punjab problem with a view to having a wider perspective.

The documents may be convenient or inconvenient to the campaigners, one way or the other.

One thing is definite. There is need for accommodation at all quarters.

An overview of Punjab in its several facets — Cultural, Economic, Educational, Geographical, Historical, Industrial, Political and Religious is provided in the introductory part of the book.

Chapter entitled 'Towards a Peaceful Punjab', though very brief, contains the essence of the issues.

A peep into the brief life sketch of the prominent Akali leaders will help to understand Sikh psyche.

Chronological events since 1809 forms Chapter 21.

Bibliography including more them 1500 entries may prove useful to readers who intend to go deeper in the matter.

A word about 1992 elections — Almost all parties and the Government can claim victory; the country, however, lost something very precious. But then who cares for larger interests! The Government can boast that it could conduct elections in spite of the boycott of the elections. Likewise the Akalis can take comfort from the fact that even in the face of unprecedented arrangements, their call for boycott had its sway over the voters which resulted in the ever lowest percentage of votes cast. The Congress can take pride in obtaining an absolute majority — the largest seats since the reorganisation of Punjab in 1966. The position of other parties, by and large, remained the same.

From a wider perspective, it is the defeat of all. The country tends to lose a considerable section of the population of Punjab in case a healing touch is not provided immediately. Let us pray for a wiser counsel.

The authors extend their gratitude to all authors and publishers whose book have been consulted and quoted.

J.C. AGGARWAL
S.P. AGRAWAL

CONTENTS

LIST OF TABLES AND MAPS

Tables

Appendix Tables

Maps

LIST OF TABLES AND MAPS

Tables

Appendix Tables

Maps

PART I

BACKGROUND AND DOCUMENTS

1

PUNJAB AT A GLANCE

Beyond the Bloodshed

If drops of blood stain a garment and render it impure,
How can minds of those who live on human blood be purified?
Says Nanak, first cleanse your heart, then utter the Name of God,
All else is but a worldly show (that does no good),
All else is but practice of falsehood.

(Translated by Khushwant Singh, Quoted in *Weekend*, January 19-20, 1991)

Land of the Golden Temple, Baisakhi, Bhakra, Bhangra and Sarson da Saag

Basic Data

1. *Area*: 50,362 sq. km. (32,87,263 sq. km.)
2. *Population*: (1991 Census) 2,01,90,795 (2.39% of total Population of India)
3. *Density of population*: 401 (267)
4. *Sex ratio*: 888 females per 1000 males (929)
5. *Literacy rate*: 57.14 (52.11) — Male 65.68 (63.86), Female 49.72 (39.42)
6. *Capital*: Chandigarh
7. *Assembly seats*: 117
8. *Lok Sabha seats*: 13
9. *Principal language*: Punjabi

Note: Figures in brackets relate to India (1991 Census).

TABLE 1.1: Population of cities (with Population of 1,00,000 and above), Sex Ratio and Crude Literacy Rate, 1991

City/UA	Total Population			Crude Literacy Rate			Sex Ratio
	Persons	Males	Females	Persons	Males	Females	
1. Ludhiana	1,012062	562880	449182	62.58	65.77	58.59	798
2. Amritsar	709456	376721	332735	64.80	68.58	60.53	883
3. Jalandhar	519530	277633	241897	67.00	70.72	62.73	871
4. Patiala (UA)	268521	140742	12779	67.90	67.82	67.99	908
5. Bat:nda	159114	85380	73734	60.38	66.17	53.67	864
6. Pathankot (UA)	147130	74147	72983	65.20	69.33	61.01	984
7. Hoshiarpur	122528	65225	57303	69.02	73.55	63.87	879
8. Moga (UA)	110868	58983	51885	58.53	62.57	53.94	880
9. Abohar	107016	57772	49244	54.81	60.93	47.63	852
10. Batala (UA)	106062	57388	48674	54.64	57.44	51.33	848

Notes:

1. Crude Literacy Rate = $\frac{\text{Number of Literates}}{\text{Total Population (Inclusive of 0-6 age group)}}$

2. UA: Stands for Urban Agglomeration.

Location

Situated in north-western corner of the country, Punjab is bounded on west by Pakistan, on north by Jammu and Kashmir, on north-east by Himachal Pradesh.

Agriculture

Three-fourths of the population is engaged in agriculture and about 83 per cent of the total geographical area of Punjab is under cultivation. The State is surplus in foodgrain especially wheat and rice. Other main foodgrains are maize, gram, barley and pulses. Major cash crops are oilseeds, sugarcane, cotton and potato. With only 1.54 per cent geographical area of the country it contributes about 55 per cent wheat and 95 per cent rice to the Central Pool.

Irrigation and Power

Bhakra Nangal Dam, Bhakra Canals, Harikar Barrage with a new lined canal called Sirhind Feeder and remodelling of Madhopur Headworks into Barrage are the important irrigation works implemented since 1947. Madhopur-Beas Link was constructed to transfer surplus waters of Ravi to Beas. A similar project, Sutlej-Beas Link Project, has been completed.

Pong Dam on Beas is an important hydro-electric project. First power house comprising three units of Mukerian Hydel Project was commissioned in October 1983. First unit of stage-I of Ropar Hydel Project was commissioned in September 1984 and the second unit of stage II was commissioned in March 1985. First micro-hydel project at Nidampur was commissioned in October-December 1986. A 10 mw rice straw plant, first of its kind in India is under construction at Jalkheri in Patiala district.

The state achieved cent per cent electrification in May 1976.

Industry

Coach factory	Hasanpur near Kapurthala
Computers and Electronics	Mohali
Cycle parts	Ludhiana
Engineering goods	Batala

Fertiliser	Nangal
Furniture	Kartarpur
Hosiery	Ludhiana
Machine goods	Batala
Oil engines	Batala
Sewing Machines	Ludhiana
Silk	Chharta near Amritsar
Sports	Jalandhar
Toys	Hoshiarpur
Woollen	Dhariwal

Education

(i)	Universities and Institutions Deemed as Universities	04
(ii)	Arts, Commerce and Science Colleges	171
(iii)	Engineering and Technology Colleges	03
(iv)	Medical Colleges (M.B.B.S. only)	05
(v)	Teacher Training Colleges	18
(vi)	Higher Secondary (10+2) New Pattern	387
(vii)	High/Post Basic Schools	2353
(viii)	Middle/Senior Basic Schools	1413
(ix)	Primary/Junior Basic Schools	12357
(x)	Teacher Training Schools	02
(xi)	Polytechnic Institutes	09
(xii)	Technical Industrial Arts and Crafts Schools	97

Note: Data of Sl.No. (i) to (xii) relate to the year 1989-90.

Source: *Educational Statistics* 1989-90, Ministry of Human Resource Development, Department of Education, New Delhi.

Important Places of Tourist Interest

Amritsar : Golden Temple; Jallianwala Bagh; Gobindgarh Fort; Gurudwara Shahid (Temple of Martyr); Gurudwara Baba Atal; Rambagh Public Gardens, Hari-ke-Pattan Durgiana Mandir.

Anandpur : Place of Panj Piare (the Five Loved Ones), Hola Mohalla.

Beas: Dera of Radha Soami Satsang.

Jalandhar : Devi Talab.

Kartarpur : Gurudwara Than Sahib.

Manji Sahib: 'Tirsar' (the Arrow Lake) Gurudwara.
Ropar : Ruins of Harappan period.
Sirhind: Fatehgarh Gurudwara.
Taran Taran: Tank of Salvation.

Districtwise Population (1991)

District	Population
1. Amritsar	25,01,731
2. Ludhiana	24,25,868
3. Jalandhar	20,33,994
4. Patiala	19,04,321
5. Gurdaspur	17,65,834
6. Faridkot	17,25,212
7. Sangrur	17,01,663
8. Firozpur	15,99,501
9. Bathinda	15,54,948
10. Hoshiarpur	14,30,210
11. Rupnagar	9,05,629
12. Kapurthala	6,41,884

A Prosperous yet Bleeding Punjab

As the home of Harappan Culture, Punjab has been the cradle of one of the oldest civilizations of the world. The word 'Punjab' is made up of two words — 'Punj' meaning five and 'Ab' meaning water. Thus it derives its name from the geographical fact that five rivers flew through it in the pre-partition (1947) days. These five rivers — Jhelum, Chenab, Ravi, Beas and Sutlej, flowing through its territory, bestowed upon it innumerable bounties. As such, it is no wonder that Punjab was regarded as the granary of India. As a result of partition, it was divided into two the western and the eastern Punjab. The western portion became part of Pakistan and the eastern that of India. So, out of the original five rivers, only two rivers, Beas and Sutlej are now exclusive to the divided Punjab on the Indian side. River Ravi passes through Indian side of Punjab and then flows through west Punjab now in Pakistan present West Punjab (Pakistan). Haryana, Himachal Pradesh and East Punjab (now called Punjab) were parts of undivided Punjab. Geographical necessity made Punjabis one of the most sturdy and enterprising people, not only in India but also outside the country. Perpetually exposed to invaders, the people of Punjab acquired martial traits for sheer survival. The Indian army is proud of the Punjabi Jawans who have always been noted for their bravery on the battle-field. Besides, the fertile soil induced Punjabi farmers to work very hard. In course of time, it became the harbinger of Green Revolution. Its overflowing granaries went a long way in making India self-sufficient in food-grains.

The people of Punjab have undergone terrible ordeals. Like phoenix, the mythological Chinese bird, they have risen again and again from the embers, every time younger and more zestful. Their courage, endurance and fortitude are unparalleled.

Some idea of the prosperity of Punjab *vis-a-vis* other States in India can be had from the fact that, according to the latest available statistics, it tops in more than one area of economic development. In 1987-88 its per capita income was Rs. 5,477 as against the national average of Rs. 3,284. Its per capita consumption of electricity and fertiliser is the highest. All its villages are electrified.

Apart from agriculture, Punjab produces industrial items such as bicycles, cycle parts, sewing machines, hand tools, machine tools, auto parts, electronic items, sports goods, surgical equipment, hosiery, fasteners, textiles, vegetable oils, etc.

Important multi-purpose projects such as the Bhakra-Nangal Pong Dam, Mukerian Hydel Project and Ropar Thermal Plant are also situated in Punjab.

All these have made the people affluent, both through agricultural as well as industrial production.

The whole of Punjab is strewn with monuments and places bearing the memory of one struggle or the other.

The people of Punjab, notwithstanding their ordeals, love music and melody in its most rustic forms — vibrant, reflecting both their power and prosperity. Its history and legends abound about people who loved life in all its manifestations.

A publication of the Punjab Government Tourist Department has described Punjab as follows :

> Intense people. Music and melody. Gaiety and colour. History and legends. Power and plenty. Rich, swaying fields and vibrant farmers

This is Punjab

Punjab combines old world charm with a sweep of the contemporary new tempo. Sleepy little villages, living, as if, the pages of history books, still dot the countryside complete with the village well and the bullock-cart. Battle-scarred fortresses, witness to the many tales of valour of the sons of Punjab, still stand upright in the pride of their glory. The romantic, fairytale gardens of the Mughal era and the palaces of the nobility of the days gone by vie with each other in displaying their charms and beauty. For those interested in art and archaeology, Punjab offers collections of rich treasurers.

Temples and gurudwaras echo with songs and hymns in the praise of man's creator, today, as they did in the centuries past.

The picture of contemporary Punjab is as intense as has been its long and proud date with history.

Punjab stands in the front ranks of industrial progress in India. In the field of agriculture, Punjab is regarded a synonym for the Green Revolution. The overflowing granaries of Punjab reflect the Punjabi farmers' hard work, enterprise and fast adoption of the ways of modern technology. It is interesting to see groups of colourfully-clad village folk riding merrily in the family tractor on their way to a movie house in the nearby town. Punjab today has planned cities and townships with universities, colleges and schools. There are dams and massive hydro-electric projects to generate the thousands of tubewells, run hundreds of factories and light countless homes in cities and villages.

Punjab is the home of proud martial races who guarded the north-western gates of India for centuries; who fought countless foreign invaders, who built and nourished kingdoms and played a vital role in India's history. Today, as in the past, Punjabis make some of the finest soldiers in India.

2

THE SIKHS

Sikhism and the Ten Gurus

To have a proper perspective of the state of affairs in Punjab, it would be necessary to have a look at the psyche of the Sikhs who constitute about 60 per cent of the population of Punjab.

The word 'Sikh' goes back to the Sanskrit word 'Shishya' meaning a disciple or one under training. Through 'Aprabhansa' the term changed to Sikhs. In Punjab, the word 'Sikh' came to be used for disciples of Guru Nanak Dev (1469-1539) and his nine spiritual successors, while Sikhism denominates the faith they have professed.

Sikhism had its birth in Punjab (undivided) and most of the followers lived there. Yet many migrated to other parts of India and countries abroad. Wherever they live, they are easily recognizable. The distinguishing characteristics are their five 'Kakori' — words starting with 'Ka', the first consonant of Nagari Varnmala. They are (1) 'Kesh' — unshaven hair (2) 'Kara' — the iron bracelet worn on hand, (3) 'Kachcha' — lower undergarment, (4) 'Kirpan' — sword, and (5) 'Kangha' — hair comb. All these are valued by them as signs of their faith—an essential part of the Sikh way of life.

The first year in Sikhism is 1469, the year in which, the founder of the faith, Guru Nanak Dev, was born in the village of Talwandi — Rai Bhoe (now in Pakistan), 60 km south-west of Lahore and now named as Nankana Sahib. Even as a boy, Nanak was the favourite of both the Hindus and Muslims in the village. At the tender age of 27, he embarked on his long preaching — Odysseys (udasis). In his preachings, he rejected distinctions between man and man, high or low, by reason of creed or caste. He did not refute any religion and its followers nor he aimed at bringing together diverse identities. Accompanied by a Muslim follower, named Mardana, he went to all the four corners of India and beyond—from the high Himalayas in the north to Shri Lanka in the south, for 26 continuous (1494-1520 A.D.) years, spreading the massage of love, faith and equality.

At the end of his 'udasis', Guru Nanak settled at Kartarpur on the right bank of river Ravi. Here a community of disciples grew around him. 'Langar' (community kitchen), which he had himself founded was its main characteristic. Here all sat together to share common meal. 'Seva' — self-giving services for common cause as a pious duty was another speciality. The community was called 'Sangat'. Guru's words (bani) was taken as the voice of God and sung in its own style. Following is one of the hymns by Guru Nanak:

Religion lieth not in the patched coat, the yogi wears.
Not in the staff he bears, nor the ashes on his body
Religion lieth not in the rings in his ears
Not in a shaven head, nor in the blowing of conch shell
If thou must the path of true religion see,
Among the World's impurities, be of impurities free.

Impurity of the heart is greed
Of tongue, untruth
Impurity of the eyes is coveting
Anothers wealth, his wife, his comliness.
Impurity of ears is listening to calumny.

In Punjab, Guru Nanak is still remembered as King of holy men, Hindu's Guru and, Musalman's Pir. (*Baba Nanak Sah Fakir, Hindu ka Guru, Musalman ka Pir*).

Guru Nanak bypassed his own sons in favour of one of the disciples as his successor. His successor was named 'Angad'—a limb of his own body. The process was repeated until the time of the Tenth Guru, Guru Govind Singh. Light passed from one body to another, as if all were one spirit though different in body.

The second Guru, Guru Angad (1538-1552) originated Gurumukhi script, which drew on Sanskrit, Persian and local dialect of the region.

The third Guru Amar Das (1553-1574) shifted to Govindwal. He set up 22 'manjis' or preaching districts. Emperor Akbar visited him and was so much impressed by the simple and pious way of life at Govindwal that he assigned the revenue of several villages to the Guru's daughter as a marriage gift. Guru Amar Das also campaigned against 'Purdah' and 'Sati' customs and laid down simple ceremonies for birth, marriage and death. In this way, the Sikh faith began developing features of a distinct social group.

Baisakhi, the first day of Baisakh (second month of the Hindu Calendar) was declared by him as the day of annual gathering of the Sikhs.

Guru Ram Das (1534-1588) whose period of holy ministry was comparatively, brief (1574-1581) is noted for founding the holy pool called Amritsar. Guru Arjun Dev the fifth Guru (1581-1606) invited the famous Muslim Saint Mian Mir of Lahore to lay the corner stone of the Golden Temple (Hari Mandir) in 1589. He also founded three other towns – Taran Taran, Hargovindpur and Kartarpur—which are held sacred by the Sikh to this date. *Adi Granth* was installed in the inner sanctum of Hari Mandir (Golden Temple), on August 16, 1604 A.D.

The *'Adi Granth'* is a vast treasure house—an anthology of hymns. In parts, it is some sort of Hindi or Hindi combined with words from Sanskrit, persian and even Arabic. Sayings of saints—Kabir, Surdas, Farid and Nanak—all find a place in the Granth.

Guru Arjun Dev's death (May 30, 1606 A.D.) by torture under Emperor Jehangir's orders, gave a martial form to the history of Sikhism. His son, Guru Hargovind (1606-1644) the sixth Guru, wore a warrior's equipment at his succession ceremony. He put two swords, one on either side, as symbols of his spiritual and temporal duty. Realising fully how peaceful means had failed to check Mughal's injustice and tyranny, he took recourse to the sword as a legitimate alternative. He also constructed Akal Takht (The throne of Timeless God) in the Golden Temple complex. He also founded the city of Kiratpur in the Shivaliks. Guru Hari Rai (1645-1661) and Guru Hari Krishna (1661-1664) following Guru Hargovind, carried out their duties from Kiratpur. Guru Hari Rai was friendly to Dara Shikoh (the eldest son of Emperor Shahjahan) and had Sufi leanings.

Guru Tegh Bahadur (1621-1675 A.D.) the ninth Guru whose period of gurudum lasted between 1664-75, had to lay down his life to defend the people's right of choice of religion. On the spot where he was beheaded (November 11, 1675), under orders of Mughal Emperor Aurangzeb, stands Gurudwara Sisganj in Delhi.

Guru Gobind Singh (1666-1706), the tenth Guru and the last Sikh Guru, and the son of Guru Tegh Bahadur who became guru in 1675, created the martial order of the Khalsa (the Pure). This was done in a democratic way at Anandpur on March 30, 1699. The five Sikhs who offered their heads at the Guru's call, were initiated as the first five members of this order and called as "Panj Piyars" (the five Beloved). Out of these five, three were the 'untouchables' and the other two drawn from different communities. They were given the surname 'Singh' meaning 'lion' and were ever to wear the five emblems of the faith.

Another permanent feature made by Guru Gobind Singh was to install '*Granth Sahib*' as the Guru of Sikhs. Personal Guruship was thus sealed, an act which had far reaching implications, both in religion and social field. From now onwards '*Granth Sahib*' became the main source to shape cultural and intellectual environment of the Sikhs.

Thus, beginning as a spiritual faith, Sikhism gradually developed into a cohesive and well knit order with a social outlook, so much so that within half a century of Guru Gobind Singh's passing away, it had become a major political force, and in another 70 years, it became a Sikh Kingdom. With the decline of the Mughal power several Sikh Sardars became the owners of large tracts of land called 'misals'. Such twelve principal 'misals' were later welded into a single Khalsa State of Maharaja Ranjit Singh (1780-1839). He captured Lahore (July 7, 1797 A.D.) and annexed the provinces of Multan, Peshawar and Kashmir — a real Sikh Kingdom.

But the kingdom could not survive for long. Within ten years of Maharaja Ranjit Singh's death, it was annexed to the British India. With this came the downfall of the Sikh spirit.

The commitment of the Sikhs to the cause of Indi's freedom was decisive and their contribution note-worthy. Who does not remember Shaheed Bhagat Singh and the Jalianwala Bagh massacre?

The partition of Punjab in 1947, which divided the Sikh population into two halves, was a severe blow to their progress. But by their native qualities of tenacity and enterprise, they soon rehabilitated themselves in Independent India.

Golden Temple, Amritsar

The Golden Temple (Hari Mandir) is regarded as the 'holiest of the holiest' shrine of the Sikh faith. The city of Amritsar is treated as the religious capital of the Sikhs as Varanasi is for the Hindus, Mecca for the Muslims, Jerusalam for the Jews and Christians and Sarnath for the Buddhists. The Golden Temple enshrines, in its inner sanctum, the 'Guru Granth Sahib', — the holy book of the Sikhs.

The upper half of the temple is copper plated covered with about 400 kg of gold leaves, and hence the name Golden Temple. The Temple is also known as Darbar Sahib (Court Divine) or Hari Mandir (Temple of the Lord).

Guru Ram Das, (1534-1588), the fourth guru is noted for founding Amritsar — ('Amrit' meaning 'nectar' and 'Sar' meaning 'tank' — the tank of nectar). Initially, Amritsar was limited to a 'talao' or the tank in the village named Tung. In the centre of the tank, stands the Golden Temple. The foundation of the temple was laid by a Muslim saint Mian Mir of Lahore, a friend and admirer of Guru Arjun Dev, the fifth Guru who completed the construction of the Temple.

Guru Arjun Dev raised money for the building of the temple. All Sikhs were asked to donate 'dasvandh' (one tenth) of their income in the name of Guru. On the completion of the project, Guru Arjun Dev, to immortalise his sentiments on this unique occasion, wrote the following:

By bathing in the tank of Ram Das
All the sins that man committeth shall be done away
And he shall become pure by his ablutions
The perfect Guru has given us this boon
"Each day in the divine tank take bath
The name divine is holy water
Taking dips into it brings fulfilment of all objectives"

— reads *Adi-Granth*, the main Sikh Scripture.

Legends and myths surround the past history of the site where now stands the Golden Temple. 'Bhavisya Purana' makes a reference to the 'Amar Kund' between the river Ravi and Beas. It is believed that the tank became the bone of contention between the demons and the gods.

According to another legend, it is believed that Lord Rama spent a few years of his exile in the forests surrounding the tank. Tradition has it that Pandavas had taken water from this very tank to sprinkle on Bhima to bring him back to life. It is also believed that Lord Buddha was so much impressed by the scenic beauty and serenity of this place that the recommended it to the Bhikshus for their hermitage. Yet another legend associates the place with the visits of Guru Nanak Dev, the founder of Sikh faith.

The Temple has grown as the nucleus of Sikhism and has attracted, day after day, crowds of worshippers. Pilgrims flock to the temple from all parts of the country and even overseas, specially on occasions such as Diwali, Baisakhi and the birthdays of the Gurus.

The Temple has four entrances opening in the four directions symbolising that it is open to all people, whichever part of the world they may hail from. The form and architecture of the Temple combine a sense of beauty with grace and peace abounding. The main Temple (Hari Mandir) is reached by a causeway over the arches of abridge. The exclusive architectural features of the Temple, the shape of the domes and turrets, became the archetype for Sikh Temples and Gurudwaras that were erected subsequently at various places.

Ahmad Shah Abdali, a foreign invader, is said to have demolished the Temple as may as seven times, the last being in the year 1764 A.D.

Golden Temple came up in the three phases of construction and reconstruction.

Year 1588 A.D. to year 1604 A.D. marks the first phase. The second phase of reconstruction ranged between the year 1764 A.D. to 1776 A.D. Major changes in design and renovation took place in the third phase — the era of Maharaja Ranjit Singh. After his many victories, Ranjit Singh came to Amritsar in January 1810. The guns of the fort of Gobindgarh saluted him on arrival. At night he rode through illuminated streets. At Hari Mandir he offered a prayer of thanks-giving to his Gurus.

Before Maharaja Ranjit Singh's ascendance to power, Amritsar was divided among nearly a dozen families owning different parts of the city. Any one who aspired to be the leader of the Khalsa and Maharaja of Punjab had to take Amritsar to make good his title. Maharaja Ranjit Singh took the city piecemeal, over-whelming the Sardars one after the other.

Maharaja Ranjit Singh took bath in the tank at Hari Mandir and made a grant for the Temple to be rebuilt in marble and covered with gold leaf. The inscription above the entrance of the central shrines reads :

The great Guru in His wisdom looked upon Maharaja
Ranjit Singh as his chief servitor.
And Sikhs in their benevolence bestowed
On him the privilege of serving the people.

(dated *Sambat* 1887)

Maharaja Ranjit Singh was the last of the independent Indian rulers. The Britishers failed to annex his territory, during his life time. He was persuaded to sign a treaty of friendship with the British at this historic city of Amritsar. *Akal Takht* (Immortal Throne): adjacent to the Golden Temple is the marble paved square in which stands the Akal Takht. It was established in the form of a raised platform by the Sixth Guru Hargobind in 1609 A.D. He used to sit on this seat and conduct the affairs of the Sikh faith. As such, Akal Takht is still regarded as the supreme seat of the Sikh religious authority. From time to time, many *Hukmnamas* (orders) have been issued from this seat on matters — political, social and religious, confronting the Sikh faith. It is also the repository of the various weapons used by the Gurus. The weapons are on display every evening.

The first storey of the building was constructed in 1774 A.D. The remaining part of the present structure was added during the reign of Maharaja Ranjit Singh. The gilded dome at the top was built by Hari Singh Nalwa at a later date. As it stands now, it is a five storeyed building with a dome at the top.

The interiors of the first and second floors of the shrine are tastefully embellished with scenes depicting the lives of the Sikh Gurus.

The Golden Temple Complex

The entire architectural complex, as it stands now, comprises the Golden Temple (Darbar Sahib), the pool of Nectar (sarovar of Amrit) and the Akal Takht (Immortal Seat of Learning). Many new structures were added in the first half of the 20th century, beginning with the widening of the outer 'parikrama' (circumambulatory path) in 1928-29. Other additions included the Guru Ram Das Sarai, Akal Rest House, Nanak Nivas, Teja Singh Samundri Hall, Manji Sahib and Diwan Hall. The main building (Hari Mandir or Golden Temple) is surrounded by a central domical structure, and kiosks at the cordinal sides. The building has been put on a square platform in the centre of a square tank, crossed over in the western side by a causeway terminating into a double storeyed entrance pavilion with an imposing archway. The sides of the square platform of the Temple serve as the *parikrama.* A similar function is served by the paved banks of the tank. The tank is surrounded by a series of columnaded verandahs. The arched pavilion serves as the 'darshani deorhi' (entrance gateway) for an access into the causeway leading to the temple.

There are four monumental buildings in the precincts of the temple and the tank, each in the centre of the four sides. The western one is not a gateway structure but the famous Akal Takhat. It is separated by a courtyard from the rest. The two other buildings, each one with a domical top and appurtenances of the kiosks and similar other architectural features, serve as the entrance to the precincts of the Temple and the tank. Of these gateways, northern one serves as the main gateway. The four gateways of the Temple are very novel. They symbolise the spirit of openness and the spirit of a casteless society which Sikhism stands for. The implication is the accessability of the Temple to people of all castes, classes, creeds and sexes. The four gates also provide a continuous view 'darshan' of the *Guru Granth Sahib* installed inside, while undergoing the process of 'Pradakshina' or 'Parikarma'.

Jaswant Rao Holker, a Maratha chief made a handsome offering at the Hari Mandir and flattered Maharaja Ranjit Singh as the only hope of the Hindus in India. The Nizam of Hyderabad sent Ranjit Singh a bejewelled canopy which he presented to the Golden Temple. Every thing connected with 'Granth' and 'Temple' is held in veneration. They are addressed as 'Granth Sahib' and 'Durbar Sahib'. All devotees rest their forehead on the ground and kiss its threshold before entering the building. Visitors cover their heads and take off their shoes before ascending the steps of the Temple (Hari Mandir).

The 'Granth Sahib' is preserved with great care. Ragis (classical singers) and instrumentalists keep a kind of regular service before it all the day. The devotees bring their offerings and cast them on a sheet laid in front of the 'Granth Sahib'. Visiting devotees also take a dip in the tank and consider themselves sanctified after the bath. Amongst the Sikh faith, it is considered as an act of virtue to contribute something to the adornment of the 'Durbar Sahib'.

The devotees also undertake 'Karseva' or the cleansing operation for the tank every two or three decades to remove the sediments left by millions of pilgrims who take bath in the holy water. Hundreds and thousands of devotees from all over India and abroad come to Amritsar to participate in the holy work.

3

UNDIVIDED PUNJAB

General Description

Punjab *(Panjāb)*. – In its strict etymological sense the Punjab, or 'land of the five rivers', is the country enclosed and watered by the *Jhelum, Chenāb, Rāvi, Beās*, and *Sutlej*; but the Province as now constituted includes also the table-land of Sirhind between the Sutlej and the Jumna to the south of the former river, the Sind-Sāgar Doāb or wedge of country between the *Jhelum* and the *Indus*, and west of the latter river the two tracts which form Dera Ghāzi Khān and part of Miānwāli District. The Province lies between 27° 39′ and 34° 2′ N. and 69° 23′ and 79° 2′ E., and with its Native States has an area of 133,741 square miles, being larger by one-tenth than the British Isles, and comprising a tenth of the area of the Indian Empire. Of the total area 36,532 square miles belong to Native States under the political control of the Punjab Government, and the rest is British territory. The population in 1901 was 24,754,737 (or whom 4,424,398 were in the Native States), or 8.4 per cent of the whole population of the Indian Empire.

Boundaries

On the north the Himālayan ranges divide the Punjab from Kashmir and the North-West Frontier Province. On the west the Indus forms its main boundary with the latter Province, except that the Punjab includes the strip of riverain which forms the Isa Khel *tahsil* of Miānwāli District, west of that river. Its south-western extremity also lies west of the Indus and forms the large District of Dera Ghāzi

---

Source: *Imperial Gazetteer of India, Punjab Series*, Vol. I, Superintendent of Government Printing, Calcutta, 1908.

Khān, thereby extending its frontier to the Sulaimān range, which divides it from Baluchistān. On the extreme south-west the Province adjoins Sind, and the Rājputāna desert forms its southern border. On the east, the Jumna and its tributary the Tons divide it from the United Provinces of Agra and Oudh, its frontier north of the sources of the latter river being contiguous with Chinese Tibet.

Physical Divisions

The province falls into five main physical divisions. Three of these – the Himālayan region, the Himālayan submontane which stretches from the Jumna to the Salt Range, and the arid plateaus of that range – are small in area, but the submontane is the most fertile and wealthiest in the Punjab. The other two are the arid south-western plains, and the western portion of the Indo-Gangetic Plain west which extends as far eastward as Lahore. Both these divisions are of vast extent, but infertile towards the south, where they encroach on the plains of Sind and Rājputāna.

The Doābs

The Punjab proper comprises five *Doābs*, or tracts lying between two rivers. These received their names from the Emperor Akbar, who formed them by combining the first letters of the names of the rivers between which they lie. They are: the Bīst Jullundur, also called the Sāharwāl Doāb, lying between the Beās and the Sutlej; the Bāri, between the old bed of the Beās and the Rāvi; the Rechna (Rachin-āb, or Rachin-ao), between the Rāvi and the Chenāb; the Chinhath, between the Chenāb and the Bihat (another name for the Jhelum), also called the Chaj; and the Sind-Sāgar, between the Indus and the Jhelum or Bihat.

Mountain System

The whole Central Punjab is a vast alluvial plain; but the north-east of the Province is formed of a section of the *Himālayas*, stretching up to and beyond the great central ranges so as to include the Tibetan cantons of Lāhul and Spiti. The *Salt Range*, with the plateaux which lie to the north between it and the Indus, forms its north-western angle, and the *Sulaimān* Range forms the southern half of the western frontier of the Province. These are the only mountain systems of importance; but a few insignificant outliers of the *Arāvalli* system traverse Gurgaon District in the extreme south-east, and terminate in the famous Ridge at Delhi.

River System

All the seven great rivers of the Punjab rise in the Himālayas, and after long courses, sometimes of several hundred miles, amid snow-clad ranges, they debouch on the plains. The slope of the low country is to be south and south west, and is very gradual, seldom exceeding a feet in the mile; and this determines the course of the rivers. In the process of time each stream has cut for itself a wide valley, which lies well below the level of the plain, and whose banks mark the extreme limits of the course on either side. Within this valley the river meanders in a narrow but ill-defined and ever-shifting show nothing but saltworts (*lāna, lāni, & c*), such as *Haloxylon recurvum, Salsola foetida, Suaeda*, & c. The type is, however, changing with the spread of cultivation. In the low grounds near the Rāvi there is a good deal of *kikar* (*Acacia arabica*), which may possibly be indigenous in this part of the Punjab and in Sind.

Fauna

Wolves and wild cats are the principal beasts of prey. 'Ravine deer' (Indian gazelle) are fairly numerous, but *nīlgai* and antelope are confined to the banks of the Rāvi on the Lahore border. Wild hog are becoming scarce as cultivation advances.

Climate and Temperature

The climate is very dry and the temperature in summer is oppressive. From May to the middle of October, and especially in June and July, the heat during the day is intense, but, except on the frequent occasions when heavy dust-storms blow, the nights are comparatively cool. The District is fairly healthy. Pneumonia is common in the winter, caused by the intense cold and dryness of the air. Fevers are prevalent, as the majority of the population live along the banks of the rivers and in the canal tracts.

Rainfall

The rainfall is generally scanty, the annual average ranging from 8 inches at Pākpattan to 10 inches at Montgomery. The average number of rainy days is twenty-three between April and October, and eight during the winter.

Earliest History

The Punjab was undoubtedly the seat of the earliest Aryan settlements in India, and the *Rig Veda* was probably composed within its borders. In one of its earliest hymns, the Vipāsa (Beas) and Sutudri (Sutlej) are invoked by the sage Visvamitra to allow the host of the Bharatas to cross them dryshod. And in the later Vedic period. The centre of Aryan civilization lay further to the south-east, between the Sutlej and the Jumna, in the still sacred land of *Kurukshetra* round Thanesar, the battle-field of the *Mahabharata*, while Indrapat near Delhi still preserves at least the name of Yudhishthira's capital, Indraprastha.

TABLE 3.1: Communitywise Population of Punjab (undivided), 1891 and 1901

Community	1891	1901
Hindus	10,122,473	10,344,469
Sikhs	1,851,070	2,102,896
Jains	45,615	49,983
Buddhists	6,236	6,940
Zoroastrians	370	477
Muhammadans	11,198,270	12,183,345
Christians		
(a) European and Eurasian	28,971	28,611
(b) Native	19,561	37,980
Jews and unspecified	57	36

Source: *Imperial Gazetteer of India Punjab*, Vol. 1, Superintendent of Government Printing, Calcutta, 1908.

TABLE 3.2: Population of Punjab (Present Areas), 1901 to 1991

Year	Population
1901	75,44,790
1911	67,31,500
1921	71,52,811
1931	80,12,325
1941	96,00,236
1951	91,60,500
1961	1,11,35,069
1971	1,35,51,060
1981	1,67,88,916
1991	2,01,90,795

TABLE 3.3: Divisions and Districts of Punjab, 1909

Division	Districts
I. Delhi	1. Hissar
	2. Rohtak
	3. Gurgaon
	4. Delhi
	5. Karnal
	6. Ambala
	7. Simla
II. Jullundur	1. Kangra
	2. Hoshiarpur
	3. Jullundhur
	4. Ludhiana
	5. Ferozpur
III. Lahore	1. Montgomery
	2. Lahore
	3. Amritsar
	4. Gurdaspur
	5. Sialkot
	6. Gujranwala
IV. Rawalpindi	1. Gujarat
	2. Shahpur
	3. Jhelum
	4. Rawalpindi
	5. Attock
V. Multan	1. Mianwali
	2. Jhang
	3. Multan
	4. Muzaffargarh
	5. Dera Ghazvi khan

Native States of Punjab

1. Patiala
2. Jind — These were called Phulkian States
3. Nabha
4. Bahawalpur State
5. Sirmor State
6. Simla Hill States
7. Kapurthala State
8. Malerkotla State
9. Mandi State
10. Chamba State
11. Faridkot State

4

BIFURCATED AND TRIFURCATED PUNJAB

Brief History before August 15, 1947

Ancient Punjab formed part of the vast Indo-Iranian region. In the later years to come it saw the rise and fall of the various powers like the Mauryans, Bactrian Greeks, Sakas, Kushans and Guptas. The medieval Punjab saw the supremacy of the Muslims. The first Muslim dynasty was followed by the Ghoris, the Slaves, the Khalijs, the Sayyids, the Lodhis and the Mughals (*India* 1990). However, with the dwindling power of the Mughals, in the eighteenth century, several (Misls) confederacies came into existence. Maharaja Ranjit Singh (1780-1839 A.D) popularly known as *Sher-e-Punjab* consolidated the numerous petty states and Misls into a strong kingdom of the Sikhs. By the year 1809, almost the whole of the Punjab came under his sway. His kingdom extended from the river Sutlej to the Khyber Pass and the Sulaiman mountains. Soon after his death, the entire edifice crumbled on account of internal intrigues of the Sikh leaders and British mechanisations. After the abortive Anglo-Sikh Wars, Punjab was finally annexed to the British empire in 1849. Punjab became a part of independent India with the independence of India in 1947. The people of Punjab played a leading role in the struggle for independence.

Partition of Punjab

Before taking up the present state of the Punjab crisis, it would be worthwhile to have a quick glance in its historical perspective. The demand for the reorganisation of Punjab was first made in 1930 before the Round Table Conference, as a counter-proposal to the demand of Pakistan by the Muslim League rather than on the linguistic considerations. The demand was reiterated in 1942 before the Cripps Mission and thereafter before the Sapru Committee in 1945 and the Cabinet Mission in 1946.

The country was partitioned under the 3rd June, 1947 Partition plan formulated by Lord Mountbatten. The erstwhile Punjab was devided into East Punjab and West Punjab as a result of Sir Cyrill Radcliffe Award of 12 August, 1947.

Reorganisation of States

East Punjab came to the share of India. On 15th July, 1948 the former 'Indian States' of Patiala, Nabha, Kapurthala, Jind, Faridkot, Malerkotla, Nalagarh and Kalsia which were located within the geographical confines of the province were constituted into 'Patiala and East Punjab States Union' (PEPSU). Subsequently as a result of the reorganisation of States in 1956 PEPSU was merged into East Punjab.

In November, 1966, East Punjab was trifurcated on the recommendations of a three-member Punjab Boundary Commission with Justice J.C. Shah as Chairman. The three States created were Punjab, Himachal Pradesh and Haryana. The reorganisation took place on the linguistic basis.

TABLE 4.1: Chief Ministers of Punjab, 1947 to 1992

1947 August	Gopi Chand Bhargava	Congress
1949 April	Bhim Sen Sachar	Congress
1949 October	Gopi Chand Bhargava	Congress
1951 June	President's Rule	
1952 April	Bhim Sen Sachar	Congress
1956 January	S. Pratap Singh Kairon	Congress
1964 June	Gopi Chand Bhargava	Congress
1964 July	Ram Kishan	Congress
1966 July	President's Rule	
1966 November	Giani Gurmukh Singh	Congress
1967 March	Justice Gurnam Singh	Akali Dal
1967 November	S. Lachman Singh Gill	Akali Dal
1968 August	President's Rule	
1969 February	B. Gurnam Singh	Akali Dal
1970 March	S. Prakash Singh Badal	Akali Dal
1972 March	Giani Zail Singh	Congress
1977 June	S. Prakash Singh Badal	Akali Dal
1980 February	President's Rule	
1980 July	S. Darbara Singh	Congress
1983 October	President's Rule	
1985 September	Surjit Singh Barnala	Akali Dal
1987 May	President's Rule	
1992 February	Beant Singh	Congress

Since the Anandpur Resolution of 1977, the demand for the bifurcation of the already twice bifurcated and mutilated Punjab has been gaining momentum from a section of the Sikhs.

After its bifurcation in 1947 the State had been called by various names such as the Indian Punjab, East Punjab and Punjab (India) but now it is referred to simply as Punjab—East Punjab was renamed Punjab and it is so referred to in the Constitution.

IAP 4.1: Sketch Map of Punjab (Not to Scale)
Bifurcated East Punjab on November 1, 1966

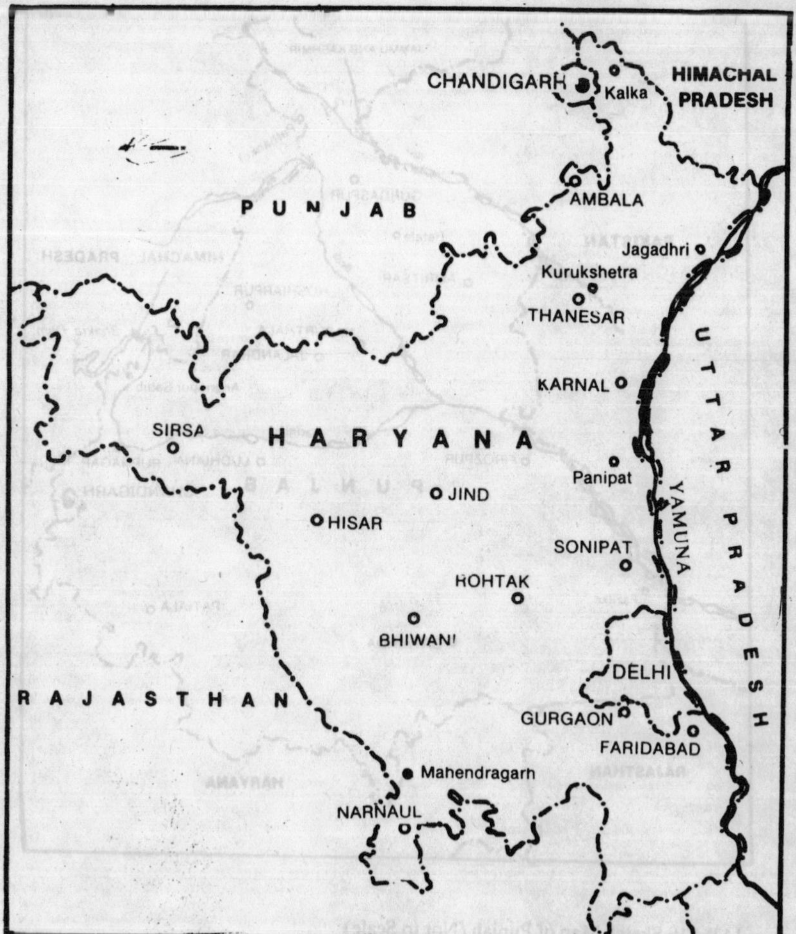

MAP 4.2: Sketch Map of Haryana (Not to scale)

MAP 4.3: Sketch Map of Himachal Pradesh (Not to scale)

5

SIKHS' DEMANDS/PERCEPTIONS DURING THE BRITISH RULE IN INDIA

The following documents throw considerable light on the origin of the Punjab crisis and are therefor appended:

1. Memorandum on Sikh Representation submitted to the Simon Commission, 1927.
2. The Nehru Report, 1928.
3. Sikh's Memorandum to Sir Cripps, 1942.
4. Sikh's Negotiations with Shri Jinnah---Extracts of a communication from Sir B. Glancy to Marquess of Linlithgow, 1942.
5. Efforts at Sikh-Muslim Reconciliation : Extracts of a communication from the Marquess of Linlithgow to Sir B. Glancy (Punjab), 1942.
6. Master Tara Singh on the concept of Azad Punjab, June 1943.
7. Jinnah's offer to Autonomy, 1944.
8. Shiromani Akali Dal's Resolution, March 22, 1946.
9. Master Tara Singh's Letter to Secretary of State, May 25, 1946.
10. Letter from the Secretary of State to Master Tara Singh, June 11, 1946.
11. R.A. Butter's Views in the House of Commons, July 15, 1947.
12. Sir Cyrill Radcliffe Award, August 12, 1947.
(*See* Chapter 6)

i. Memorandum on Sikh Representation submitted to the Simon Commission, 1927*

"While anxious to maintain their individuality as a separate

---

* Sikh Representation before the Indian Statutory Commission, May 1928

community they [the Sikhs] are always ready to cooperate with their sister communities for the development of a united nation.

They would, therefore, be the first to welcome a declaration that no considerations of caste or religion shall affect the matter of organisation of a national government in the country. They are prepared to stand on merit alone, provided they, in common with others, are permitted to grow unhampered by any impediments, in the way of reservation for any other community."[1]

If, however, separate representation was to continue, the memorandum demanded that in the Punjab Legislature communal proportions should be fixed as follows – 40 per cent Muslim, 30 per cent Hindu, and 30 per cent Sikh. Claim was made for Sikh representation in Sindh (if it was made into a separate province), Delhi, and the North-West Frontier Province – Quoted by Khushwant Singh.

The signatories to the memorandum were Shivdev Singh Oberoi (president of the Chief Khalsa Diwan and members of the Council of States), Harbans Singh of Attari (secretary, Chief Khalsa Diwan), Raghbir Singh Sandhawalia, Sunder Singh Majithia and Mohan Singh Raise of Rawalpindi.

ii. The Nehru Report, 1928

While the Simon Commission was at work, the Indian National Congress tried once more (as in 1916) to present the British Government with a draft constitution agreeable to Indians. In February 1928 it called a conference of members of all important Indian parties "to consider and determine the principles of the constitution for India." The moving spirit behind the conference was Motilal Nehru; his son, Jawaharlal, was secretary. The Sikhs were represented by Mangal Singh Gill. The Nehru Report recommended the abolition of separate electorates but agreed to reservation of seats for Muslims at the Centre and in the provinces in which they were a minority; the only other people for whom this concession was recommended were non-Muslims of the North-West Frontier Province. Mangal Singh did not press for special rights for his community in his home state or at the centre.

The committee met for over two months. At first Mangal Singh insisted that, if the Muslims were given separate rights, the Sikhs would ask for one-third representation in the Punjab and 5 per cent at the Centre. And, if weightage was abolished, he would accept representation on the basis of population with the right to contest other seats. The final decision to give up all communal representation was taken under the inspiration of Dr. Ansari, (Author's interview with Mangal Singh Gill) — Quoted by Khushwant Singh.

iii. Sikhs' Memorandum to Sir Cripps, 1942

The Sikh All-Parties Committee to Sir S. Cripps[2] Cmd. 6350

31 March, 1942

Dear Sir Stafford Cripps,

May we begin by stating that after giving careful consideration of the proposals which have now been published from the point of view of: (1) India's integrity and (2) the Sikh position, we find them unacceptable because: (1) instead of maintaining and strengthening the integrity of India specific provision has been made for separation of Provinces and constitution of Pakistan and (2) the cause of the Sikh community has been lamentably betrayed.

Ever since the British advent our community has fought for England in every battlefield of the Empire and this is our reward, that our position in the Punjab, which England promised to hold in trust and which we occupied a predominant position, has been finally liquidated.

Why should a Province that fails to secure a three-fifths majority of its Legislature, in which a religious community enjoys statutory majority, be allowed to hold a plebiscite and be given the benefit of a bare majority ? In fairness this right should have been conceded to communities who are in permanent minority in the Legislature.

Further, why should not the population of any area opposed to separation be given the right to record its verdict and to form an autonomous unit ?

We are sure you know that Punjab proper extended up to the banks of the Jhelum excluding Jhang and Multan Districts, and that the Trans-Jhelum area was added by the conquest of Maharaja Ranjit Singh and retained by the British for administrative convenience. It would be altogether unjust to allow the extraneous Trans Jhelum population, which only accidentally came into the

Province, to dominate the future of the Punjab proper.

We give below the figures which abundantly prove our contention. From the boundary of Delhi to the banks of the Ravi river the population is divided as follows: Muslims forty-five lakhs five thousand, Sikhs and other non-Muslims seventy-six lakhs forty-six thousand.

From the Delhi boundary to the banks of the Jhelum river excluding Multan and Jhang districts : Muslims eighty-two lakhs eighty-eight thousand, Sikhs and other non-Muslims ninety-three lakhs forty-eight thousand.

To this may be added the population of the Sikh State of Patiala, Nabha, Jind, Kapurthala and Faridkot, which is about twenty-six lakhs. Of this the Muslims constitute barely twenty per cent and this reduces the ratio of Muslim population still further.

We do not wish to labour the point any more. We have lost all hope of receiving any consideration. We shall resist however by all possible means separation of the Punjab from All-India Union. We shall never permit our Motherland to be at the mercy of those who disown it.

Yours sincerely,
BALDEV SINGH, President, Sikh All-Parties Committee.
TARA SINGH
JOGENDRA SINGH
UJJAL SINGH
MOHAN SINGH (ex-Adviser to the Secretary of State for India).

We append herewith a note which gives some particulars of the position of our Community in the Punjab.

Enclosure to No. 467

On behalf the Sikhs we wish to place the claims of the Sikh community in the proposed scheme of His Majesty's Government for the governance of India. We begin by giving a historical background of our case.

The Sikhs an important and distinct community mainly concentrated in the Punjab of which they were the Rulers until 1849. Sikhism recognises no caste and strictly enjoins upon those who profess it to treat all human beings as equal.

Sikhs play an important role in the economic and civic life of the country and a leading part in its defence. In the British Punjab with their 3-3/4 million population (13.5 per cent of the whole) the Sikhs pay 25 per cent of the land revenue and 40 per cent of the land revenue and water rates combined, the main source of the Provincial Exchequer. They maintain at their own expense over 400 schools and 4 colleges open to all communities and class without distinction. The percentage of literacy among the Sikhs is higher than in any other community in the Punjab. They have got a large number of Sikh shrines with big landed estate attached to them which are the centres of Sikh culture and tradition.

The authors of the Montford Report recognised the importance of the Sikhs and "the difficulty of denying to the Sikhs in the Punjab a concession which is granted to Mohammedans."[3]

The Simon Commission states : "Sikhism remained pacific cult until the political tyranny of the Mussalmans and the social tyranny of the Hindus converted it into a military creed. It is a striking circumstance that this small community contributed no less than 80,000 men" (actually 89,000 combatant recruits in addition to 32,500 already serving when the war broke out) "to serve in the Great War, a larger portion than any other community in India."[4]

With a population of over 6,000,000 in India the share of Sikhs in the defence forces of the country has always been out of all proportion to their population. The Sikhs are perhaps the only community which is making an organised war effort by the establishment of the "Khalsa Defence of India League" to maintain its glorious traditions in the Army. We do realise that with our past traditions and the excellent fighting material that can be found in the Sikh districts, we should have done still better in mobilising out manpower, but we are constrained to remark that nothing has been done by Government to rouse the enthusiasm of the Sikh community in the way of recognition of its status in the sphere of the Central Government or of providing effective safeguards for it in the Punjab, to which it was entitled on account of its unrivalled position, historical, political and economic.

The Sikhs were deeply disappointed at the differential treatment meted out to them under the so-called "communal award" of 1932. In spite of their unique position in the Punjab they were not given the same weightage in the Legislature as the Moslem minorities were given in other Provinces. By way of illustration it may be stated that

Muslims with 14.8 per cent population in the United Provinces were given 30 per cent seats in the Provincial Assembly as against 18.8 per cent seats to the Sikhs in the Punjab with their 13.5 per cent population. Their influence in the administration and political life of the Punjab was further weakened in the formation of the Provincial Cabinet. Whereas in the days of dyarchy out of three Punjabees appointed as Ministers and Members of the Governor's Council there was one Sikh from 1921 to 1926 and one Sikh out of four Punjabees from 1926 to 1937, since the advent of the Provincial autonomy there has been only one Sikh out of a total of six Ministers, It will thus be observed that in the sphere of the supreme Executive of the Province, the representation of the Sikhs was reduced from 33 per cent in 1921 to 25 per cent in 1926 and to 16 per cent in 1937.

This progressive deterioration of the share of Sikhs in the Punjab Cabinet is strongly resented by the community as it has led to encroachment of their religious and cultural rights and the waning of their influence on the political and economic life of the country.

We submit that under the existing constitution the strength of the Sikhs in the Punjab Cabinet should be maintained normally at 33 per cent and in no case below 25 per cent so that there may always be at least two Sikh Ministers in the Cabinet. We also feel that so long as communal electorates continue to be the method of representation in the Legislature, Cabinet should be formed on a coalition basis in the true sense of the word. We may here point out that when ministries were functioning in all Provinces, in the United Provinces where the percentage of the Muslim population is nearly the same as that of the Sikhs in the Punjab, there were two Moslem Ministers in a Cabinet of six.

In the sphere of the Central Government, the Sikh community in spite of its important stake in the country, its sacred shrines scattered all over India and the valuable services that the Sikh soldiers and technicians are rendering, has been unjustly treated. The Sikhs have suffered a great disillusionment by the deliberate neglect of their claims and omission of any reference to the Sikh minority by British statesmen and the Viceroy of India in their statements made from time to time during the last ten years on the Indian question. It seems as if in their opinion, Muslims alone or the depressed classes sometimes, constitute the important minorities of India.

Although for seventeen years a Punjabee has been appointed on the Viceroy's Council, no Sikh has ever been considered for such an appointment. Even at the time of the last expansion of the Executive Council, the claims of the Sikhs were entirely ignored.

In this connection we should like to invite attention to the decisions of the Allahabad Unity Conference which were arrived at between Hindus, Muslims and Sikhs in November 1932. Resolution Number 4 regarding Cabinets read as follows : 1. "In the formation of the Cabinet of the Central Government, so far as possible, members belonging to the Muslim, *Sikh* and other minority communities of considerable numbers forming the Indian National shall be included by convention." 2. "Further during the first ten years in the formation of the Central Government, *a seat shall be offered to a member of the Sikh community*."

Resolution No. 7 read as under : II. "It is agreed that in the Central Legislature out of the total elected seats allotted to British India 3 per cent shall be reserved for Muslims, 4-2/3 per cent or 14 seats out of 300, for Sikhs".

It will thus be observed that leading Indians of different communities recognised the importance of the Sikh minority and agreed to accommodate it in the Central Cabinet, and also to give it nearly 5 per cent representation in the Central Legislature.

We favour immediate transfer of power to Indian hands, entrusting all portfolios including defence to Indians with experience of public life.

We feel that in this way alone, the moral and material resources of India can be tapped to the fullest extent and Indians can participate in the war with full vigour and enthusiasm.

The Sikhs stand for national unity and the integrity of India. They would like the provinces to enjoy as wide a measure of autonomy as may be compatible with good government in the country as a whole but they also feel that any weakness at the centre will expose India to internal and external dangers.

They are strongly opposed to the vivisection of India into two or three rival dominions or sovereign states as is contemplated in the British proposals. They feel that such a step would lead to a state of perpetual strife and civil war in the country.

If the object is to give self-determination to the provinces in the matter of accession to the "Union of India", the right to stand out and break the unity of India should not be exercised by a bare majority but by at least 65 per cent of Indian members present at the meeting of the provincial assembly when the resolution is considered. A plebiscite on the issue of secession is certain to lead to inter-communal riots of a most serious character and magnitude and should in no case be resorted to.

We are constrained to remark that the proposed scheme does not make any provisions for safeguarding the interests of the Sikh minority. The decisions of the constitution-making body are to be by a bare majority and no provision is made for recourse to arbitration by the aggrieved party as was even assured by Mahatma Gandhi in his statement on the Congress scheme of Constituent Assembly.

The Treaty which is proposed to be negotiated between the constitution-making body and His Majesty's Government for protecting the religious and racial minorities in accordance with undertakings given by the British Government, will have no sanction behind it. Besides, we are not sure how political rights which relate mainly to a share in the Legislature and the administration of the country will be incorporated in the Treaty. The Treaty might cover the cultural, religious and linguistic rights of minorities as such Treaties in European countries after the last Great War did. But the undertakings given to the Sikhs by His Majesty's Government from time to time relate to the position and status of the Sikhs in the governance of the country and not merely regarding the exercise of their religious or cultural rights.

The Sikhs therefore feel that they cannot attain their rightful position or effectively protect their interests unless the Punjab is distributed into two Provinces with the river Ravi roughly forming the boundary between them.

We might invite attention to the All-India Moslem League Resolution of the Lahore session held in March, 1940, which is popularly known as the Pakistan Resolution, "that no Constitution would be workable in this country or acceptable to the Muslims unless it is designed on the following basic principle, *viz.*, that geographically contiguous units are demarcated into regions which should be so constituted *with such territorial readjustments as may be necessary that the areas in which the Muslims are numerically in a majority,* as in the north-western and eastern zones of India, should be grouped to constitute independent States in which the constituent units shall be autonomous and sovereign."

A careful reading of the Resolution discloses the fact that the Muslim League itself visualised the re-adjustments of areas and the inclusion in their separate state of only those areas in which the

Muslims were in a majority.

The population of the Punjab is so distributed that the two western divisions of Rawalpindi and Multan are predominantly Muslims and the two eastern divisions of Ambala and Jullundur area predominantly non-Muslims. The three central districts of Amritsar, Gurdaspur and Lahore have a balanced population. The separate figures of population for each district of the Punjab are attached as appendix to this statement. If a new Province of a contiguous area of the two divisions of Ambala and Jullundur *plus* the three districts of Lahore, Gurdaspur and Amritsar is carved out, it will have a total population of 12,151,000 (according to 1931 census) with non-Muslims forming 63 per cent and Muslims 37 of the population. The other Province to the west of the river Ravi comprising the Multan and Rawalpindi divisions *plus* the three districts of Shiekhupura, Sialkot and Gujranwala will have a total population of 11,429,000, with Muslims forming 77.3 per cent and non-Muslims 22.7 per cent of the population.

The Sikhs do not want to dominate but they would certainly not submit to the domination of a community which is bent upon breaking the unity of India and imposing their personal laws and culture on the other sections of the population.

We submit that in any interim arrangement or in the permanent scheme the following safeguards should be provided either in the Treaty which might be enforceable or in the Constitution itself :

No. 1. By delimiting the present Provincial boundaries of the Punjab, a new Province comprising of Ambala and Jullundur division with the three districts of Amritsar, Gurdaspur and Lahore be constituted.

No. 2. The Sikh minority in the Provinces be given the same weightage and measure of protection as the Muslim minority.

No. 3. So long as communal electorates exist, Provincial Cabinets should be formed on a coalition basis.

No. 4. The Sikhs should be given 5 per cent representation in the Central Legislature.

No. 5. A Sikh should always be given a seat in the Cabinet of the Central Government.

No. 6. A Defence Advisory Committee should be set up for advising the Indian Defence Minister and a Sikh should be given a seat on that Committee.

No. 7. The position of the Sikhs in the Defence Forces of India should be maintained in keeping with their past traditions and strength in those forces.

No. 8. The share of the Sikhs should be fixed in Provincial and All-India Services on the lines it has already, been provided or may be provided for the Muslims.

No. 9. Religious laws of Sikhs enacted may only be amended by the votes of majority of the Sikh members in the legislature.

No. 10. No restrictions should be imposed by the State in the exercise of the religious rights of the Sikhs in the matter of eatables and religious performances.

No. 11. The State should provide for teaching of Punjabi in Gurmukhi script where a certain fixed number of scholars is forthcoming.

Baldev Singh, President.

iv. Sikhs' Negotiations with Jinnah, 1942

Extracts of a Communication from Dr. B. Glancy (Punjab) to the Marquess of Linlithgow, 1942 MSS. EUR. F. 125/91

Govt. House, Lahore, 13 November, 1942

Private and Personal
D.O. No. 417-F.L.

Dear Lord Linlithgow,

There is little of any great importance to bring to Your Excellency's notice since we met at Rawalpindi last month. Any active support of Congress appears to be on the decline, though there have been a few minor demonstrations on the part of students and others from time to time. The Sikh community as a whole has wisely continued to abstain from any participation in the Congress crusade. There is no doubt that "Sikander-Baldev Singh Pact"[5] has been a powerful factor for good and that it has exercised a distinctly pacifying effect on the Sikh community. There are signs that Baldev Singh is inclined to attach increasing value of his appointment as a Minister and that he is less likely to run out of the ropes. Communal relations have on the whole been less strained and social gatherings have been held at Lahore on the occasions of the Id and the Diwali with the object of bringing the various communities together; the Sikhs are about to organize a similar event in commemoration of Guru Nanak's birthday. This happy state of affairs is in danger of disturbance when Mr. Jinnah pays his forthcoming visit to the Punjab, Lyallpur, Jullundur and Lahore are included in his programme, and it is only to be expected that his tour will give rise to further disquieting cries for "Pakistan" and counter-attacks on the part of non-Muslims. Sikandar, who would of course be much relieved if Jinnah's visits were cancelled, has chosen this time to float his scheme, of which I have already informed you for the possible dismemberment of the Province. The main object of his exposition is to point out the practical difficulties that lie in the way of partition, and in this he has not been without success. The scheme has not been popular with Muslims and it is of course intensely disliked by Hindus. *Sikh leaders have been professing to take the idea seriously and some of them have been attempting negotiations with Jinnah the intention being apparently to see whether they can get more out of Jinnah or Sikandar; steps have been taken to point out to some of them in the course of friendly discussions that they are not likely to secure any practical benefit from dealings with Jinnah and that the various elements in the Province would be better advised to try and settle their difficulties among themselves. I do not think that responsible reasonably-minded Sikhs have any serious desire to see the Province dismembered as long as they are likely to be given a fair deal.*

v. Efforts at Sikh-Muslim Reconciliation

Extract of a Communication from The Marquess of Linlithgow to Sir B. Glancy (Punjab), 1942 MSS. EUR.F. 125/91

Viceroy's Camp, Chiklod, Bhopal, 24 November, 1942

Private and Personal

My Dear Glancy,

Many thanks for your private and personal d.o. No. 417—F.L.[6] of the 13th November, and for the news contained in it. I am glad that Baldev Singh is settling down and, as you know, I have always attached very great importance to the Sikander-Baldev Singh Pact, and hoped sincerely that it will continue to pay a good dividend. I should think that you have got out of Jinnah's tour pretty lightly on the whole! I have read his speech at Lyallpur and, of course, on the main Pakistan issue he has not the slightest mention of making any move whatever. But I think that most people, too, appreciate Sikander's difficulties with the very awkward balance which he has to maintain between Muslim, Sikh, and Hindu in the Punjab, and realise the motives that prompt his occasional appeals against the Qaid-e-Azam and also his alternative schemes for dismemberment. *I get the impression of closer contact between the Muslims and the Sikhs, and you touch on that indirectly in paragraph 1 of your letter. It is an aspect of the general problem on which you may care to comment at some later date.*

vi. Master Tara Singh on the Concept of Azad Punjab, June 1943

In the Azad Punjab, the boundaries, should be fixed after taking into consideration the population, property, land revenue and historical traditions of each of the communities. If the new demarcations are affected on the above principles, then the Azad Punjab comprises of Ambala, Jullundur, Lahore division and out of Multan division Lyallpur district, some portions of Montgomery and Multan Districts. (*Indian Annual Register,* 1943, Vol. 1, p. 298.)

vii. Jinnah's Offer of Autonomy, 1944

Field Marshall Viscount Wavell to Mr. Amery L/PO/10/21

The Viceroy's House, New Delhi, 15 August, 1944

Private and Secret

Many thanks for your letter of 1st August.[7] The approaching discussion between Gandhi and Jinnah, which is announced for 19th August in Bombay, is giving rise to much speculation. There has for the past few days been a truce in the Press from recriminations likely to prejudice a settlement. But Hindu objections to the Raja-gopalachari formula are still strong. Most educated Hindus dislike the Pakistan idea intensely and find it difficult to forgive Gandhi for going back on his earlier statements about it. Shyama Prasad Mookerjee and others have been in touch with Gandhi since he returned to Sevagram, and Mookerjee is reported to have said that he felt much encouraged—a statement which the Muslims find disquieting. *Jinnah has reverted to his proposal for some kind of special autonomy for the Sikhs within Pakistan;* but the Sikhs did not like this before and there is no reason to suppose that they will like it now. I am told that Tej Bahadur Sapru attempted to advise Gandhi the other day, and took the line that he must base himself on the 1935 Constitution and the Cripps offer. If he failed to do so, Jinnah would be free to range over the entire field of constitutional possibilities and would make most extravagant demands. Gandhi said that these were most complicated matters which Sapru must leave him to consider in his own way. Sapru is said to have left Sevagram in a very bad temper. I am sure that Gandhi's real object is to get the Working Committee out of detention and that he will go a very long way (with the usual mental reservations) in dealing with Jinnah to secure the co-operation of the Muslim League. Having drafted an agreement of some kind he may tell Jinnah that he is at a disadvantage because the Working Committee, who alone can commit the Congress, are in detention, and may suggest a joint approach to the Viceroy to secure their release. Gandhi would of course be acting only in his personal capacity and would, as usual, keep various lines of retreat open. I think it unlikely that Jinnah will rise to this fly, but it is a possible that he may do so. Bhulabhai Desai recently wrote to Liaqat Ali Khan suggesting not a constitutional settlement but an alliance between the Congress and the League for the duration of the war.

viii. Shiromani Akali Dal's Resolution, March 22, 1946

"Whereas the Sikhs being attached to the Punjab by intimate bonds of holy shrines, property, language, traditions and history claim it as their homeland and holy land which the British took as a trust from the last Sikh ruler during his minority and whereas the entity of the Sikhs is being threatened on account of the persistent demand of Pakistan by the Muslims on the one hand and of danger of absorption by the Hindus on the other, the executive committee of the Shiromani Akali Dal demands the preservation and protection of the religious, cultural and economic and political rights of the Sikh population and their important sacred shrines and historical gurudwaras with provision for the transfer and exchange of population and property."[8]

ix. Master Tara Singh's Letter to the Secretary of State for India, 25 May, 1946

"Since the British Cabinet Mission recommendations for the future constitution of India have been published, a wave of resentment and indignation has run throughout the Sikh community. The reasons are quite obvious. The Sikhs have been entirely thrown at the mercy of the Muslims. Group 'B' comprises Punjab, the north-west Province, Sind and Baluchistan and the representation given to each community will be : Muslims 23, Hindus 9 and Sikhs 4. Can anybody expect from this Assembly, constituted as it is, any consideration or justice for the Sikhs ? The Cabinet Mission recognises the genuine and acute anxiety among the Sikhs lest they should find themselves subjected to a perpetual Muslims majority rule. If the British government is not aware of Sikh feelings, the Sikhs will have to resort to some measures to convince everybody of the Sikh anxiety in case they are subjected to perpetual Muslim domination. The Cabinet Mission has not only put under Muslim domination the non-Muslim areas of the Punjab and Bengal but the whole province of Assam where the non-Muslims are in an overwhelming majority. This has been evidently done to placate the Muslims. It appears that Sikhs have been studiously debarred from having any effective influence in the province a group or general union. I refer to section 15 (ii) and Section 19(vii) in which it has been definitely provided that the majority of both Hindus and Muslims is necessary for certain purposes. The Sikhs are entirely ignored, though they are as much concerned as the other communities.

This is how I read the recommendations of the Cabinet Mission, but as the issues are very grave and momentous, the Sikh representatives assembled here today to consider the situation created have advised me to seek clarification from you and find out if there is any hope of such amendments as may save the Sikhs from perpetual domination.

So I put three questions:

1. What is the significance of recognising the Sikhs as one of the main communities?

2. Suppose the majority of Section B frames a constitution under section 19(v) but the Sikh members do not agree, does it mean a deadlock of does the opposition of the Sikh members mean simply discussion ?
3. Is there any hope of obtaining for the Sikhs the same rights as is given to the Muslims and the Hindus under section 15(ii) and 19(iii) ?

x. Letter from the Secretary of State to Master Tara Singh, 11 June, 1946

Thank you, for your letter of May 25. The anxieties of the Sikhs were kept permanently in mind when we were drafting the Cabinet Mission statement, and I can certainly claim that of the various alternatives open to us the best one from the Sikh point of view was chosen. You will, I am sure, admit that, if India had been divided into two sovereign states or if Punjab was partitioned, either of these decisions would have been far less acceptable to Sikhs than the one which was actually reached.

I have considered carefully the detailed points you have raised at the end of your letter. I fear the Mission cannot issue any addition to, or interpretation of, the statement. There is, however, no intention whatever to prejudice the position of the Sikhs in Punjab or in the north-west group, nor do I think their position has been prejudiced, for, it is inconceivable that either the Constituent Assembly or any future government of Punjab will overlook the special place of the Sikhs in province. The estimate of the importance of your community would never depend on the number of seats that you hold in the Constituent Assembly. The Viceroy has told me that he will be glad, in view of the anxieties you have expressed on behalf of your community, to discuss the position of the Sikh specially with the leaders of the main parties when the Constituent Assembly has been formed. He hopes he may be able to persuade them, if persuasion is needed, that the interests of the Sikhs should on no account be overlooked.

If you and Sardar Baldev Singh would care to see the Cabinet Mission and Viceroy in the first week of June, we shall be glad to see you.

Source: P. Sitaramayya, *The History of the Indian National Congress*, Vol. II; Mitra's, *Register*, 1946, Vol. I, pp. 202-203.

xi. R.A. Butler's Views in the House of Common, July 15, 1947

"The British had the happiest possible relations with the Sikh community and, of all the martial races of the world, the Sikhs probably had built up the greatest reputations. The only situation which could mitigate the plight of the Sikhs was that the Boundary Commission should so define the boundary that the maximum portion of the Sikhs should be included within one conglomerate whole (*Tribune,* July 16, 1947).

NOTES

1. Sikh Representation before the Indian Statutory Commission, May 1928.
2. The text of this letter and its enclosure were transmitted by Lord Linlithgow to Mr Amery in telegram 209-S.C. of 18 April, MSS, BUR.F. 125/22.
3. Report on Indian Constitutional Reforms, 1918 para. 163, Cd. 9109.
4. Report of the Indian Statutory Commission, Vol. 1, 1930, paraa 44, Cmd. 3568.
5. Since the 1937 elections, when the Unionist Party won a clear majority in the Punjab Legislature, its leader — Sir Sikandar Hyat Khan had held office as Premier with a Cabinet consisting of 3 Muslims, 2 Hindus and 1 Sikh. By the so-called Sikander-Baldev Singh Pact, announced on 15 June, 1942, the Premier promised certain concessions to the Sikh Community in return for which Baldev Singh, who now entered the Ministry, undertook to support the Unionist Government in the interests of communal unity and the defence of the country.
6. No. 176.
7. No. 618.
8. V.P. Menon, *Transfer of Power is India,* 1957.

6

SIR CYRIL RADCLIFFE AWARD, 1947

Introduction

Punjab was bifurcated in accordance with the recommendations of the Punjab Boundary Award of August 12, 1947.

The Punjab Boundary Commission was constituted by the announcement of the G.G.,d/the 30th June, 1947, Reference No. D.50/7/47-R. The members of the Commission thereby appointed were :

Mr. Justice Din Muhammad
Mr. Justice Muhammad Munir
Mr. Justice Mehr Chand Mahajan
Mr. Justice Teja Singh

Sir Cyril Radcliffe was subsequently appointed Chairman of this Commission.

The terms of reference of the Commission, as set out in the announcement, were as follows :

"The Boundary Commission is instructed to demarcate the boundaries of the two parts of the Punjab on the basis of ascertaining the contiguous majority areas of Muslims and non-Muslims. In doing so, it will also take into account other factors."

The Commission was asked to arrive at a decision as soon as possible before the 15th of August, 1947.

After preliminary meetings the Commission invited the submission of memoranda and representations by interested parties. Numerous memoranda and representations were received.

The public sittings of the Commission took place at Lahore, and extended from Monday, the 21st of July 1947, to Thursday the 31st of July 1947, inclusive, with the exception of Sunday, the 27th July. The main arguments were conducted by Counsel on behalf of the Indian National Congress, the Muslim League and the Sikh members of the Punjab Legislative Assembly; but a number of other interested parties appeared and argued before the Commission.

Partition Proceedings, Vol. VI, Alipore, 1950

Introductory Observations by Sir Radcliffe

The task of delimiting a boundary in the Punjab is a difficult one. The claims of the respective parties ranged over a wide field of territory, but in my judgement the truly debatable ground in the end proved to lie in and around the area between the Beas and Sutlej rivers on the one hand and the river Ravi on the other. The fixing of a boundary in this area was further complicated by the existence of canal systems, so vital to the life of the Punjab but developed under the conception of a single administration and of systems of road and rail communication, which have been planned in the same way. There was also the stubborn geographical fact of the respective situations of Lahore and Amritsar, and the claims to each or both of those cities which each side vigorously maintained. After weighing to the best of my ability such other factors as appeared to me relevant as affecting the fundamental basis of contiguous majority areas, I have come to the decision set out in the schedule which thus becomes the award of the Commission. I am conscious that there are legitimate criticisms to be made of it; as there are, I think, of any other line that might be chosen.

I have hesitated long over those not inconsiderable areas east of the Sutlej river and in the angle of the Beas and Sutlej rivers in which Muslim majorities are found. But on the whole I have come to the conclusion that it would be in the true interests of neither state to extend the territories of the West Punjab to a strip on the far side of the Sutlej and that there are factors such as the disruption of railway communications and water systems that ought in this instance to displace the primary claims of contiguous majorities. But I must call attention to the fact that the Dipalpur Canal, which serves areas in the West Punjab, takes off from Ferozepur headworks and I find it difficult to envisage a satisfactory demarcation of boundary at this point that is not accompanied by some arrangement for joint control of the intake of the different canals dependent on these headworks.

I have not found it possible to preserve undivided the irrigation system of the Upper Bari Doab Canal, which extends from Madhopur in the Pathankot Tehsil to the western border of the district of Lahore although I have made small adjustments of the Lahore-Amritsar district boundary to mitigate some of the consequences of this severance; nor can Hydro-electric Scheme which supplies power in the districts of Kangra, Gurdaspur, Amritsar, Lahore, Jullundur, Ludhiana, Ferozepur, Sheikhupura and Lyallpur. I think it only right to express the hope that, where the drawing of a boundary line cannot avoid disrupting such unitary services as canal irrigation, railways and electrical power transmission, a solution may be found by agreement between the two States of some joint control of what has hitherto been a valuable common service.

I am conscious too that the award cannot go forward satisfying sentiments and aspirations deeply held on either side but directly in conflict as to their bearing on the placing of the boundary. If means are to be found to gratify to the full those sentiments and aspirations. I think that they must be found in political arrangements with which I am not concerned and not in the decision of a boundary line drawn under the terms of reference of the Commission.

New Delhi (Signed) CYRIL RADCLIFFE
12th August, 1947

Boundary Award

1. The boundary between the East and West Punjab shall commence on the north at the point where the west branch of the Ujh river enters the Punjab province from the State of Kashmir. The boundary shall follow the line of that river down the Western boundary of the Pathankot Tehsil to the point where the Pathankot, Shakargarh and Gurdaspur Tehsils meet. The tehsil boundary and not the actual course of the Ujh river shall constitute the boundary between the East and West Punjab.

2. From the point of meeting of the three tehsils above-mentioned, the boundary between the East and West Punjab shall follow the line of the Ujh river to its junction with the river Ravi and thereafter the line of the river Ravi along the boundary between the

tehsils of Gurdaspur and Shakargarh, the boundary between the tehsils of Batala and Shakargarh, the boundary between the tehsils of Ajnala and Shahdara, to the point on the river Ravi where the district of Amritsar is divided from the district of Lahore. The tehsil boundaries referred to, and not the actual course of the river Ujh or the river Ravi, shall constitute the boundary between the East and West Punjab.

3. From the point on the river Ravi where the district of Amritsar is divided from the district of Lahore, the boundary between the East and West Punjab shall turn southwards following the boundary between the tehsils of Ajnala and Lahore and then the tehsils of Tarn Taran and Lahore, to the point where the tehsils of Kasur, Lahore and Tarn Taran meet. The line will then turn down the eastern boundary of village Panhuwan to its junction south-westward, along the boundary between the tehsils of Lahore and Kasur to the point where the boundary meets the north-east corner of village Theh Tharolian. It will then run along the eastern boundary of that village to its junction with village Chalhianwala, turn along the northern boundary of that village, and then run down its eastern boundary to its junction with village Waigal. It will then run along eastern boundary of village Waigal to its junction with village Kalia, and then along the southern boundary of village Waigal to its junction with village Panhuwan. The line will then run with village Gaddoke. The line will then turn down to the eastern border of village Gaddoke to its junction with village Nurwala. It will then turn along the southern boundary of village Gaddoke to its junction with village Katluni Kalan. The line will then run down the eastern boundary of village Katluni Kalan to its junction with villages Kals and Mastgarh. It will then run along the southern boundary of village Katluni Kalan to the north-west corner of village Kals. It will then run along the western boundary of village Kals to its junction with village Khem Karan. The line will then run along with western and southern boundaries of village Khem Karan to its junction with village Maewala. It will then run down the western and southern boundaries of village Maewala, proceeding eastward along the boundaries between village Mahaidepur on the north and villages Sheikhupura, Kuhna, Kamalpuran, Falehwala and Mahewala. The line will then turn northward along the western boundary of village Sahjra to its junction with villages Mahaidepur and Machhike and Sahjra and then proceed along the boundary between village Rattoke and Sahjra to

the junction between village Rattoke, Sahjra and Mabbuke. The line will then run north-east between the village Rattoke and Mabbuke to the junction of villages Rattoke, Mabbuke and Gajjal. From that point the line will run along the boundary between villages Mabbuke and Gajjal, and then turn south along the eastern boundary of villages Mabbuke to its junction with village Nagar Aimanpur. It will then turn along the north-eastern boundary of village Nagar Aimanpur, and run along its eastern boundary to its junction with village Masteke. From there it will run along the eastern boundary of village Masteke to where it meets the boundary between the tehsils of Kasur and Ferozepur.

For the purpose of identifying the villages referred to in this paragraph, I attach a map of the Kasur tehsil authorised by the then Settlement Officer, Lahore District, which was supplied to the Commission by the Provincial Government.

4. The line will then run in a south-westerly direction down the Sutlej river on the boundary between the districts of Lahore and Ferozepur to the point where the districts of Ferozepur, Lahore and Montgomery meet. It will continue along the boundary between the districts of Ferozepur and Montgomery to the point where the boundary meets the border of Bahawalpur State. The district boundaries, and not the actual course of the Sutlej river, shall in each case constitute the boundary between the East and West Punjab.

5. It is my intention that this boundary line should ensure that the canal headworks at Sulamanke will fall within territorial jurisdiction of the West Punjab. If the existing delimitation of the boundaries of Montgomery district does not ensure this, I award to the West Punjab so much of territory concerned as covers the headworks, and the boundary shall be adjusted accordingly.

6. So much of the Punjab Province as lies to the West of the line demarcated in the preceding paragraphs shall be the territory of the West Punjab. So much of the territory of the Punjab Province as lies to the east of that line shall be the territory of the East Punjab.

(Signed) K.V. SUNDARAM
Officer on Special Duty

7

SIKHS' DEMANDS/PERCEPTIONS, 1947 TO 1966

Documents in this Chapter

1. Master Tara Singh's Statement, September 21, 1947.
2. Dar Commission, 1948.
3. Master Tara Singh's Statement, February, 1948.
4. Rejection of the Demand by Minority Committee, November 12, 1948.
5. Memorandum by the Sikh Members to the Constituent Assembly, November 15, 1948.
6. Master Tara Singh's Statement, 1949.
7. Shiromani Akali Dal Manifesto, 1951.
8. Population of the Hindus and Sikhs in Punjab and PEPSU, 1951.
9. States Reorganisation Commission, 1955
10. Master Tara Singh's Reaction on States Reorganisation Commission, 1955
11. Regional Plan, 1957.
12. Das Commission 1961.
13. Nehru-Fateh Singh Talks, February 8, 1961.
14. Master Tara Singh's Statement, September 1961.

Master Tara Singh's Statement, September 21, 1947

. . . The Hindus and the Sikhs will rise and fall together. Their fates are inextricably linked . . . . (*Hindustan Times*, September 21, 1947)

Dar Commission, 1948

The formation of linguistic provinces is sure to give rise to a demand for the separation of linguistic groups elsewhere. Claims have already been made by the Sikhs, Jats and others and these demands will in course of time be intensified and become live issues if once the formation of linguistic provinces is decided upon. (*Dar Commission Report*, 1948)

Master Tara Singh's Statement, February 1948

. . . Master Tara Singh, however, did not make a demand for a separate and independent sovereign state. He made it clear that it would be a part of the federal unit which will have to give financial aid and help in the defence. (*Tribune*, February 29, 1948)

Rejection of the Demand by Minority Committee, 1948

The question relating to the treatment to be accorded to the Sikhs was referred to a Committee of the Constituent Assembly which included Jawaharlal Nehru, Vallabhai Patel, Dr. Rajendra Prasad and Dr. Bhim Rao Ambedkar. This Committee appointed a ten-man sub-committee to evolve an agreed formula in respect of all communal questions affecting the East Punjab. The sub-committee recommended that "in view of the fact that seats in the House of People and the Legislative Assemblies of the States had been reserved for other religious minorities, provisions for reservation of (seats for religious minorities of) the East Punjab and other States should also be made if and where demanded." The Minority Committee, however disapproved the suggestion of the reservation of seats for religious minorities, and consequently no seats were reserved for the Sikhs in any legislature. (*Hindustan Times*, November 8, 1948 editorial)

Memorandum by the Sikh Members to the Constituent Assembly, 1948

On November 4, 1948 the Sikh members of the East Punjab Assembly, except Sardar Pratap Singh Kairon presented a 13-point memorandum to the Constituent Assembly. The important demands were as under:

1. Representation be given to the Sikhs on the basis of 1941

census without excluding Sikhs who had migrated to other provinces.

2. They should be given five per cent representation in the centre and reservation of seats in other provinces.
3. One Sikh minister and one Deputy minister be taken in the Central Cabinet.
4. Posts of the governor and the premier of the East Punjab should go alternately to a Hindu or a Sikh.
5. Fifty per cent representation in the Provincial Cabinet and the Assembly be reserved for them.
6. Gurgaon district and Loharu State should be separated from the East Punjab.
7. Forty per cent seats in services should be reserved for Sikhs.
8. If the above demands were rejected, Sikhs should be allowed to form a new province of seven districts including Ambala.

(*Hindustan Standard*, Calcutta, November 15, 1948)

Master Tara Singh's Statement, 1949

The demand for a 'Punjabi Suba' was made in 1948 by Master Tara Singh, the most prominent Akali leader. He said, "We have a culture different from the Hindus. Our culture is Gurumukhi culture and our literature is also in the Gurumukhi script . . . we want to have a province where we can safeguard our culture and our tradition.

Other Akali leaders also made similar declarations. Jathedar Pritam Singh, a prominent Akali leader, in his address to All India Sikh Students Federation, said that the Sikhs had a different culture, dress, living and a different code of behaviour and as such must have a separate province to themselves. (*Akali Patrika*, 2(1), October 11, 1949, Jullundur)

Shiromani Akali Dal Manifesto, 1951

"The true test of democracy, in the opinion of the Shiromani Akali Dal, is that the minorities should feel that they are really free and equal partners in the destiny of their country: (a) to bring home this sense of freedom to the Sikhs, it is vital that there should be a Punjabi speaking language and culture. This will not only be in fulfilment of the pre-partition Congress programme and pledges, but also in entire conformity with the universally recognised principles governing formation of provinces. (b) The Shiromani Akali Dal is in favour of formation of provinces on a linguistic and cultural basis throughout India, but it holds it is question of life and death for the Sikhs for a new Punjab to be created immediately. (c) The Shiromani Akali Dal has reason to believe that a Punjabi speaking province may give Sikhs the needful security. It believes in a Punjabi speaking province as an autonomous unit of India." (*The Spokesman*, August 29, 1951)

Population of Hindus and Sikhs in Punjab and PEPSU, 1951

TABLE 7.1: Population of Hindus and Sikhs in Punjab and PEPSU, 1951

North-Western Districts	Hindus (%)	Sikhs (%)	Northern & South-eastern Districts	Hindus (%)	Sikhs (%)
(a) *Punjab*			(a) *Punjab*		
Hoshiarpur	73.2	26.2	Hissar	91.3	7.7
Jullundur	43.6	56.5	Rohtak	98.5	0.7
Ludhiana	37.4	61.7	Gurgaon	82.1	0.7
Ferozepur	38.7	59.6	Karnal	90.3	8.9
Amritsar	27.7	70.7	Ambala	72.2	24.5
Gurdaspur	45.5	46.5			
(b) *Pepsu*			(b) *Pepsu*		
Patiala	52.1	47.1	Sangrur	65.4	33.4
Barnala	21.0	71.0	Mohindergarh	99.0	0.6
Bhatinda	21.6	73.1	Kohistan	89.0	9.0
Kapurthala	35.5	63.6			
Fatehgarh Sahib	33.6	65.2			

	Hindus	Sikhs	Others
(1) Punjab	63.5	33.4	3.1
(2) Pepsu	48.8	49.3	1.9
(3) Punjab and Pepsu	62.3	35.0	2.7

* India (Republic), Census Commissioner, *Census of India 1951*, Vol. VII, I, Part II-A. In 1956, States of Punjab and Pepsu were merged, and some of their districts were combined.

States Reorganisation Commission, 1955

Chairman: Shri S. Fazl Ali.
Members. Shri H.N. Kunzru; Shri K.M. Panikkar.
Secretary: Shri P.C. Chaudhuri.

APPOINTMENT

The States Reorganization Commission was constituted under the Ministry of Home Affairs vide their Resolution No. 53/69/53-Public dated December 29, 1953.

TERMS OF REFERENCE

The Commission will investigate the conditions of the problem, the historical background, the existing situation and the bearing of all important and relevant factors thereon.

CONTENTS

Introductory; *Part I*: The conditions of the Problem: State of the Indian Union; Rationale of Reorganization; Time for Reorganization; *Part II*: Factors Bearing on Reorganization: Cost of Change; Unity and Security of India; Language and Culture; Financial Viability; Requirements of National Development Plans; Regional Planning and Balanced Economy; Smaller *vs.* Larger States; Some Other Factors; *Part III*: Proposals for Reorganization: Basic Pattern of the Component Units; Madras; Kerala; Karnataka; Hyderabad; Andhra; Bombay; Vidarbha; Madhya Pradesh; Rajasthan; The Punjab; Delhi; Uttar Pradesh; Bihar West Bengal; Assam; Manipur; Orissa; The Reorganised Units; *Part IV*: Administrative and Allied Matters: Safeguards for Linguistic Groups; The Integration of Services; Financial and other Administrative Measures; The Unity of India; Notes and Summary; Note on Himachal Pradesh, Note on Uttar Pradesh; Summary of Conclusions and Recommendations; Appendices I and II.

RECOMMENDATIONS

The problem of the reorganization of States is urgent as with large-scale planning the country has to think in terms of enduring political units. The integration of State has removed the main hurdle in the way of rationalization of the existing units. Further deferment of a general reorganisation will cause dissatisfaction and disappointment.

In proposing any changes in the existing structure, due

consideration should be given to the unsettling consequences of reorganization. The changes proposed should be such as would compensate, in terms of the welfare of the people, for the administrative dislocation and the heavy burden on the administrative and financial resources of the country which they entail.

In the interests of the national unity, it is necessary that the administrative and political structure of the country should be based on the primacy of the nation.

The administrative set-up in strategic area should be determined primarily by consideration of national security. Where border areas are not under the direct control of the Centre, it would be safer to have relatively large and resourceful States.

It is neither possible nor desirable to reorganize States on the basis of the single test of either language or culture; a balanced approach, which takes all relevant factors into account, is necessary.

Financial viability has an important bearing on reorganization proposals, but it has to be considered along with other relevant factors.

Some degree of dislocation in the working of the next plan is likely to be caused by any scheme of reorganization; this dislocation, however, should be considered along with the possible advantages of reorganization. Steps should also be taken to minimise the unsettling effects of reorganization.

The States cannot be so reorganized as to conform to economic regions. Nor can the principle of economic self-sufficiency within an administrative unit be regarded as a clear criterion. Consistently with these principles it would be desirable to avoid as far as possible wide disparities in resources between the various States.

The wishes of the people should be regarded as an important factor bearing on reorganization but they have to be considered along with other relevant factor.

The facts of the existing situation are more important than the previous historical associations of differences areas. Undue importance cannot be attached, therefore, to historical arguments.

Geographical contiguity of the units is important from the point of view of administrative convenience. Other geographical factors have to be regarded secondary.

The existing constitutional disparity between the different constituent units of the Indian Union should disappear as a necessary consequence of reorganization.

In respect of three of the Part 'C' States, namely Himachal Pradesh, Kutch and Tripura, the Central Government should retain supervisory powers for specified period to maintain then present pace of development.

Such of the existing Part 'C' States as can not be merged in the adjoining areas for security and other imperative considerations should be administered by the Centre as "territories".

The component units of the Indian Union should thus consist of two "categories":

(a) "States" forming primary federating units of Indian Union; and
(b) "Territories" which are 'Centrally' administered.

THE PUNJAB

There is no case for dividing the present Punjab State. PEPSU and Himachal Pradesh should, however, be merged in the Punjab.

Loharu Sub-Tehsil of Hissar District, should be transferred to Rajasthan.

Himachal Pradesh should be represented in the Punjab Cabinet by at least one member.

Master Tara Singh's Reaction to States Reorganisation Commission, 1955

Master Tara Singh denounced the report as a 'decree of Sikh annihilation'.

Source: 1. *States Reorganisation Commission Report*, 1955;
2. *The Spokesman*, October 19, 1955.

Regional Plan, 1957

Outline of the Regional Committees in the Punjab

1. There will be one legislature for the whole of the reorganised State of the Punjab, which will be the sole law-making body for the entire State, and there will be one Governor for the State, aided and advised by Council of Ministers responsible to the State Assembly for

the entire field of administration.

2. For the more convenient transaction of the business of Government with regard to some specified matters, the State will be divided into two regions, namely, the Punjabi-speaking and the Hindi-speaking regions.

3. For each region there will be a regional committee of the State Assembly consisting of the members of the State Assembly belonging to each region including the Ministers from that region but not including the Chief Minister.

4. Legislation relating to specific matters will be referred to the Regional Committees. In respect of specified matters proposals may also be made by the Regional Committees to the State Government for Legislation or with regard to question of general policy not involving any financial commitments other than expenditure of a routine and incidental character.

5. The advice tendered by the Regional Committees will normally be accepted by the Government and the State Legislature. In case of difference of opinion, reference will be made to the Governor whose decision will be final and binding.

6. The Regional Committees will deal with the following matters:

(i) Development and economic planning, within the framework of the general development plans and policies formulated by the State legislature;

(ii) Local self-governments, that is to say, the constitutional powers of municipal corporation, improvement trusts, district boards and other local authorities for the purpose of local self-government of village administration including Panchayats;

(iii) Public Health and Sanitation, local hospitals and dispensaries;

(iv) Primary and secondary education;

(v) Agriculture;

(vi) Cottage and small-scale industries;

(vii) Preservation, protection and improvement of stock and prevention of animal diseases, veterinary training and practice;

(viii) Ponds and prevention of cattle trespass;

(ix) Protection of wild animals and birds;

(x) Fisheries;

(xi) Inns and Inn-keepers;

(xii) Markets and fairs;
(xiii) Co-operative societies; and
(xiv) Charities and charitable institutions, charitable and religious endowments and religious institutions.

7. Provision will be made under the appropriate Central Statute to empower the President to constitute regional committees and to make provision in the rules of business of Government and the rules of procedure of the Legislative Assembly in order to give effect to the arrangements outlined in the preceding paragraphs. The provisions made in the rules of business and procedure for the proper functioning of regional committees will not be altered without the approval of the President.

8. The demarcation of the Hindi and Punjabi regions in proposed Punjab State will be done in consultation with the State Government and the other interests concerned.

9. The Sachar Formula will continue to operate in the area comprised in the existing Punjab State and in the area now comprised in the *Pepsu* State, the existing arrangements will continue until they are replaced or altered by agreement later.

10. The official language of each region will, at the district level and below, be the respective regional language.

11. The State will be bilingual recognising both Punjabi (in Gurmukhi script) and Hindi (in Devnagari script) as the official languages of the State.

12. The Punjab Government will establish two separate departments for developing Punjabi and Hindi languages.

13. The general safeguards proposed for linguistic minorities will be applicable to the Punjab like other States.

14. In accordance with and in furtherance of its policy to promote the growth of all regional languages the Central Government will encourage the development of the Punjabi language.

Das Commission, 1961

BACKGROUND

Fasts by Akali Leaders, 1961

In 1957, the Akalis did not contest the Second General Elections, as they had reached on understanding with the Congress Party.

However, this understanding proved to be short-lived. The political activities of the Akali Dal were resumed in 1959. In 1959-60, the elections to the Shiromani Gurudwara Prabandhak Committee (SGPC) were held. SGPC is a statutory body set up in 1925 to control and supervise the management of Sikh Gurudwaras. The members are elected exclusively by the Sikh electorate. Master Tara Singh, a veteran Akali leader, master-minded the victory of his group. He exhibited by his victory that he represented the Sikh community in the real sense of the word. The Akali Dal launched their 'morchas' in 1961. About fifty thousand Akalis were said to have courted arrest in support to Punjabi Suba. Master Tara Singh recruited Sant Fateh Singh to his fold. Master Tara Singh and his lieutenant Sant Fateh Singh undertook fast unto death to achieve the formation of Punjabi Suba. Both of them broke their fasts without achieving Punjab Suba. However, Master Tara Singh was promised by the Centre that a Commission would be appointed to inquire into the discrimination against Sikhs.

APPOINTMENT AND RECOMMENDATIONS

On August 28, 1961 Pt. Jawaharlal Nehru announced the constitution of the Das Commission comprising S.R. Das, retired Chief Justice of India as chairman and Dr. C.P. Ramaswamy Aiyer and M.C. Chagla, members.

The Commission examined the grievances of the Sikh community under four heads,namely:

(i) Constitutional and Legal,
(ii) Political and Social,
(iii) Public Services, and
(iv) Government patronage to business and industry.

The Commission concluded: that there was no cause of discrimination against the Sikhs in Punjab.

The appointment and findings of the Commission failed to satisfy the aspirations of the Akali Dal.

Nehru-Fateh Singh Talks, February 8, 1961

Sant Fateh Singh accompanied by S. Harbans Singh Gujral and S. Gurbax Singh met the Prime Minister in his room.

Death of Feroze Gandhi Condoled

Sant Ji condoled the death of Shri Feroze Gandhi and for a minute both the leaders remained silent. Sant Ji expressed his grief over this loss to the country and added that as a mark of respect to the memory of the deceased, he had stopped the Jatha of Satyagrahis on the evening of this sad death.

The Prime Minister said that he had been anxious to meet Sant Fateh Singh but he did not like to bother him earlier as he wanted him to recover fully after his fast.

Punjab being discriminated against

Sant Fateh Singh said that he was very happy to meet Prime Minister and he was sure that the problem of the Punjab could be solved by the Prime Minister alone. He added that difference of opinion could be removed by discussions and by trying to understand each other's point of view. The peace and stability needed to be restored to Punjab, could be done through the efforts of the Prime Minister. He further added that he was not a politician but had dragged himself into this movement on account of his belief that in the formation of linguistic States, Punjab is being discriminated against.

P.M.'s tribute to Punjabis

The Prime Minister agreed with Sant Ji and said that he himself thought the same way – "Legitimate grievances of any party or people should, of course, be considered and removed by negotiation". He however, regretted that Punjab had already suffered a great deal on account of partition and the present difference of opinion was rather unfortunate. He said that the Punjabis were very hard working people and as such they had made remarkable success in so short a time. He had before his eyes both Punjabis and Bengalis who had suffered because of the partition of their States. Punjabis have recovered much more quickly from this set-back by dint of their hard labour, with the result that though Punjab was today comparatively a small State, it was better of, both economically and otherwise, than many other bigger States.

At this stage Sant Fateh Singh requested the Prime Minister that Sant Ji's colleagues may also be called in. The Prime Minister readily agreed to this suggestion and they were called in. S. Harbans Singh Gujral and S. Gujral and S. Gurbax Singh joined the talks from this stage.

Malicious propaganda against Sikhs

Sant Fateh Singh said that in his view peace, stability and economic progress could only be achieved in the Punjab if Punjabi Suba was formed. The Sikhs feel that the Government have some suspicions about their integrity and accusations were being made by responsible Congress Ministers and others of their being in league with some foreign countries and Pakistan etc. and, therefore, their genuine and just demand of a Unilingual Speaking State is being denied to them.

Master Tara Singh's Statement, September 1961

"If we face the problem open-mindedly then the situation can be summed up in three sentences :

(1) A national principle has been accepted that to make the people feel the flow of freedom states should be created on the continuity of language affording full scope for development of one national language in one state.
(2) This principle has been implemented in other parts of India and even in Punjab an area has been demarcated which the government experts feel is a Punjabi-speaking area.
(3) This Punjabi-speaking area, with any adjustments that the expert opinion may deem necessary, is not being afforded the status of a state, simply because the Hindus do not agree to it."

Tara Singh pleaded: "If I have committed a mistake, correct me. If I have done the right thing, march with me. If I have acted treacherously, punish me." (*The Spokesman*, November 6, 1961)

8

PARLIAMENT COMMITTEE ON THE DEMAND FOR PUNJABI SUBA, 1965

Chairman:	Sardar Hukam Singh
Members	
Lok Sabha:	Dr. M.S. Aney; Shri Mani Ram Bagri; Chowdhury Brahm Perkash; Shri Surendranath Dwivedy; Sardar Dhanna Singh Gulshan; Shri Hem Raj; H.H. Maharaja Karni Singhji of Bikaner; Shri Lahri Singh; Sardar Surjit Singh Majithia; Shri K.D. Malaviya; Shri H.N. Mukerjee; Shri Krishna Chandra Pant; Shri Sadhu Ram; Shri Amar Nath Vidyalankar.
Rajya Sabha:	Shri Bansi Lal; Shri Uttam Singh Dugal; Shri Jogendra Singh; Shri Dahyabhai V. Patel; Shri Sadiq Ali; Kumari Shanta Vasisht and Shri Atal Behari Vajpayee.
Secretary	Shri S.L. Shakdher.
Dy. Secretary:	Shri M.C. Chawla.

Appointment

On September 6, 1965, the Minister of Home Affairs (Shri Gulzari Lal Nanda) made a statement in Lok Sabha in which he referred to the several steps which had been taken in recent years to arrive at an amicable arrangement for meeting the needs of the Punjabi and Hindi-speaking regions of the Punjab State and said that "the whole question (of formation of a Punjabi-speaking State) can be examined afresh with an open mind". He had added that "Government would be prepared to have further talks on the subject. We may hope that a

---

Source: Report, Lok Sabha, New Delhi, 1966, iii, 90 p.

co-operative solution would be discovered based on goodwill and a reasoned approached". A similar statement was made in the Rajya Sabha on the same date by the Minister of State in the Ministry of Home Affairs (Shri Jai Sukhlal Hathi).

Subsequently, on the September 23, 1965, the Minister of Home Affairs (Shri Gulzarilal Nanda) recalling his earlier statement of the September 6, 1965, announced in Lok Sabha Government's decision "to set up a Committee of the Cabinet to pursue this matter further" and added "I would request you (the Speaker, Lok Sabha) and the Chairman, Rajya Sabha, to set up for the same purpose a Parliamentary Committee of members of both Houses of Parliament presided over by you". Concluding his Statement, he expressed his confidence that "the efforts of this Cabinet Committee and of the Parliamentary Committee will lead to a satisfactory settlement of the question. A similar statement was made by the Minister of Home Affairs in Rajya Sabha also on the same date.

Terms of Reference

To arrive at an amicable arrangement for meeting the needs of the Punjabi and Hindi speaking regions of the Punjab State.

Contents

Composition of the Committee; Report; Introduction; Evolution of the Demand for Punjabi Suba; Working of the Regional Formula in Punjab; Demand for Haryana State; Merger of Hill Areas of Punjab in Himachal Pradesh; Conclusions and Recommendations; Notes by Members; Appendices from I to X.

Recommendations

Cooperative Solution

It was the earnest desire of the Committee to find a cooperative solution of the vexed linguistic problem facing Punjab which would be universally acceptable to all. After perusing the large number of memoranda/representations received by the Committee and hearing the various view-points expressed by the different witnesses representing the various shades of opinion, it soon became evident that it was not possible to arrive at any 'cooperative solution' which would be unanimously acceptable to all without reservations. Nor is unanimity possible or necessary on all matters in a democratic set up. The next best thing was for the Committee to look for a solution which would be acceptable to the largest number of people and which would also be in the best interests of not only the people and the State of Punjab but also in the best interests of the country as a whole from the point of view of affinity between the various communities and the economic and cultural well being of the people.

Various Alternatives

(a) *Status quo:* The bulk of the evidence before the Committee suggest the reorganisation of the State on linguistic basis. Even the Chief Minister of the Punjab State admitted that the present position needed a change and *status quo* in its entirely was not possible. But a section of the people from the Punjab convassed before the Committee that the *status quo* might be maintained in the Punjab. In support of this argument, it was urged that the Punjab was not a unilingual State but a bilingual State with the people speaking both Hindi and Punjabi spread over throughout the State, although in varying percentages. Another argument advanced in favour of the *status quo* was that any division of the State would adversely affect the economy of the State and the resulting units would not be financially viable. A third argument advanced in favour of the *status quo* was that any reorganisation of the State would not be in the interests of the security of the country and would weaken the defences of India.

The Committee have carefully considered all the arguments advanced for and against the reorganisation of the existing State of Punjab. The witness who appeared before the Committee could not satisfactorily prove to them as to how the linguistic reorganisation of the State of Punjab would adversely affect the economy of the area or the defence of the country. The Committee has no authentic data before them to show that it would be so. The Committee requested the Ministry of Home Affairs. Government of India, to furnish a note or a paper on the viability of the proposed Punjabi-speaking State from the point of view of defence and the finance but the Government expressed their inability to comply with request as the former did not like to involve themselves either way 'in a controversy' (vide D.O. No. 38/3/66-S.R. dated the 11th March, 1966 from Shri B.S. Raghavan Deputy Secretary, Ministry of Home Affairs to Shri M.C. Chawla, Deputy Secretary, Lok Sabha Secretariat). Although this Committee are not an expert body on matters relating to the defence and finance but it should be self-evident that security or defence of the country should not be affected by a mere linguistic reorganisation of the State. Defence is a Central Subject and the State Governments have nothing to do with it. On the contrary, it should strengthen the defence of the country, if there are on the borders people whose political and economic aspirations are fully satisfied and they can devote all their energies towards the task of nation-building and development, instead of frittering away their energies in political agitations or the like. While the Committee agree that financial viability should be considered as an important factor while creating a unit, nevertheless having regard to the economic progress of the State so far (which judged from the per capita income in each region of the State, which is the highest in the whole country) it can be safely visualised that the human and material resources (both tapped and untapped) of the State are sufficient to make each unit economically viable. Looked at from another aspect, it was urged before the Committee that no State in the Union is at present economically viable, as most of the States are dependent on the Union Government for grants and loans. Be that as it may, the arguments of viability has no force in denying a well-recognised and well-established principle of formation of States on linguistic basis which has been universally applied in the rest of the country.

As regards the State being bilingual, it had been already recognised in the Regional Formula that there were two distinct regions, namely, the Punjabi Region and Hindi Region. In each region were included the predominantly Punjabi-speaking and the Hindi-speaking districts respectively. Thus, the State was already divided into a distinct Punjabi Region and the Hindi Region. People of neither region are satisfied with the *status quo*. As overwhelming majority of the memoranda received by the Committee and of the witnesses who appeared before them were in favour of the two regions being made full-fledged States with suitable adjustment of boundaries which could be done by a Boundary Commission or any other expert body appointed for the purpose.

In the opinion of the Committee, maintenance of *status quo* in the

State would cause further unrest among the people. Past experience has shown that the present bilingual State of Punjab has been the scene of internal disorder, agitations and counter-agitations. Any make-shift arrangement is not likely to provide a lasting solution to this vexed question. The Committee, therefore, feel that it is high time that some permanent and satisfactory solution of the problem is found.

An apprehension was expressed before the Committee by a section of the Punjabi-speaking Region who was opposed to the bifurcation of the existing State of Punjab that in the event of creation of a new Punjabi State, a large scale migration of population and capital, and consequent human suffering, might take place. The Committee's attention was also drawn in this connection to the "Questionnaire Reports of the Committees of the Constituent Assembly of India (Third series), page 222 (serial No. 19 of the Questionnaire) regarding the proposed provinces of Andhra, Karnataka, Kerala and Maharashtra" which was issued by the Linguistic Provinces Commission set up under the aegis of the Constituent Assembly of India (known as Dar Commission) where in the Commission posed this specific question and asked for public opinion as to the steps that should be taken for its prevention. The Committee note that this particular aspect was not ultimately touched upon by that Commission. Similar fears were expressed at the time of the formation of the Andhra State and Maharashtra and Gujarat States but experience has shown that they did not materialise. Obviously, such fears are ill-convinced and ill-founded. This is more so in the present case especially when Hindus and Sikhs have close ethnic, racial, religious and cultural relationship.

(b) *Strengthening of Regional Committees:* A view was expressed before the Committee that the present State of Punjab might remain united and more powers could be given to Regional Committees, but it was not specifically stated as to how such Committees could be given more powers or what the nature of those powers was. A vague suggestion was made that the decisions of the Regional Committees could be final in respect of the subjects entrusted to them. In fact, it was also mooted that they might function something like "Sub-Legislatures", but what the powers and functions of "Sub-Legislatures" would be was never specified. As has been stated in detail in chapter third of this report, the working of the Regional Committees has been an utter failure. Suffice it to say that no body, including the Ministers of the Punjab, was satisfied with the working of these Committees and, in fact that the sooner they were scrapped the better. The Committee, therefore, feel that the idea of continuing Regional Committees in any form should be given up.

(c) *Reorganisation on Linguistic Basis:* It would not perhaps be out of place to refer here to the following passage from the Report of the Linguistic Provinces Commission (Dar Commission, 1948) which enunciates the cardinal principle for the formation of linguistic provinces, which rests upon two alternative grounds: "–upon the theory that these linguistic groups are sub-nations and as such contracting parties to the constitution from which the Federation and the Centre derive their existence and power; alternatively it rests upon the administrative advantage, which may result from bringing together people speaking one language, in imparting education and in the working of courts, legislatures, governmental machinery and democratic institutions".

The only alternative which found the largest measure of support was that the present State of Punjab should be reorganised on a linguistic basis on which basis all the States in the country had been formed. This will not only satisfy the political and economic aspirations of the people of the respective areas but also end once for all the political controversy on a vexed question in this strategic border area and help remove the tension prevailing for the last so many years.

A suggestion was made that the question of formation of a Punjabi-speaking State might be referred to the people of Punjab for decision by a referendum and the wishes of the people ascertained. Apart from the fact that no such references were held for the reorganisation of the rest of the States in the country on linguistic basis, such a course is neither feasible nor desirable. The wishes of the people are easily known through their elected and representative bodies and other leaders of public opinion.

After carefully considering all the view points represented before the Committee and taking all relevant factors into consideration, the Committee have come to the conclusion that it would be in the larger interests of the people of these areas and the country as a whole that the present State of Punjab be reorganised on linguistic basis. The Punjabi Region specified in the First Schedule to the Punjab Regional Committees Order, 1957, should form a unilingual Punjabi State, the hill areas of the Punjab included in the Hindi Region of the

Punjab which are contiguous to Himachal Pradesh and have linguistic and cultural affinity with that Territory should be merged with Himachal Pradesh. The remaining areas of the Hindi-speaking Region of the Punjab should be formed as a separate unit called the Haryana State. The distribution of population and density of population in the: (i) Hill area, (ii) Haryana area, and (iii) other areas of the existing State of Punjab are indicated in Appendix X. In case there are any boundary adjustments to be made among the three States of Punjab, Himachal Pradesh and Haryana, a Committee of experts be set up immediately to suggest the necessary adjustments.

A view was expressed before the Committee that a Vishal Haryana Prant be formed by bringing together of certain areas of Rajasthan, Uttar Pradesh, Delhi and the Haryana areas of the Punjab. The Committee have refrained from expressing opinion on these view-points or suggestions nor have they applied their mind to these proposals as the Committee consider that these matters do not fall within the scope of their competence. A suggestion was also made that the Haryana area of the Punjab might be joined with Delhi, as originally it was detached from Old Delhi Province. Here too the Committee cannot make any recommendation. The Committee leave it to the Government to consider in due course whether, after retaining New Delhi Municipal Committee area intact under the direct administration of Central Government it is feasible to join Delhi Municipal Corporation areas with the Haryana Prant which the Committee have proposed in this report.

The question of parts of Rajasthan being added to the new Punjabi State or the Haryana State was considered to be beyond the competence of the Committee and hence the Committee did not examine it.

The Committee trust that all the various political and other elements in the country in general, and Punjab in particular, will accept the solution proposed in a cooperative spirit and work for the harmony and prosperity of the heroic people inhabiting the present State of Punjab.

9

PUNJAB BOUNDARY COMMISSION, 1966 AND CREATION OF HARYANA AND HIMACHAL PRADESH

Terms of Reference

On 23 April, 1966 a three-member Punjab Boundary Commission (Chairman Justice Jayantilal Chhotalal Shah, Members: S. Dutt, and M.M. Philip) was set up to recommend :

(i) The adjustment of the existing boundaries of the Hindi and Punjabi regions of the present State (Punjab) to secure linguistic homogeneity and also;
(ii) To indicate boundaries of the Hill areas of the present State which were contiguous to Himachal Pradesh and had cultural and linguistic affinities.

The Commission was required to apply the linguistic principle with regard to the census figure of 1961 and other relevant considerations. The Commission was asked to take into consideration other factors, namely :

1. Administrative convenience.
2. Economic well-being.
3. Geographical contiguity; and
4. Facility of Communication.

The Commission submitted its report on 31 May, 1966.

Recommendations

131. In recommending adjustment of the boundary, due

consideration must undoubtedly be given to the effective maintenance of irrigation and power distribution systems. The proposed division of the State of Punjab necessitates division of the irrigation and power distribution systems, and that must be done keeping in mind the paramount purpose of ensuring linguistic homogeneity. The points of division suggested by the Chief Engineer (Projects) which may avoid serious dislocation of the irrigation system is to fix the boundary line at certain points indicated by him, but acceptance of the scheme would completely upset the principle of linguistic homogeneity. Another Engineer suggested that the canal systems should be located intact, canal by canal, in the State they serve and not cut, particularly not towards or near the tail ends, for the effect of such cutting on the inhabitants depending on canal irrigation in the tail end areas of another state may result in serious consequences. He said that if it is not at all practicable to leave the whole canal system in one State, the division should be at only those points from below which fairly high discharge still flows, so that satisfactory distribution of water to cultivators served by the irrigation canals beyond these points may be ensured. He then suggested that in respect of the Upper Bari Doab Canal from Ravi river, the Eastern Canal from Beas River and Sirhand Canal no division was necessary. He suggested that division of the Bhakra Main branch should be made at certain points near Tohana. About Narwana Branch, he suggested that a suitable point for division could be at Tangri south of Ambala. He also said that electric power supply Grids should be cut, if necessary, at certain fixed points to ensure that no untoward result would ensure therefrom, and since there were two Grids in Punjab: (i) 132000 Volts Jogindernagar, Amritsar, Ludhiana, Ropar and Bhakra Grid and (ii) 220000 Volts Bhakra, Ganguwal, Kotla, Dhulkot, Panipat and Delhi Grid, to ensure effective supplies to consumers it would be advisable to retain the first Gird in one State as a whole and to divide the second Grid at any of the sub-stations Ganguwal, Kotla, Dhulkot or Panipat. He suggested that division at any other point will greatly complicate the supplies of power to the State for which the control of the Grid line is in other hands. These suggestions which contain several alternatives may also seriously upset the linguistic principle.

132. The Chief Engineer, Electricity Board, was of the view that the proposed reorganisation of the present State of Punjab was likely to create serious impact on the future set up of the Punjab State

Electricity Board, and recommended that Joint Electricity Board with separate Chief Engineers for Distribution System for the consuming States and a common organisation for planning, execution and operation of major works, (not covered by Distribution System) should be constituted. In his opinion, broadly speaking, there should be a common Board with subjects like generation, transmission works, their planning, design, procurement, execution, research and operation etc. under Central Agencies, and distribution workers and their operation should be dealt with by respective Chief Engineers who would be *ex officio* members of the Board, but responsible to the respective States for carrying out the works according to the budget requirements. The Joint Board as proposed, in the view of the Chief Engineer, would meet all the technical requirements of the Region and be in the interest of coordinated power development and power consumption, and meet the regional interests of the respective States.

133. The sources of water supply and power lie in a majority of cases within the hilly areas of Himachal Pradesh, and the beneficiaries of water and power will hereafter in respect of some channels of supply, be the Punjabi-speaking, the Hindi-speaking States, Delhi and Rajasthan. Though Himachal Pradesh derives no direct irrigation benefit from the waters of the rivers having their sources in its territory, its claim to have a voice in the maintenance of reservoirs, disposal of waters and distribution of power cannot be ignored.

134. A legalistic approach to a complex problem on the just solution of which depends the prosperity of many territorial units, would be impermissible. Having carefully considered the problem, we are of the view that constitution of Joint Boards, one for Irrigation and another for power, of the beneficiary States and the State which is the source of supply of water and power, having authority to lay down policies and execute them, consistently with the legitimate need of the State concerned, under the supervision of the Central Government may be a practical solution of the problem raised by the division of the territory into separate units in which the canal and power supply lines are situated.

135. We recommend that:

1. (i) The Districts Simla, Kulu, Kangra, Lahaul-Spiti;
   (ii) Development Blocks Gagret, Amb and Una (excluding the village Kherabagh, Samipur, Bhabhaur and Kalsch and

village Kosri from Tehsil Una (District Hoshiarpur);

(iii) Tehsil Nalagarh (District Ambala);

(iv) Enclaves Dalhousie, Balun and Bukloh in Chamba District which are hill areas and have cultural affinity with the people of Himachal Pradesh;

should be merged with Himachal Pradesh.

2. That districts Gurdaspur (excluding Dalhousie, Balun and Bukloh), Amritsar, Kapurthala, Jullundur, Ferozepore, Bhatinda, Patiala, Ludhiana, and Tehsils Barnala, Malerkotla and Sangrur (District Sangrur), Tehsil Ropar (District Ambala), Tehsils Dasuya, Hoshiarpur and Garhshankar, and Development Blocks Anandpur, Nurpurbedi and villages Kherabagh, Samipur, Bhabhaur and Kalseh from Una Block and village Kosri in Una Tehsil will form the Punjabi-speaking State; and
3. That District Hissar, Mohindergarh, Gurgaon, Rohtak and Karnal, and Tehsils Narwana and Jind (District Sangrur) and Tehsil Kharar (including Chandigarh Capital Project), Naraingarh Ambala, and Jagadhri will form the Hindi-speaking State.

Adjustments of the boundaries of the three States should be made on the division of territory as set out.

136. In conclusion we would like to make a few general observations.

Agitation for setting up separate linguistic States in the territory of Punjab raised its head more than 18 years ago. It is unfortunate that strong passions have been aroused on that problem. The Punjab has been at the forefront among the States of India in war and peace. It has been the sword arm of the country in times of war; and in times of peace it has led all other States in agricultural production, and parts of the State are humming with small scale industry. We fervently hope that after the dust of conflict has settled, the people of Punjab to whichever State they belong will in healthy rivalry achieve higher targets of production, agricultural and industrial, and bring about all-round prosperity and contribute to a higher standard of living for all our people. The people of Punjab share the common aspirations and ideals with the rest of our people, and we trust that nothing will be done in either State to prejudice the linguistic preferences of the minorities residing within their territory. It is on the cultivation of a tolerant attitude towards the claims of others within the constitutional framework that democracy flourishes, and we share the optimism with many others that the people of Punjab will maintain the democratic ideal.

31-5-1966

Sd/- (J.C. SHAH)
Chairman,
Punjab Boundary Commission
*Sd/- (S. DUTT),
Member,
Punjab Boundary Commission
Sd/- (M.M. PHILIP),
Member,
Punjab Boundary Commission
Subject to my note on Kharar-Chandigarh.
Sd./- S. DUTT.

***Note on Kharar-Chandigarh by S. Dutt**

I regret that I am unable to agree with the recommendations which my colleagues propose to make about Kharar tehsil including Chandigarh. In my view, Kharar tehsil as a whole, with the exception of Kalka Police Station, should be merged with the proposed Punjabi State; the area of Kalka Police Station should be merged with Himachal Pradesh. I give my reasons below:

2. Kharar is a tehsil of Ambala district with a total population of 332.361 according to the 1961 Census, of whom 183,452 (55.2 per cent) are Hindi-speaking and 148,908 (43.9 per cent) are Punjabi-speaking. The total rural population of the tehsil is 200,425 of whom 112,723 (56.2 per cent) are Punjabi-speaking and 86,777 (43.3 per cent) are Hindi-speaking. The urban population totals 131,936 — 15.1 per cent Punjabi-speaking and 73.3 per cent Hindi-speaking. The majority of the urban population belong to Chandigarh Capital Project area (89,000). The other three towns are Kharar with a population of 8,216, Kurali (6,390), Manimajra (9,901) and Kalka (18,668). It will thus be seen that while in the whole of Kharar tehsil the Hindi-speaking people are in a majority (55.2 per cent) in the rural areas the Punjabi-speaking people hold the

majority (56.2 per cent).

3. Under the Sachar Formula of 1949 Kharar tehsil was placed in the Punjabi region. It did not then include Pinjore Police Station which in 1961 had a population of 28,635. Pinjore, which formerly formed part of the Pepsu, was included in the Kharar tehsil after Pepsu's merger with the Punjab. Under the Punjab Regional Committees Order, 1957, Chandigarh was made bilingual and therefore it was not included either in the Punjabi-speaking or in the Hindi-speaking region. The rest of the Kharar tehsil was divided between the two regions. Indeed, Kharar is the only tehsil in Punjab which was divided between the Hindi and the Punjabi regions under the Regional Committee Order. The Hindi areas of tehsil Kharar consist of 17 villages in Zail Mubarakpur and the areas of the Pinjore Police Station and Kalka Police Station; the rest of the tehsil exclusive of the Chandigarh Capital Project area forms part of the Punjabi-speaking region. Both the language areas of the tehsil are contiguous with the Chandigarh capital, but it appears that the latter is surrounded on three sides by the areas included in the Punjabi region and on the remaining side on the south-east by the area included in the Hindi region. A further point need to be mentioned. Although Chandigarh Capital Project is bilingual for the purpose of election of the Legislative Assembly it forms part of the Chandigarh Assembly Constituency. This Constituency includes, besides Chandigarh, the area of the Kharar tehsil also.

President's Assent to the Recommendations of the Boundary Commission

The recommendations of the Punjab Boundary Commission with some modifications were incorporated into the Punjab Reorganization Bill, which was duly approved by both Houses of Parliament. The President gave his assent on 18 September, 1966. As per recommendations of the Boundary Commission, the Punjabi-speaking areas went to Punjab — that Districts of Gurdaspur (excluding Dalhousie, Balum and Bukloh), Amritsar, Kapurthala, Jullundur, Ferozepur, Bhatinda, Patiala, Ludhiana and Tehsils Barnala, Malerkotla and Sangrur (District Sangrur), Tehsil Ropar (District Ambala), Tehsils Dasuya, Hoshiarpur and Garhshankar and Development Blocks Anandpur, and villages Kherabagh, Samipur, Bhabhaur and Kalseh from una Block and village Kosri will form the

Punjabi-speaking States.

The Hindi-speaking areas that went to Haryana were — district Hissar, Mohindergarh, Gurgaon, Rohtak and Karnal and Tehsils Narwana and Jind (District Sangrur) and Tehsil Kherar (including Chandigarh Capital Project) Naraingarh, Ambala and Jagadhri. The Hilly areas were given to Himachal Pradesh. These were:

(i) Districts Shimla, Kulu, Kangra, Lahaul Spiti.
(ii) The Development Blocks Gagret, Amb and Una (excluding the villages Kherabagh, Samipur, Bhabhaur and Kalseh) and village Kosri from Tehsil Una (District Hoshiarpur).
(iii) Tehsil Nalagarh (District Ambala).
(iv) Enclaves Dalhousie, Balum and Bukloh in Chamba District which are hill area and have cultural affinity with the people of Himachal Pradesh should be merged with Himachal Pradesh.

Reactions to the Punjab Reorganisation Act

The Punjab Reorganization Act was welcomed in Haryana. At the time of the publication of the Report, Sant Fateh Singh had gone abroad. He on his return from foreign tour, opposed the reorganization, claiming that "the Punjab Boundary Commission Report smacks of communalism" and declared that "Chandigarh at no cost will be allowed to remain out of Punjabi Suba". A similar stand was taken by Master Tara Singh. In an Akali Conference Tara Singh said that "the new Punjabi Suba was yet another move to enslave the Sikhs". (*The Hindu*, 23 September, 1966).

The Akali Dal (Master Tara Singh) held demonstrations to mark its utter disapproval of the scheme of reorganization of Punjab resulting in the formation of a "lame" Punjabi Suba and reiterated its demand for a Sikh Homeland. Copies of the Punjab Reorganization Bill were burnt at the meeting organized by Dal.

The Jana Sangh dissociated itself and boycotted all functions organized in connection with the formation of the Punjabi Suba. The Communist Party was also dissatisfied with the bifurcation of Punjab and on making Chandigarh a Union Territory, which in its opinion, actually formed part of the Punjabi-speaking areas.

The Reorganization Bill became an Act on 18 September, 1966. The Act provided for bifurcation of Punjab into Punjabi Suba and Haryana from November 1966.

10

ANANDPUR SAHIB RESOLUTION, 1977

Text of Anandpur Sahib Resolution Authenticated by Sant Harchand Singh Longowal

The Draft of the New Policy Programme of the Shiromani Akali Dal

Adopted by the Working Committee at its meeting held at Sri Anandpur Sahib on 16-17 October, 1973 to be approved by the General House of the Akali Dal at its Session at Ludhiana on 28-8-1977 (*Later passed in the form of 12 Resolutions*).

Giani Ajmer Singh,
Secretary,
Shiromani Akali Dal
1-8-77

Educational Targets of the Khalsa Panth

The Shiromani Akali Dal aims at grooming the Sikhs into a strong and sturdy Nation, highly educated, fully aware of its fundamental rights, very well versed in various arts and ever ready to honour the more outstanding of its sons.

The Shiromani Akali Dal regards the educationists, scientists, philosophers, poets, writers an artists of the Sikh Nation as its most prized asset.

The Shiromani Akali Dal would extend at all help to the students from rural and backward classes to acquire higher education.

There has been much confusion and misunderstanding about the text of the resolution adopted by the Working Committee of the Akali Dal at Anandpur Sahib. The Shiromani Akali Dal has been consistently making efforts to clear the spirit and the content of the resolution. Now, an authentic English version is being issued for the benefit of non-Punjabi knowing country-men.

(Sant) Harchand Singh Longowal
President, Shiromani Akali Dal

FOREWORD

The Shiromani Akali Dal undoubtedly, is a great organisation whose coming into existence has been a matter of pride for the Sikhs. Its entire history is a glorious record of struggle and agitations, victories and achievements of which it can be justly proud of. The past record of the party vouchsafes that whosoever has ever tried to confront it, he did have to perish ultimately. The most momentous part played by it in the Freedom Struggle of the country would ever form an indelible part of the history written in letters of gold.

Shiromani Akali Dal has been guiding the Sikhs according to exigencies of the situation for their rights and for a respectable status in the set-up of the country. Its objective has been exaltation of the Sikh Panth and for the achievement of this lofty ideal Shiromani Akali Dal has been adopting different and varied means.

Keeping in view the anti-Sikh policies of the Congress government and the political, social and economic conditions pulsating in the country, the Shiromani Akali Dal, has decided to redraw the aims and objectives of the Sikh Panth and to give a more vigorous lead for their achievements so that they by so doing it may serve the larger interests of the Panth, the Punjab as also the country and thus live up to the expectations of the Sikhs.

For such a purpose, a sub-committee of Sikh intellectuals and thinkers was formed by the Shiromani Akali Dal at a meeting of its Working Committee held on 11-12-1972 to draw up the draft of 'Policy-Programme', with the General Secretary of the Party, S. Surjit Singh Barnala, as its Chairman, and S. Gurcharan Singh Tohra, M.P. President, Shiromani Gurdwara Prabandhak Committee, Jathedar Jivan Singh Umranangal, S. Gurmit Singh, ex-Minister, Dr. Bhagat Singh, ex-Minister, S. Balwant Singh, ex-Finance Minister, S. Gian Singh Rarewala, S. Prem Singh Lalpura, S. Jaswinder Singh Brar, General Secretary, Shiromani Akali Dal, S. Bhag Singh, ex-M.L.A., Major General Gurbux Singh Badhni and S. Amar Singh Ambalvi, Advocate, as its members.

This Sub-Committee had eleven sittings beginning with the first at Amritsar, on 23-12-1972. Most of the meetings were held at Chandigarh for its peaceful and congenial atmosphere.

All the members of the Sub-Committee evinced keen interest in its working and engaged themselves in very interesting and useful discussions which were a treat to watch and partake of. A unanimous report was ultimately drawn up after very close deliberations on each and every aspect of the matters and more suitable of their aspects. Actuated by feelings of love for the Sikhs Panth, more of its eminent Army Generals, legal experts, doctors, political thinkers, experienced politicians and religious leaders joined together to lend their helping hands to draw up this plan for a more glorious future of the Panth. During their discussions a very happy balance of love for the Panth and the Country was all too evident, as also the keenness to safeguard the interest of the Sikhs and the Country.

When the meticulously drawn up report of S. Surjit Singh sub-committee was presented in the meeting of the Working Committee of Shiromani Akali Dal held at Shri Anandpur Sahib, the sacred and historic seat of the Tenth Lord, it was approved, after close discussions extending over two days, for placing it before the General House.

This draft, is, therefore, being sent to you to enable you to study it in depth so that the meeting of the General House may be benefited by your valued opinion.

With Panthic Love and regards,

Office of	*Yours humbly,*
Shiromani Akali Dal,	Ajmer Singh,
Sri Amritsar,	*Secretary,*
1-8-1977	*Shiromani Akali Dal*

RESOLUTIONS

Adopted, in the light of the Anandpur Sahib Resolution, at the open session of the 18th All India Akali Conference held at Ludhiana on 28-29 October, 1978 under the Presidentship of Jathedar Jagdev Singh Talwandi are as under and it was after the passing of these Resolutions that Shiromani Akali Dal started the struggle therefor.

Resolution 1

Moved by S. Gurcharan Singh Tohra, President Shiromani Gurdwara Prabandhak Committee and endorsed by S. Prakash Singh Badal, Chief Minister, Punjab.

The Shiromani Akali Dal realized that India is a federal and republican geographical entity of different languages, religions and cultures. To safeguard the fundamental rights of the religious and linguistic minorities, to fulfil the demands of the democratic traditions and to pave the way for economic progress it has become imperative that the Indian constitutional infrastructure should be given a real federal shape by redefining the Central and State relations and rights on the lines of aforesaid principles and objective.

The concept of total revolution given by Lok Naik Sh. Jayaparkash Narain is also based upon the progressive decentralization of powers. The climax of the process of centralization of powers of the States through repeated amendments of the Constitution during the Congress regime came before the countrymen in the form of the Emergency, when all fundamental rights of all citizens were usurped. It was then that the programme of decentralization of powers ever advocated by Shiromani Akali Dal was openly accepted and adopted by other political parties including Janata Party, C.P.I.(M), A.D.M.K. etc.

Shiromani Akali Dal has ever stood firm on this principle and that is why after very careful considerations it unanimously adopted a resolution to this effect first at All India Akali Conference, Batala, then at Shri Anandpur Sahib which has endorsed the principle of State autonomy in keeping with the concept of federalism.

As such, the Shiromani Akali Dal emphatically urges upon the Janata Government to take cognizance of the different linguistic and cultural sections, religious minorities as also the voice of millions of people and recast the constitutional structure of the country on real and meaningful federal principles to obviate the possibility of any danger to National unity and the integrity of the country and further, to enable the states to play a useful role for the progress and prosperity of the Indian people in their respective areas by the meaningful exercise of the powers.

Resolution 2

The momentous meeting of the Shiromani Akali Dal calls upon the

Government of India to examine carefully the long tale of the excesses, wrongs, illegal actions committed by the previous Congress government, more particularly during Emergency, and try to find an early solution to the following problems :

(a) Chandigarh originally raised as a Capital for Punjab should be handed over to Punjab.
(b) The long standing demand of the Shiromani Akali Dal for the merger in Punjab of the Punjabi speaking areas, to be identified by linguistic experts with village as an unit, should be conceded.
(c) The control of Head Works should continue to be vested in Punjab and, if need be, the Reorganization Act should be amended.
(d) The arbitrary and unjust Award given by Mrs. Indira Gandhi during the Emergency on the distribution of Ravi-Beas waters should be revised on the universally accepted norms and principles, thereby justice be done to Punjab.
(e) Keeping in view the special aptitude and martial qualities of the Sikhs the present ratio of their strength in Army should be maintained.
(f) The excesses being committed on the settlers in the Terai region of U.P. in the name of Land Reforms should be vacated by making suitable amendments in the Ceiling Law on the Central guidelines.

Resolution 3

(*Economic Policy Resolution*)

The chief sources of inspiration of the economic politics and programme of the Shiromani Akali Dal are the secular, democratic and socialistic concepts of Sri Guru Nanak Dev and Sri Guru Gobind Singh Ji. Our Economic programme is based on three basic principles:

(a) Dignity of Labour.
(b) An economic and social structure which provides for the uplift of the poor and depressed sections of society.
(c) Unabated opposition to concentration of economic and political power in the hands of the capitalists.

While drafting its economic policies and programme, the Shiromani Akali Dal in its historic Anandpur Sahib Resolution has laid particular stress on the need to break the monopolistic hold of the capitalists foisted on the Indian economy by 30 years of Congress rule in India. This capitalistic hold enabled the central government of assume all powers in its hands after the manner of Mughal Imperialism. This was bound to thwart the economic progress of the states and injure the social and economic interests of the people. The Shiromani Akali Dal once again reiterates the Sikh way of life by resolving to fulfil the holy words of Guru Nanak Dev :

"He alone realizes the True Path who labours honestly and shares the fruits of that Labour."

This way of life is based upon three basic principles:

(i) Doing honest labour,
(ii) Sharing the fruits of this labour, and
(iii) Meditation on the Lord's Name.

The Shiromani Akali Dal calls upon the Central and the State Government to eradicate unemployment during the next ten years. While pursuing this aim special emphasis should be laid on ameliorating the lot of the weaker sections, Scheduled and depressed classes, workers, landless and poor farmers and urban poor. Minimum wages should be fixed for them all.

The Shiromani Akali Dal urges upon the Punjab Government to draw up such an economic plan for the State as would turn it into the leading province during the next ten years, by raising per capita income to Rs. 3,000 and by generating an economic growth rate of 7% per annum as against 4% at National level.

The Shiromani Akali Dal gives first priority to the redrafting of the taxation structure in such a way that the burden of taxation is shifted from the poor to the richer classes and an equitable distribution of National income is ensured.

The main plank of the economic programme of the Shiromani Akali Dal is to enable the economically weaker sections of the Society to share the fruits of National income.

The Shiromani Akali Dal calls upon the Central Government to make an international air-field at Amritsar which should also enjoy the facilities of a dry port. Similarly a Stock Exchange should be opened at Ludhiana to accelerate the process of industrialisation and economic growth in the State. The Shiromani Akali Dal also desires that suitable amendments should be made in the Foreign Exchange rules for free exchange of foreign currencies and thereby removing the difficulties being faced by the Indian emigrants.

The Shiromani Akali Dal emphatically urges upon the Indian Government to bring a parity between the prices of the agricultural produce and that of the industrial raw materials so that the discrimination against such states which lack these materials may by removed.

The Shiromani Akali Dal demands that exploitation of the producers of the cash crops like cotton, sugarcane, oil-seeds etc. at the hands of the traders should be stopped forthwith and for such a purpose arrangements for the purchase of these crops by the government, at remunerative prices should be made. Besides, effective steps should be taken by the government for the purchase of cotton through the Cotton Corporation.

The Shiromani Akali Dal strongly feels that most pressing National problem is the need to ameliorate the lot of millions of exploited persons belonging to the scheduled classes. For such a purpose the Shiromani Akali Dal calls upon the Central and State Governments to earmark special funds. Besides the State Governments should allot sufficient funds in their respective budgets for giving free residential plots both in the urban and rural areas to the scheduled castes.

The Shiromani Akali Dal also calls for the rapid diversification of farming. The shortcomings in the Land Reforms Laws should be removed, rapid industrialization of the State ensured, the credit facilities for the medium industries, expanded and unemployment allowance given to those who are unemployed. For remunerative farming perceptible reduction should be made in the prices of machinery like tractors, tubewells as also the inputs etc.

Resolution 4

This huge session of the Shiromani Akali Dal regards the discrimination to which the Punjabi language is being subjected in the adjoining States of Himachal, Haryana, Delhi and Jammu and Kashmir etc. It is firm demand that in accordance with the Nehru

Language Formula the neighbouring States of Punjab should give second language status to the Punjabi language because a fairly large sections of their respective population are Punjabi-speaking.

Resolution 5

The meeting reiterates the claims of the refugees who had migrated to Jammu and Kashmir as a result of the partition of the country, no compensation has been provided to them even after such a long time and these unfortunate refugees are rotting in the campus ever since then.

This Akali Dal Session therefore forcefully demands that their claims should be soon settled and immediate steps should be taken to rehabilitate them even if it involves an amendments in Section 370.

Resolution 6

The 18th session of the All India Akali Conference takes strong exceptions to the discrimination to which the minorities in other States are being subjected and the way in which their interests are being ignored.

As such, it demands that injustice against the Sikhs in other States should be vacated and proper representation should be given to them in the government services, local bodies, state legislatures through nomination, if need be.

Resolution 7

The 18th session of the All India Conference notes with satisfaction that mechanization of farming in the country handled to increase in the farm yield and as a result the country is heading towards self sufficiency.

However, the session feels that poor farmers are unable to take to mechanisation because of the enormity of the cost involved.

As such, the Shiromani Akali Dal urges upon the Government of India to abolish the excise duty on tractors so that with the decrease in their prices the ordinary farmers may also be able to avail of farm machinery and contribute to the growth of gross agricultural produce of the country.

Resolution 8

The meeting of the Shiromani Akali Dal appeals to the Central and State Governments to pay particular attention to the poor and labouring masses and demands that besides making suitable amendments in the Minimum Wages Act, suitable legal steps should be taken to improve the economic lot of the labouring class to enable it to lead a respectable life and play a useful role in the rapid industrialization of the country.

Resolution 9

This session seeks permission from the Government of India to instal a broadcasting station at Golden Temple, Amritsar, for the relay of 'Gurbani Kirtan' for the spiritual satisfaction of those Sikhs who are living in foreign lands.

The session wishes to make it clear that the entire cost of the proposed Broadcasting Project would be borne by the Khalsa Panth and its over all control shall vest with the Indian Government. We have every hope that the government would have no hesitation in conceding this demand after the consideration.

Resolution 10

The huge Session of the Shiromani Akali Dal strongly urges upon the Government of India to make necessary amendments in the following enactments for the benefit of the agricultural classes who have toiled hard for the larger national interests :

1 By suitable amendment in the relevant clause of the Hindu Succession Act, a woman should be given rights of inheritance in the properties of her father-in law instead of the father's.
2. The agricultural land of the farmers should be completely exempted from the Wealth Tax and the Estate Duty.

Resolution 11

The vast session of the Shiromani Akali Dal strongly impresses upon the Government of India that keeping in view the economic backwardness of the scheduled and non-scheduled castes provisions proportionate to population should be made in the budget for utilization for their welfare. A special ministry should be created at the Central as a practical measures to render justice to them on the basis of the reservation.

The Session also calls upon the government that in keeping with the settlement already no discrimination should be made between the Sikh and Hindu Harijans in any part of the country.

Resolution 12

The Congress government is called upon to vacate the gross injustice discrimination done to Punjab in the distribution of Ravi-Beas waters. The Central Government must also give approval for the immediate establishment of six sugar and four textile mills in Punjab so that the state may be able to implement its agro-industrial policy.

BASIC POSTULATES OF THE SHIROMANI AKALI DAL

As adopted by the Working Committee of the Shiromani Akali Dal at its meeting held at Sri Anandpur Sahib on 16-17 October, 1973.

(A) *Postulates*

1. The Shiromani Akali Dal is the very embodiment of the hopes and aspirations of the Sikh Nation and as such is fully entitled to its representation. The basic postulates of this Organisation are Human progress and ultimate unity of all human beings with the Spiritual Soul.
2. These postulates are based upon the three great principles of Guru Nanak Dev Ji, namely, a Meditation on God's Name, dignity of labour and sharing of fruits of this Labour. (Nam Japo, Kirat Karo, Wand Chhako)

(B) *Purposes*

This Shiromani Akali Dal shall ever strive to achieve the following aims:

1. Propagation of Sikhism and its code of conduct and denounciation of atheism.

2. To preserve and keep alive the concept of distinct and independent identity of the Panth and to create an environment in which national sentiments and aspirations of the Sikh Panth will find full expression, satisfaction and growth.
3. Eradication of Poverty and Starvation, by increased production and more equitable distribution of wealth and the establishment of a just social order sans any exploitation.
4. Vacation of discrimination on the basis of caste, creed or illiteracy in keeping with basic principles of Sikhism.
5. Striving for the removal of diseases and ill-health, denouncement of use of intoxicants and enlargement of facilities for physical well-being to prepare and enthuse the nation for the national defence.

First Part

The Shiromani Akali Dal considers in its primary duty to inculcate among the Sikhs, religious fervour and a pride in their rich religious heritage for which it proposes to pursue the following programmes :

(a) Reiteration of the unity (Oneness) of God, meditation on His Name, recitation of *Gurbani*, renewal of faith on the ten Holy Sikh Gurus and the Holy *Sri Guru Granth Sahib* and other appropriate measures for such a purpose.

(b) Grooming accomplished preachers, *Ragis, Dhandis*, and poets in the Sikhs Missionary College for a more effective propagation of Sikhism, Sikh Philosophy, belief in Sikh code of conduct and *Kirtan* etc. at home and abroad, in schools and colleges, in villages and in cities as indeed at every place.

(c) Baptising the Sikhs (*Amrit Prachar*) on a vast scale, with particular emphasis on schools and colleges of which the teachers and the taught shall be enthused through regular study circles.

(d) Reinculcate the religious practice of 'DASWAND' among the Sikhs. (Giving on tenth of one's earnings for the welfare of the Community).

(e) Generating feelings of respect for the Sikh intellectuals, writers, preachers, *granthis*, etc., who also in turn, would be enthused to improve upon their accomplishments while conforming to the basic Sikh tenets and traditions.

(f) Streamlining the Gurdwara administration by giving better training to their workers. Appropriate steps would also be taken to maintain Gurdwara buildings in proper condition. For such a purpose, the party representatives in the Shiromani Gurdwara Prabandhak Committee and local Committees would be directed time to time to pull their weight.

(g) Making appropriate arrangements for the error free publication of Gurbani; promoting research work in the ancient and modern Sikh history as also its publication; rendering *Gurbani* in other languages and producing first rate literature on Sikhism.

(h) Taking appropriate steps for the enactment of an All India Gurdwara Act with a view to introduced improvements in the administration of the Gurdwaras throughout the country and to reintegrate the traditional preaching sects to Sikhism like Udasis and Nirmalas with the mainstream of Sikhism without in any way encroaching on the properties of the respective individuals 'maths'.

(i) Taking such steps as may be necessary to bring the Sikh Gurdwaras all over the world under a single system of administration with a view to run them according to the basic Sikh norms and to pool their sources for the dissemination of Sikhism on a wider and more impressive scale.

(j) Striving for free access to all those holy Sikh Shrines, including Nankana Sahib from which the Sikh Panth has been separated, for pilgrimage and proper upkeep.

Political Goal

The political goal of the Panth without doubt, is enshrined in the commandments of the Tenth Lord, in the pages of Sikh history and in the very heart of the Khalsa Panth, the ultimate objective of which is the pre-eminence of the Khalsa.

The fundamental policy of the Shiromani Akali Dal is to seek the realization of this birth right of the Khalsa through creation of congenial environment and a political set up.

For attainment of this Aim

1. The Shiromani Akali Dal is determined to strive by all possible means to :

(a) Have, all those Punjabi speaking areas deliberately kept out of Punjab, such as Dalhousie in Gurdaspur District; Chandigarh, Pinjore-Kalka and Ambala Saddar etc. in Ambala District; the entire Una tehsil of Hoshiarpur District; the 'Desh' area of Nalagarh; Shahabad and Gulha blocks of Karnal District; Tohana Sub-tehsil, Ratia block and Sirsa tehsil of Hissar District and six tehsils of Ganganagar District in Rajasthan; merged with Punjab to constitute a single administrative unit where the interests of the Sikhs and Sikhism are specifically protected.

(b) In this new Punjab and in other States the Centre's interference would be restricted to Defence, Foreign relations Currency and General Communication; all other departments would be in the jurisdiction of Punjab (and other states) which would be fully entitled to frame own laws on these subjects for administration. For above departments of the Centre, Punjab and other States contribute in the proportion to representation in the Parliament.

(c) The Sikhs and other religious minorities living out of Punjab should be adequately protected against any kind of discrimination.

2. The Shiromani Akali Dal would also endeavour to have the Indian Constitution recast on real federal principles, with equal representation at the Centre for all the States.

3. The Shiromani Akali Dal strongly denounces the foreign policy of India framed by the Congress party. It is worthless, hopeless and highly detrimental to the interests of the country, the National and the mankind at large. Shiromani Akali Dal shall extend its support only to that foreign policy of India which is based on the principles of peace and national interests. It strongly advocates a policy of peace with all neighbouring countries, especially those inhabited by the Sikhs and their sacred shrines. The Akali Dal is of the firm view that our foreign policy should in no case play second fiddle to that of any other country.

4. The Shiromani Akali Dal shall raise its firm voice against any discrimination to any Sikh (or even other) employees of the Central or State Governments. The Shiromani Akali Dal shall also endeavour to maintain the traditional position of the Sikhs in all the wings of defence departments and the Panth would pay particular attention to the needs of the Sikh Armymen. The Shiromani Akali Dal would also see that 'kirpan' is accepted as an integral part of the uniform of the Sikhs in Army.
5. It shall be the primary duty of the Shiromani Akali Dal to help rehabilitate the ex-servicemen of the Defence Department in the civil life and or such a purpose it would extend them every help to enable them to organize themselves so that they are able to raise their voice in an effective way of giving adequate concessions and proper safeguards for a life of self-respect and dignity.
6. The Shiromani Akali Dal is of the firm opinion that all those persons males or females—who have no been convicted of any criminal offences by a court of law, should be at liberty to possess all types of small arms, like revolvers, guns, pistols, rifles, carbines etc., without any licence, the only obligation being their registration.
7. The Shiromani Akali Dal seeks ban on the sale of liquor and other intoxicants and shall press for prohibition on the consumption of intoxicants and smoking on public places.

Economic Policy and Programme of the Shiromani Akali Dal

As adopted by its Working Committee on 17th October, 1973 at its meeting held at Sri Anandpur Sahib :

Although the mainstay of the Indian economy is agriculture and all those political powers who claim to raise social structure on the basis of justice cannot afford to ignore this fact, yet this is hard fact that the levers of economic powers, continue to be in the hands of big traders, capitalists and monopolists. Some marginal benefits might have accrued to other classes, but the real benefits of economic growth have been reaped by these categories during the last 26 years after Independence. The political power has also been misappropriated by these classes which are wielding the same for their own benefits. As such, any peaceful attempt to usher in a new era of social justice would have to break the economic and political strongholds of these categories of the people.

The Shiromani Akali Dal strongly advocates that the growing gulf between the rich and the poor, in the urban and rural areas both, should be abridged but, it is of the firm opinion that, for such a purpose, the first assault would have to be made on the classes who have assumed all the reins of economic power in their hands. In rural areas, the Akali Dal is determined to help the weaker classes, like the scheduled castes, backward classes, landless tenants, ordinary labourers, the poor and middle class farmers. For such a purpose, it stands for meaningful land reforms which envisage a ceiling of 30 standard acres and the distribution of excess land among the poor farmers.

The motto of the Shiromani Akali Dal is to provide employment for all, requisite food and clothing for all, a house to live in, suitable transport and to create means to fulfil all those necessities of a civilized life without which life appears incomplete.

As such, the economic policy of the Shiromani Akali Dal shall endeavour to achieve the following objectives :

Agriculture Sector

During recent years the agriculture sector has witnessed land reforms and green revolution. The Shiromani Akali Dal undertakes to enrich the green revolution by an increase in yield per acre. It shall also ensure perceptible improvement in the standard of living of all rural classes, more particularly of the poor and the middle class farmers, as also the landless labourers. For such a purpose it plans to work on the following lines:

(a) Introducing land reforms and measures for increasing agricultural production with a view to remove the growing gap between the rich and the poor. For such a purpose the existing legislation on land ceiling would have to be revised and a firm ceiling of 30 standard acres per family would have to be enforced with proprietory rights to the actual tillers. The excess land would be distributed among the landless tenants and poor farmers, while the cultivable government land unused shall be distributed among the landless classes, especially the scheduled castes and tribes. While distributing such lands the interests of Harijans and landless labourers would be particularly taken care of. The Akali Dal would also consider the possibilities of allowing the tenants to service loans by mortgaging land under their plough, as also prohibiting the scheduled castes/tribes and backward classes from mortgaging the land distributed among them.

(b) The Shiromani Akali Dal shall work for the modernization of farming and would also try to enable the middle class and poor farmers to seek loans and inputs made available by different agencies.

(c) The Shiromani Akali Dal shall try to fix the prices of the agricultural produce on the basis of the returns of the middle class farmers. Such prices would be notified well before the sowing seasons and only the State governments would be empowered to fix such prices.

(d) The Shiromani Akali Dal stands for complete nationalization of the wholesale trade in foodgrains through the establishment of State agencies.

(e) The Shiromani Akali Dal strongly opposes the demarcation of food zones and the attendant restriction on the movements of foodgrains. The whole country should be the single food zone.

The party shall make special efforts to bring the Thein Dam and the Bhartiya Thermal plants to a speedy completion so that increased and cheaper power and irrigation facilities are made available. Definite efforts would be made for the establishment of an Atomic power station in the state.

Co-operative societies would be set up in the rural areas. In all those areas where canal water is not available small irrigation projects would be taken in hand.

Industrial Sector

The Shiromani Akali Dal strongly advocates that all key industries should be under the public sector.

It is of the opinion that consumer industries should be immediately nationalized to stabilize the prices of the consumer goods and to save the poor consumer from exploitation at the hands of the industrialists and the middlemen.

The public sector industries should be established in such a way that the imbalance between different States is removed.

A planned effort to establish agro-industries in the rural areas should be made to relieve the growing population pressure in the urban areas. The industrial management should be democratized by enabling the workers to have a say in the management and by fair distribution of profits between the industrialists and the workers. The credit agencies, especially the nationalized banks, should be directed to invest a fixed ratio of their deposits in the rural areas. Every industrial unit beyond worth one crore assets should be brought under the public sector. The Akali Dal stands for progressive nationalization of Transport.

The Public Sector units should be fully autonomous and manned by competent young executives drawn from a central pool of talent.

Economic Policy

The Shiromani Akali Dal demands that the whole tax structure be revised in such a way that the evasion of taxes and the flow of black money is completely eradicated. It stands for a straight forward system of taxation. The present infrastructure of taxation weighs heavily against the poor and enables the rich to bypass it. The party stands for a more realistic policy in this respect so that the black money running a parallel economy may be usefully employed.

Workers, Middle Class Employees and Agricultural Labour.

For their benefits the Shiromani Akali Dal would try its best :

1. To fix need based wages for industrial workers.
2. To bring progressive improvement in the standard of living of government employees.
3. To re-assess the minimum wages of agricultural labour and to standard of living for them.
4. To take necessary steps to provide roofed accommodation for standard of living for them.
5. To take necessary steps to provide roofed accommodation for the rural and urban poor.

Unemployment

The Shiromani Akali Dal stands for full employment in the country. For such a purpose it is of the firm opinion that the Govt. must provide immediate employment to the educated and trained persons, otherwise reasonable unemployment allowance should be paid to them. This amount should be shared by the Centre and the state government. The minimum rates of such an allowance should be as under :

1. Matric and or trained hands	Rs. 50 per month
2. B.A.	Rs. 70 per month
3. M.A.	Rs. 100 per month
4. Engineers and Doctors	Rs. 150 per month
5. Other trained Labour	Rs. 50 per month

All persons above the age of 65, should be given old-age pension.

Weaker Section and Backward Classes

The Shiromani Akali Dal shall try to improve the economic conditions of the backward classes and weaker sections of society by extending them facilities for education, employment and other concessions, to enable them to come at par with other sections of society. Foodgrains at cheaper rates would be made available to them.

Educational and Cultural

The Shiromani Akali Dal aims at grooming the Sikhs into a strong and sturdy Nation highly educated, fully aware of its fundamental rights, very well-versed in various arts and ever ready to honour the more outstanding of its sons. For such a purpose :

1. The Shiromani Akali Dal regards the educationalists, scientists, philosophers, poets, writers and artists of the Sikh Nation as its most prized asset.
2. The Shiromani Akali Dal stands for compulsory and free education up to matric standard.
3. To check the growing rate of unemployment, Shiromani Akali Dal would try to introduce such courses of study as would enable their students to get immediate employment on completion of a course.
4. The Shiromani Akali Dal shall make arrangements for the education of the rural and weaker classes and would also make provisions for the higher education of the more promising students among them.

5. Punjabi would be a compulsory subject for all students up to the matric standard.
6. Special attention would be paid to the science and technical field of education, with particular emphasis on the study of Nuclear physics and space science in the University.
7. The Shiromani Akali Dal shall try to improve the standard of games and bring them on level with international standards.

Sd/-
Giani Ajmer Singh
Secretary,
Shiromani Akali Dal

Dated 1-8-1977

11

WHITE PAPER ON PUNJAB, 1984

Background: Operation Blue Star

The growing militancy of Sant Bhindranwale (devotion to Sikh Panth by his followers) led to Operation Blue Star – a military term, on June 5, 1984.

Operation Blue Star had five components:

1. To clear the Golden Temple and "neutralise" Bhindranwale.
2. To simultaneously raid extremist hide-outs in 34 gurdwaras all over the state.
3. To start mop-up operations in villages and roundup extremists.
4. To safely escort the Akali leaders within the Golden Temple complex.
5. To take over BSF pickets along the Indo-Pak border so as to prevent any infiltration or exist.

A 36-hour Statewide curfew was clamped from 9 p.m. on June 4, 1984 and all road, rail and air traffic suspended. The fight between the Sikh militants entrenched in the Golden Temple and the army started in the morning of 5th June. "We will not surrender". "We will fight to the last man", said the 37 year old Bhindranwale in what was apparently his last interview with a journalist. "No might in the world can make as bow our head" (An eye-witness account by Brahma Chillaney, Correspondent, Associated Press (AP) of America, Appendix F. *Tragedy of Punjab*.

Among the dead were Sant Bhindranwale and two former Indian Army Generals, who were leading the Sikh militants. According to unconfirmed reports a large number of about 1,000 Sikh militants and 200 army men lost their lives in the Operation Blue Star.

The Operation Blue Star sent waves of shocks among the Sikh

community. Many sections of the public and legislators wanted the Government of India to come out with the factual position. The Government of India, issued a White Paper on the Punjab Agitation on 10 July, 1984.

Summary of the White Paper

During the last three years Punjab has been the scene of a series of agitations. Four distinct factors were noticeable at work:

- The agitations sponsored by the Shiromani Akali Dal:
- A stridently communal and extremist movement which degenerated into open advocacy of violence and sanction for the most heinous crimes against innocent and helpless citizens and against the State:
- Secessionist and anti-national activities; and
- Involvement of criminals, smugglers, other anti-social elements and Naxalites who took advantage of the situation for their own ends.

2. The secessionist agitations and terrorist groups took advantage of the cover of agitations provided by the Akali Dal leadership to pursue a systematic plan of stockpiling of arms and ammunition in places of worship and of misusing the sacred precincts of the Golden Temple and other gurdwaras to direct and commit acts of murder, sabotage, arson and loot. Simultaneously a determined effort was made to drive a wedge between Hindus and Sikhs.

3. Gradually a secessionist and anti-national movement with the active support of a small number of groups operating from abroad, dominated the scene. The Akali Dal leadership surrendered the initiative and control over the agitation to the terrorists and was unwilling to negotiate a settlement on the basis of any reasonable framework offered by Government.

4. Government made every possible effort to bring about a settlement. Till the very last moment discussions were held with the Akali Dal leaders who were found to be more rigid than before.

5. The subversive activities of terrorists had assumed menacing proportions in the context of India's security environment. The influence of external forces, with deep-rooted interest in the disintegration of India, was becoming evident. In these circumstances

the Army was called in to meet the challenge to the security, unity and integrity of the country.

Demands of the Shiromani Akali Dal and Government Response

The Akali Dal sponsored an agitation in support of a set of demands submitted to Government in October, 1981. Some of these demands had their origin in a resolution, generally known as the Anandpur Sahib Resolution, adopted by the Akali Dal in October 1973. This resolution asked for the immediate merger with Punjab of Punjabi speaking Sikh populated areas in Haryana, Rajasthan and Himachal Pradesh besides Chandigarh. It also sought a fundamental change in the Centre-State relations, restricting the role of the Centre to defence, foreign affairs, telecommunications, currency and railways. The authenticated version of the resolution, issued in November 1982, emphasized the constitution of "a single administrative unit where the interests of Sikhs and Sikhism are specially protected."

2. The Prime Minister met the representatives of the Akali Dal on October 16, 1981 and thereafter again on two occasions in November 1981 and April 1982. The process of consultation and discussion initiated thus has not been interrupted by the Government since then. There have been several rounds of talks, both open and secret, as well as tripartite discussions in which leaders of Opposition parties in Parliament also participated.

3. The main issues discussed with the Akali Dal representatives fall into three broad categories, viz.,

(i) those which concern the Sikh community as a religious group:
(ii) those which relate to other States besides Punjab; and
(iii) general issues.

(i) Demands Concern the Sikh Community as a Religious Group

4. The religious demands finally put forward by the Akali Dal were:

(a) Grant of 'holy city' status to Amritsar on the pattern of Hardwar, Kashi and Kurukshetra:
(b) Installation of 'Harmandir Radio' at the Golden Temple to relay *kirtan*;

(c) Permission to Sikhs travelling by air to wear *kirpans* on domestic and international flights; and

(d) Enactment of All India Gurdwara Act.

(a) *Grant of 'holy city' status to Amritsar*

5. Government has not conferred 'holy city' status on the cities mentioned or any other city. Restrictions on the sale of meat or liquor in cities like Hardwar and Kurukshetra had been imposed by the local authorities or State Governments. On February 27, 1983 the Prime Minister announced that the sale of tobacco, liquor and meat would be banned in a demarcated area around the Golden Temple as well as the Durgiana Temple in Amritsar. Action has already been taken in pursuance of this announcement and shops selling tobacco, liquor and meat within a radius of 200 metres of Harmandir Sahib and Durgiana Temple have already been shifted. The grant of 'holy city' status as such to any city is not in consonance with the secular nature of our Constitution.

(b) *Installation of transmitter station at the Golden Temple*

6. While private radio broadcasting facilities cannot be allowed to any group, the Government of offered to arrange for direct relay of *shabad kirtan* from the Golden Temple through the Jalandhar station of All India Radio. However, the Shiromani Gurdwara Prabandhak Committee did not extend the requisite facilities to the All India Radio authorities.

(c) *Carrying Kirpans on Flights*

7. Instructions were issued in February 1983 permitting Sikh passengers to carry *kirpans* which do not exceed 22.8 cm (9″) in length and whose blade length does not exceed 15.24 cm (6″) on domestic flights. International regulations do not permit carrying of weapons on international carriers.

(d) *All India Gurdwara Act*

8. On February 27, 1983 the Prime Minister announced that Governments of the States where the gurdwaras are located and the

managements of the gurdwaras would bc consulted to arrive at thc consensus needed for enacting such a legislation.

(ii) Disputes Which Relate to Other States besides Punjab

(a) *River Waters*

9. Government were agreeable to rescinding the agreement of December 31, 1981 between the Governments of Punjab, Haryana and Rajasthan and to refer the dispute regarding the surplus waters of Ravi-Beas to a tribunal presided over by a judge of the Supreme Court under the Inter State Water Disputes Act, 1956 to determine afresh the allocation between the two States. However, the Akali Dal wanted to reopen the 1955 agreement on the basis of which arid and dry lands of the Indus basin in Rajasthan are being irrigated. It also wanted the Yamuna waters to be taken into account. The widening of the scope of the dispute relating to the Ravi-Beas waters was obviously not acceptable to Haryana and Rajasthan as well as to the Central Government.

10. The Prime Minister has assured the Akali Dal that the interest of Punjab would not be affected. She suggested that a committee of experts should go into the whole question of augmenting the availability of water in the basin. Its recommendations would receive priority consideration by Government. Even these assurances had no effect in changing the rigid position of the Akali Dal.

(b) *Territorial Issue*

11. In 1966 the Shah Commission recommended that Chandigarh be given to Haryana. However, in 1970 Smt. Indira Gandhi, as Prime Minister, announced that Chandigarh would go to Punjab. Under this decision –

(1) The Capital project area of Chandigarh would go to Punjab,
(2) A part of Fazilka Tehsil (including Abohar) of Ferozepur district of Punjab would be transferred to Haryana, and
(3) As regards other claims and counter-claims for the readjustment of inter-state boundaries a Commission would be appointed.

The above decision could not be implemented due to the change in the Government of the State.

12. Government have indicated their willingness to abide by any one of the following alternatives:

(1) Implement of the 1970 decision;
(2) Referring all disputes and claims including Chandigarh to a new Commission;
(3) Dividing Chandigarh between Punjab and Haryana with Punjab getting the major share, and referring the remaining disputes to a Commission; or
(4) Adopting any other alternative acceptable to both States.

13. Within the above framework a large number of different formulations were proposed, none of which was acceptable to the Akali Dal leadership.

14. The Prime Minister has repeatedly declared that Chandigarh would go to Punjab provided Haryana were suitably compensated. As late as on June 2, 1984 the Prime Minister in her broadcast reiterated that Chandigarh would go to Punjab provided Haryana gets its share of some Hindi speaking areas which are now in Punjab.

15. The Akali Dal is, however, adamant that Chandigarh should be transferred to Punjab immediately and other disputes referred to a Commission. Thus stalemate continues.

(iii) General Issues

(a) Centre-State Relations

16. Government set up in June 1983 a Commission under the Chairmanship of Mr. Justice Ranjit Singh Sarkaria to examine and review the existing arrangements between the Union and the States in regard to powers, functions and responsibilities in all spheres and recommend such changes or measures as may be appropriate. The Commission was to keep in view the scheme and the framework of the Constitution designed to ensure the unity and integrity of the country. Government invited the Akali Dal to make any submissions it wished before the Sarkaria Commission within its terms of reference. However, the Akali Dal insisted that Government make a specific mention of the Anandpur Sahib Resolution, which restricts

the Central role to foreign affairs, defence, currency and communications, while referring the matter to the Sarkaria Commission.

17. During discussions the Akali Dal had agreed not to press this. But subsequently Sant Harchand Singh Longowal, President of the Akali Dal reiterated the demand.

18. The Anandpur Sahib Resolution is at total variance with the basic concept of the unity and integrity of the nation as expressed in our Constitution. It cannot be accepted as a basis for discussion.

(b) *Other Demands*

19. Among their other demands, the Akali Dal representatives emphasized the following two as issues of special concern to them:

(i) Grant of second language status to Punjabi language in Haryana, Delhi, Himachal Pradesh and Rajasthan.
(ii) Stopping the uprooting of Punjabi farmers from Terai areas of Uttar Pradesh.

(i) *Second Language Status for Punjabi Language*

20. The demand for the teaching of Punjabi as a second language in areas of Haryana and Rajasthan, where there is a sizeable Punjabi speaking population, can be met within the framework of the three language formula agreed at the Chief Ministers' Conference in 1961. This was explained to the Akali Dal. Haryana, Rajasthan and Himachal Pradesh have taken action to provide facilities to teach Punjabi at the primary and the secondary stages.

(ii) *Punjabi Farmers in the Terai region of U.P.*

21. The State Government of Uttar Pradesh have denied that Sikh farmers were being uprooted from the Terai area. The State legislation is intended to prevent unauthorised occupation of tribal land. The Tharu and Buxar tribes have been dispossessed of substantial areas of land cultivated by them prior to 1947. Of the 7860 unauthorised occupants, more than 5000 were from Uttar Pradesh itself, and one common policy was being followed with regard to all such persons. Local authorities had been directed to take action only

in accordance with the principles of natural justice and within the framework of the law.

(c) *Amendment of Article 25(2)(b) of the Constitution*

22. A completely new demand was raised by the Akali Dal in January 1984 asking for an amendment of Article 25(2)(b) of the Constitution. Simultaneously an agitation was announced for burning and mutilation of copies of the Constitution of India. Even though this demand was raised, the Akali Dal was not clear about the nature of the amendment. On May 1, 1984, it was reported that SGPC President had constituted a 21-member committee of experts to suggest relevant amendments.

23. Even though Government maintain that Article 25(2)(b), far from weakening the distinct identity of the Sikh community was in fact a recognition of that identity, it wanted to allay any misgivings on this point. Accordingly the Home Minister declared on March 31, 1984 that the Government would be prepared to consult the SGPC and other representatives of the Sikh community as well as legal experts and undertake such legislation by way of amendment as may be necessary to remove such doubts.

24. The Akali Dal also wanted to link the demands for the amendment of Article 25 with the idea of a separate personal law for the Sikhs. However, no concrete proposals have been submitted.

25. The timing and manner in which the demand for amendment of Article 25 was presented are typical of the Akali Dal's approach to negotiations. When some issues appeared to have been settled, new issues were raised, thereby frustrating the possibility of a settlement The Akali Dal appeared to want to keep an agitation going on some issue or other, regardless of the consequences of such agitation which progressively grew more and more violent.

12

RAJIV GANDHI-LONGOWAL ACCORD, 1985

Prime Minister Shri Rajiv Gandhi on Punjab*

Introduction

Sir, regarding the problem in Punjab, we have been trying to get to the root of it. What we really have to fight is not the political aspect. That is where we must adjust and accommodate always, within the constraints of a united and integral India — that is where we must be flexible. At the same time, we must be very firm where there is any question of using violence towards those ends, where there is any question of using terrorism towards those ends, where there is any question of threat to our national unity or integrity and where there is a question of a section breaking away. There we will be tough. We hope the whole House will stand with us in taking both these lines simultaneously.

Sir, one party is talking about water, Chandigarh and territory. But what they are really talking about is perhaps how to sit in the Chief Minister's chair. Another group is talking about the same territory in a different way, about taking it away. We must fight the second group with everything that we have with us; and we will do that.

Prof. Dandavate raised some points which, I think, need a little explanation. I do not want to go into the full details of what has happened in the last three years, because we all know that; we have debated it a number of times. Most of the charges that he has made have been answered more than fully on the floor of this very House. It is no use going into them again and again.

---

* Extracts from the speech of Prime Minister Rajiv Gandhi in Lok Sabha, 13 May, 1985

He did raise a point of arms being smuggled into the Golden Temple complex in food trucks. But if I remember correctly, while they were in food trucks, they were inside bags of wheat and bags of food. I should like to point out that these trucks belonged to the SGPC and that these trucks were given specific clearance to go in and out by the SGPC at that time. The SGPC has not changed much since then. So, although we all want to accommodate as much as possible, there are certain things we must keep in mind. We cannot forget that these actions could not have taken place without the full help of the SGPC. If people had gone into the Golden Temple, they were sitting inside the Akal Takht, sitting there because they had the permission of the management.

I think this is a very important juncture for all of us; and as many members have pointed out, members of the Akali Dal have come out openly, may be for the first time as strongly as they have. I think this is very positive; and not only the Akali Dal, but also for the first time, we have seen a large number of Sikhs coming out and condemning these actions. I must congratulate our Sikh brothers and sisters on coming out openly against the extremists' actions, on showing courage and guts, because they will, at some stage, have to face the terrorists as well; and the whole House must congratulate all the Sikhs who have shown the guts and come forward and stood up against this. This is where we must rise above. We must help them come out of their shells. We have a choice today. We have a choice of countering a small group of extremists and terrorists and carrying the rest of the Sikhs in India with us. When I say 'with us' I do not mean, the government, I mean the House, the country. And we could very easily go wrong. A small false move, a small error in our discretion, or hastiness in our action, could turn the whole group against all of us. And that is where we need to act with the utmost restraint and utmost patience. Really we are talking of what Gandhiji taught us: non-violence to the ultimate degree. Let them provoke us. Many members pointed out that every time discussions started, every time they started moving towards conclusions, and things started going well, something was done. What was the result? That whatever procedures had been started were abandoned. Now, we have to show the guts to follow through with the action that we have initiated. We must have the guts to bring them to a conclusion and isolate the extremists. To do this we shall need the help of every single person. And this is the time when members in the Opposition, specially leaders in the Opposition, must not turn this into a political battle with the Government or against any party. It is too easy to do that. When a *bandh* is called, when public action is taken, that is what will be damaging, and that is what we must always be careful about. I am not trying to make an accusation, because it would not be good to accuse anyone. We have to convince everyone who may have any doubts about the line of action that we are taking. It is in fact the only correct line of action, and there is no real alternative.

We have seen that the traditional leaders of the Akali Dal have taken a stand to an extent. Perhaps we all wish that they would have taken a much stronger stand. But let us not forget that just a few days ago, they could not even have taken this much of a stand. We must see the positive side and see how we help them to build themselves up without in any manner damaging them. We must help them by our actions by not reacting in the way the extremists and terrorists might want to see us react. The aim of latter, all along, is that a backlash comes and the hole community is alienated from the country. That is what we must avoid here today.

It is also good to hear the Opposition Benches speak of the involvement of a "foreign hand" in these terrorist activities. I should like to remind them that whenever the Treasury Benches had raised this, the Opposition had been sarcastic. But the fact is that there is such involvement. You know it. It does not help ignoring it. At the same time, it does not help to give it too much importance and pretend that is the only problem. It is a much wider problem than that and we have to see it in all its aspects.

One of our Members said that the Punjab was leaderless. I beg to differ with him. The Akali Dal might be having leadership problems, but I do not think the Punjab is having any leadership problem.

Another Member spoke about the Akal Takht being broken down. I beg to say that this is entirely the business of the Sikhs and we should not interfere in what they want to do with their religious institutions. If they want to remove it, they are welcome to remove it. If they want to build a 24-storey structute, they are welcome to do it, provided it is within the municipal rules. They can do whatever they like.

The fact is that today there is no room for complacency. We have been facing terrorism in our country for the first time for the past two or three years. Last week, it has taken a new turn, a more serious turn. Earlier it was limited to boys with guns or machine guns going and gunning down people. Where they were visible, they could be spotted and they could be caught. This is a different type. It is laying booby traps for the people to pick up, where it is not so easy to spot the person who is doing that. Wherever terrorism has come up in this manner, in whichever country it has come up, it has not been possible to eliminate it in a very short period of time. It has always lasted quite some time before they have been able to finish it off. and we must brace ourselves to face such a situation. We must build up our machinery, whether it is intelligence, whether it is police, whether it is the administrative apparatus, whether it is some sort of civil defence structure. We must build awareness among the public, use voluntary organisations, use all our political organisations to try and identify where things are going wrong and where unusual objects are placed. People should not go and grab things and get themselves killed. This is a matter about which we much do something.

Provisions of the Accord

1. *Compensation to Innocent Persons Killed*

Along with *exgratia* payment to those innocent killed in agitation or any action after 1-8-1982, compensation for property damaged will also be paid.

2. *Army Recruitment*

All citizens of the country have the right to enrol in the army and merit will remain the criterion for selection.

3. *Enquiry into November Incidents*

The jurisdiction of Mr. Justice Ranganath Mishra Commission enquiring into the November riots of Delhi would be extended to cover the disturbances at Bokaro and Kanpur also.

4. *Rehabilitation of those Discharged from the Army*

For all those discharged, efforts will be made to rehabilitate and provide gainful employment.

5. *All-India Gurudwara Act*

The Government of India agrees to consider the formulation of an All-India Gurudwara Bill. Legislation will be brought forward for this purpose in consultation with Shiromani Akali Dal, others concerned and after fulfilling all relevant constitutional requirements.

6. *Disposal of Pending Cases*

(1) The notifications applying the Armed Forces Special Powers Act, Punjab will be withdrawn.

Existing special courts will try only cases relating to the following type of offences:

A) Waging war
B) Hijacking.

(2) All other cases will be transferred to ordinary courts and enabling legislation if needed will be brought forward in this session of Parliament.

7. *Territorial Claims*

(1) The capital project area of Chandigarh will go to Punjab. Some adjoining areas which were previously part of Hindi or the Punjabi regions were included in the Union territory. With the capital region going to Punjab the areas which were added to the Union Territory from the Punjabi region of the erstwhile State of Punjab will be transferred to Punjab and those from Hindi region to Haryana. The entire Sukhna lake will be kept as part of Chandigarh and will thus go to Punjab.

(2) It had always been maintained by Mrs. Indira Gandhi that when Chandigarh is to got to Punjab some Hindi-speaking territories of Punjab will go to Haryana. A Commission will be constituted to determine the specific Hindi-speaking areas of Punjab which should go to Haryana, in lieu of Chandigarh.

The principle of contiguity and linguistic affinity with a village as a unit will be the basis of such determination.

The Commission will be required to give its findings by December 31, 1985 and these will be binding on both sides.

The work of the Commission will be limited to this aspect and will be distinct from the general boundary claims which the other Commission referred to in Para 7.4 will handle.

(3) The actual transfer of Chandigarh to Punjab and areas in lieu thereof to Haryana will take place simultaneously on January 26, 1986.

(4) There are other claims and counter-claims for re-adjustment of daries (territories). The government will appoint (in addition to) the existing Punjab-Haryana boundary (commission) another commission to consider these matters and give its findings. Such findings will be based on a village as a unit, linguistic affinity and continuity.

8. *Centre-State Relations*

(1) Shiromani Akali Dal states that the Anandpur Sahib Resolution is entirely within the framework of the Indian Constitution, that it attempts to define the concept of Centre-State relations in a manner which may bring out the true federal characteristics of the resolution to provide greater autonomy to the state with a view to strengthening the unity and integrity of the country, since unity in diversity forms the corner-stone of our national entity.

(2) In view of the above, the Anandpur Sahib resolution in so far as it deals with Centre-State relations, stands referred to the Sarkaria Commission.

9. *Sharing of Rivers Waters*

(1) The farmers of Punjab, Haryana and Rajasthan will continue to get water not less than what they are using from the Ravi-Beas system as on 1-7-1985. Waters used for consumptive purposes will also remain unaffected. Quantum of usage claimed shall be verified by the tribunal referred to in para (2) below.

(2) The claims of Punjab and Haryana regarding the shares in their remaining waters will be referred for adjudication to a tribunal to be presided over be a Supreme Court Judge. The decision of this tribunal will be rendered within six months and would be binding on both parties. All legal and

constitutional steps required in this respect be taken expeditiously.

(3) The construction of the SYL canal shall continue. The canal shall be completed by August 15, 1986.

10. *Representation of Minorities*

(1) Existing instructions regarding protection of interests of minorities will be recirculated to the State Chief Ministers. (PM will write to all Chief Ministers).

11. *Promotion of Punjabi Language*

The Central Government may take some steps for the promotion of the Punjabi language.

This settlement brings to an end a period of confrontation and ushers in an era of amity, goodwill and cooperation, which will promote and strengthen the unity and integrity of India.

Akali Differences over Accord

Sant Harchand Singh Longowal, Akali Dal (L) president, announced at Anandpur Sahib on July 26 that the accord was "unanimously" approved by a congregation comprising former MPs, former MLAs, ex-Ministers and district and circle jathedars.

Shri G.S. Tohra, SGPC president, and Shri Prakash Singh Badal, former Chief Minister of Punjab, however, disapproved the accord and opposed every clause of the agreement singed by Shri Rajiv Gandhi and Sant Longowal.

At one stage of the four-hour meeting held in the historic gurdwara, Shri Surjan Singh Thekedar made an emotional appeal to Shri Tohra and Shri Badal to support the accord as otherwise "it would mean an end of us Sikhs".

Shri Tohra reacted by asking whether it was a crime to express his views on the accord and threatened to walk out. Party workers persuaded him to stay on. Shri Tohra said that while Sant Longowal might be a "dictator", the decision would have to be taken by the Akali Dal.

The meeting was preceded by a closed door discussion among Sant Longowal, Shri Tohra, Shri Badal and Shri Surjit Singh Barnala.

But Shri Badal and Shri Tohra told waiting newsmen that their differences persisted.

In the congregation, Shri Tohra took the position that they had not got anything out of the accord, "only ruination. Sant Longowal has acted as he has no faith in us", he remarked, adding that the accord was the result of some secret meetings.

Both Shri Tohra and Shri Badal emphasized that nothing had been done for Army deserters and for those who wee still in prison. "If deserters are punished, it will be because they are devoutly religious. If they escape punishment, they will not be obliged to the Sikh leadership which had done nothing for them", Shri Tohra argued. The abolition of special courts was also meaningless, if the cases were to go to designated courts.

Both Shri Badal and Shri Tohra pointed out that in earlier meetings held at Anandpur Sahib and Chandigarh, it had been decided that no talks would be held with the Government unless it accepted the pre-conditions. But Sant Longowal had violated this decision and gone ahead with the talks and signed the accord.

Shri Badal referred to the statement made by the Punjab Governor, Shri Arjun Singh, that 280 of the discharged deserters would be rehabilitated. Alleging that the total number of deserters was 12,000, Shri Badal wanted to know the fate of the rest.

Even on the issue of inquiry into the riots. Shri Badal felt that it had a limited scope. "I am dissatisfied with every point in the accord", Shri Badal told the congregation.

On the Anandpur Sahib Resolution, Shri Tohra alleged that it was not sent to the Sarkaria Commission in the shape in which it was adopted by the 'sangat' (congregation) at Anandpur Sahib.

On July 25, the 'united' Akali Dal rejected the accord reached between Shri Rajiv Gandhi and Sant Longowal on Punjab, describing it as a "sell out".

The meetings of the Dal and a faction of the All-India Sikh Students' Federation owing allegiance to it adopted similar resolutions rejecting the accord.

The resolution adopted at the meeting of the Dal presided by Shri Joginder Singh, father of the late Jarnail Singh Bhindranwale, dubbed Sant Longowal, Shri Balwant Singh and Shri Surjit Singh Barnala as "traitors" of the Panth. The resolution asserted that the three leaders did not represent the Sikh masses.

The resolution accused Sant Longowal of diluting the Anandpur

Sahib Resolution which, it said, was the basis of launching a "dharmyudh morcha" in 1982. Listing various sections of the accord, the resolution said that on each and every count, the interests of the Sikhs and Punjab had been sold out.

Opposition in Haryana

Meanwhile, five opposition parties in Haryana decided to launch a movement against the agreement on Punjab. Twenty-nine members of the Haryana State Assembly handed over their resignations to their leaders to be submitted to the Speaker on August 9, the Quit India Day, after a rally in Rohtak.

Announcing these decisions on behalf of the State units of the Lok Dal, BJP, Janata Party, Congress (S) and Congress (J), Shri Devi Lal, the former Chief Minister of Haryana and the president of Haryana Lok Dal, said on July 27 that the parties had further decided to observe Haryana bandh on July 31.

A statement issued after the meeting of the five parties took objection to the Punjab memorandum of settlement mainly on five counts. The opposition parties objected to the Anandpur Sahib Resolution of the Akali Dal to be referred to the Sarkaria Commission as it had been the root cause of trouble in Punjab in the past few years. They also found fault with the resettlement of Army personnel who had deserted the Army. They felt that those concessions were a serious affront to the nation's integrity.

Another objection was that the 1970 award of the late Prime Minister Shrimati Indira Gandhi on Punjab was "non-negotiable" and any change in the award could be done only with the consent of all concerned authorities to the award. It was explained that Haryana was also a signatory to the 1970 award.

Another basic objection to the settlement from the five parties was that while the 1970 award had recognized the claim of Haryana over Fazilka and Abohar, the present settlement "was absolutely vague" on those areas or any other chunk of territory which would be referred to a Commission.

A major objection also was with regard to the sharing of river waters. The statement expressed shock at the clauses of the settlement imposing a ceiling on the use of waters of Ravi-Beas system on the basis of water being used by the three States of Punjab, Haryana and Rajasthan on July 01 this year. It was stated that such distribution could give great advantage to Punjab which was using 4.2 million acre-feet now against 3.5 million acre-feet allocated to them. It was stated that Haryana was using less of the allocated water because of the non-construction of the SYL canal.

Misgivings were also expressed for non-mention in the memorandum of settlement of the control of headworks. An understanding over the control of the headworks was felt to be necessary for the share of water to the concerned States to be enjoyed without interruption.

However, the Haryana Chief Minister, Shri Bhajan Lal and the HPCC(I) president, Shri Sultan Singh complimented the Prime Minister, Shri Rajiv Gandhi for showing 'wisdom, political sagacity and promptness" in resolving the Punjab problem.

In a joint statement, the Haryana leaders thanked the Prime Minister for fully protecting the interests of their State and prescribing a time-limit for the implementation of the award. It was evident from the fact that the Ravi-Beas waters could start flowing into the Sutlej-Yamuna Link canal by August 15, 1986, and the simultaneous transfer of the Chandigarh capital project to Punjab and Hindi-speaking areas of Punjab to Haryana, they added.

Underlining that the tribunal to determine the share of various States in the surplus waters of Ravi and Beas had been asked to announce its decision within six months, they said this had all along been the stand of the Haryana Chief Minister as well as the HPCC(I).

Source: Asian Recorder, August 11-17, 1985.

13

JUSTICE E.S. VENKATARAMIAH'S REPORT ON PUNJAB-HARYANA, 1986

A Commission headed by Justice E.S. Venkataramiah (Supreme Court) was appointed on April 3, 1986, to determine and specify the Hindi speaking areas of Punjab to be given to Haryana in lieu of Chandigarh. The term of the Commission was extended till 10 June, 1986. The Commission submitted its report on June 7 and recommended the transfer of 70,000 acres of land from Punjab to Haryana in lieu of Chandigarh.

Source: India : A Reference Annual, 1987, Publications Division, Ministry of Information and Broadcasting, Government of India, 1988.

14

POLICY STATEMENTS OF GOVERNNMENT OF INDIA ON PUNJAB

Defence Minister Jagjivan Ram in the Lok Sabha on Recruitment of Sikhs in the Army, March 14, 1974

"In order to broadbase the recruitment in the various States the recruitment demands placed on the Punjab, Himachal Pradesh and Haryana have had to be reduced recently, as recruitment from these States has been much heavier than their due proportionate share in the past".

(Ranjit Roy, The Myth of the Martial Races, *Sunday*, August 18, 1974, quoted in *'History of the Sikhs'* by Khushwant Singh, Vol. 2, 1974).

Clarification by the Defence Ministry

The statement caused resentment in the minds of the Punjabi's. The Defence Ministry was constrained to explain, "There has been no change in the policy on the representation of the Sikhs in the Army and there need not be any fear or alarm that any injustice would be done to any area or community. The Sikh and the Sikh Fight Infantry Regiments are entirely reserved for the Sikhs. The Sikhs also have approximately 50 per cent reservation in the Punjab Regiment, besides having a sizeable representation in the Guards, Paras, Mahar and J&K Rifles. Further, the Sikhs have secured more than their proportionate share of representation in other arms and services like artillery, engineers and armoured corps."

(Khushwant Singh, *History of the Sikhs*)

Prime Minister Shri Rajiv Gandhi in Parliament, 1989

1. *Extracts from Rajya Sabha Speech*[1]

Sir, coming to Punjab, we have given no quarter to terrorism. We have taken a tough position, and we have worked like we have in the rest of the country on the basic principle of only talking when violence is abjured and people fall within the purview of our Constitution. We had to give up the political process that we started because those in authority would not stand firm against the forces of terrorism. We have stood firm, Sir. The people of Punjab have stood firm with us. Sir, I would like to take this opportunity to salute the martyrs and patriots of Punjab who have died for the unity and integrity of our country. I would also like to take this opportunity to thank those political parties who have worked with us, who have sacrificed with us in Punjab in fighting against terrorists and extremists. At the same time, I would like to point out that there are some who do not take this issue as seriously as they should. Sometimes I even feel that they do not look to the whole national interest in their actions, for example, after the completion of 'Operation Black Thunder', I was very dismayed when some from the Opposition parties — and when I say Opposition parties, I am not meaning members of this House or that House; I am talking of the Opposition in the country — some from the Opposition parties decried 'Operation Black Thunder'. It was sad because 'Operation Black Thunder' was not just a question of flushing out some terrorists from a holy shrine, from the Golden Temple. It was more than that. It showed the people of Punjab that the terrorists were not religious, it showed the people of Punjab that if anybody had committed sacrilege in the Holy Shrine, in the holy place, it was these terrorists and nobody else. And yet there were some amongst the Opposition who condemned that action. Then there are some who have demanded that our law delinking religion and politics should be repealed, taken away, and religion and politics should be allowed to be linked. And the sad thing is that one of those who have asked for this is a Member of this House, Sir. . . .

There has also been a demand for a Sikh State, unfortunately,

---

1 Rajya Sabha, March 3, 1989.

again by a Member of this House. . . . Now, I have a little booklet here. It is called "The Sikh Case", and it is brought out by the Bharat Mukti Morcha, Punjab. And it says on top: 'Genesis and solution of the Punjab problem'. It says here in the Foreword, right on top, first sentence: "The booklet prepared by the Punjab Unit of Bharat Mukti Morcha at the instance of Shri Ram Jethmalani, M.P., is an endeavour to place before the general public and particularly the opposition leaders the Punjab problem and to suggest a just and amicable settlement". Then towards the end of the Foreword it says: "Special thanks are due to Mr. Ram Jethmalani who read the draft and made many useful suggestions". And then beyond here it goes on to actually give some suggestions. The whole book is about 23 pages. It does not at any point talk about any killings by the terrorists. Nothing at all about that. There is only one reference to killings by terrorists, and I think I should read that out for your benefit. It is a long para: I will read just two sentences of the para. This is the only reference to killings by terrorists. It says: "The Golden Temple had been destroyed and desecrated in the past, but those who did it were outsiders. Everytime, the persons responsible for the sacrilege were exterminated. Assassination of the Prime Minister and the Army Chief of Staff should be viewed in that perspective". This is the only reference to people killed by the terrorists. Then it goes on to say: 'Solutions' here, solution and lots of things. It says: "Firstly, the solemn commitment made before Independence for creation of an autonomous Sikh State within India should be honoured". One, I am not aware of any such commitment; I am not aware of it. And what does 'Autonomous Sikh State within India' mean? This is a question I would like the Hon. Members to think about, not the opposition, all the members to think about; what does that mean and how has the Member of this House been propagating this? And his party has not taken any action on it, unless his party — I do not know what his party thinks about it. Then, Second — one more point.

The second point now. That was 'firstly' and now it is 'secondly'; point No. 1, point No. 2 are not that relevant; point No. 3 now. "Secondly, repeal all the laws separating religion and politics". Is this what we want in this House? Then it goes on to 'Permanent Solution'. The last para is 'Permanent Solution'. "There being no alternative to the formation of an autonomous State within India, the structure of such a State is what should engage the deliberations of the Opposition leaders". Is this what the Opposition leaders have been discussing and is this what the Opposition leaders want us to call them to discuss? Then it goes on; the last sentence now. ' his is on the 'autonomous State'. It says: "It must have full internal autonomy with complete control over its economy. Only defence, foreign affairs, communication and currency to be Central Subjects". . . . On both occasions, I was overwhelmed by the enthusiasm and affection that the people of Punjab showed on those occasions. And when I talked to people — I drove almost 300-400 kilometres through Punjab, stopping at almost every village that we went through and every time I stopped I talked to the people, breaking out of the security and letting the people gather around — one thing became very clear to me there — that the people of Punjab are very clearly not supporting any secessionist or fundamentalist forces in that State. The people of Punjab are looking for only one thing. They are looking for their development work to get going at full speed and the law and order to be controlled properly. During these last four years, a lot has happened in Punjab, some good, some bad. On the whole, I feel that we have made progress. I do not want to go into too many details. . . . Sir, what we have achieved in Punjab is this. We set out to do two or three things. We set out, one, to break the link, the religious and fundamentalist link with the terrorists and the criminals; second, to bring the criminals and terrorists to book; third, to bring about normalcy in Punjab, including in the political process. We have been sometimes more successful in one, sometimes more in another, sometimes less. Today, I can say with confidence that in one thing we have been successful in these past two years. We have broken the nexus between the fundamentalists, the secessionists and the youngsters who are today the terrorists and who are the criminals. It has been broken. Today, Sir, the gurdwaras no longer act as sanctuaries for the terrorists. Today, Sir, the gurdwaras no longer act as sanctuaries for the terrorists. Today, Sir, the devout are shocked and distressed by the defilement that these terrorists have done in gurdwaras. It has been exposed. The Golden Temple has been restored to its pristine purity. The full *maryada* is being observed. Recently on the Makara Sankranti Day 20,000 devotees on one day, visited the Golden Temple.

The social reform movement that had started trying to get people, trying to get ladies not to make up, change their head style and change their dress, trying to make men change their clothes and their shaving habits and other things, has all but died away, petered out

One does not hear about it any more.

Schools and colleges are back to normal. Last year over 50,000 school-leaving children took examinations.

The economy of Punjab is strong and robust despite the drought in 1987 and the very severe unprecedented floods in 1988.

The terrorists, barring one group and some individuals, have no more links with fundamentalism or religion. They are today pure and simple criminals involved in drug-trafficking, in smuggling, in looting. Amongst the people, there is wide-spread revulsion at such criminal activities.

I feel that in spite of the difficulties that we are having even today with the law-and-order position, it is an advance on where we started off in 1984, and it has come about because the people of Punjab have stood with us. It has come about because Congress with the two Communist Parties, worked solidly against tremendous odds in Punjab, not worrying about life, not worrying about sacrifice, not worrying about what lies ahead. And for that, I would like to thank the people of Punjab and the workers of the Congress in Punjab and the two Communist Parties in Punjab.

I feel that we have come a long way and the people of Punjab, after this long haul, deserve some more incentives to continue this fight and terrorism. The action will be even stronger. But to help normalise the situation in Punjab because having cleaned the terrorists out of the Gurdwaras, having separated the religious and fundamentalist linkages, we feel it is time now to start the process of normalisation. We will be watching and measuring this process at every step as we go along. If we feel the things are not going well, we will slow down. It they go worse, we will stop If they go well, we will accelerate and do things faster.

We have decided to take a number of steps to bring about normalcy in Punjab. The first step is that all Jodhpur undertrials will be released. There are some amongst Jodhpur undertrials who have other charges, who are accused of other things. The normal process of law will continue with those categories of people. . . .

We will be also requesting the Punjab Government to withdraw the cases the they have launched for objectionable speeches and objectionable writings. We will be removing the restrictions under the Foreigners Act on visiting and we will be restricting to seriously disturbed areas only the Punjab Disturbed Areas Act and the Armed Forces (Punjab and Chandigarh) Special Powers Act. Sir, TADA will be used only, very rarely. We will be withdrawing the NSA (Special Amendment) for the Punjab but the Parent Act will continue. Most important we will be trying to normalise the functioning of the Police Stations. A monitoring mechanism will be set up to see that cases are properly followed up and registered and all the corrective actions taken.

One of the most difficult areas during this period has been that development in Punjab has suffered in simple things like maintenance of roads and other infrastructure. There also have been problems and to overcome these problems, we are recommending that Development Committees be set up initially at the district level, and after watching how this works, at the sub-divisional level. The District Committee will be chaired by a D.M. and we will associate non-officials also in these Committees. I believe work has already started and the various political parties have given names of their people in each district to the Governor and the Governor is now going into the actual format and the functioning of these Committees. We will see that some devolution of powers is given to these Committees. Certainly, in the anti-poverty programmes, we can do that. In some other areas, we will try and do it. They will have an advisory role and a role as a grievance redressal machinery. This should help normalise the development process in Punjab. It should also help involve the people of Punjab after a long time in the development process.

Then, we will be setting up a village defence organisation. This will be made up mostly of non-political parties, ex-servicemen, ex-CRPF, ex-BSF and basically ex-uniformed people and their task will be to protect the villages. They will be trained and prepared to be able to cope with that and to motivate the local people to stand up in their own defence against the terrorists.

Most important of all, we will be starting the democratisation process by holding Panchayat elections starting sometime in the middle of May and hopefully ending by the middle of this year. We would like full restoration of the political process but that may be difficult till we are completely able to end violence and terrorism that is still continuing. But a beginning has been made. We will be watching and if things move well, we will continue the process following the Panchayat elections. Sir, then I have promised that I would have a Cabinet Committee to go into the problems in Punjab. They have had a number of meetings and we will be calling

Opposition parties in Punjab for talks on solution for the problems in Punjab and how to move ahead from here. Sir, there is one more point I would like a mention, linked to Punjab and it is always raised when Punjab is raised and that is the violence that followed Indiraji's assassination in Delhi. We have been accused on a number of occasions of inaction on the Delhi riots. I would like to clarify that there has been no inaction on the part of the Government. There has been action on the part of the Government. . . .

Sir, we have registered 225 cases with over 2,300 accused. Most of them are still in the judicial process. Sir, you know what our judicial process is like but we have faith in our judicial system. It is sometimes slow but always grinds to a proper conclusion. Eleven cases have concluded with conviction, over 90 people have been convicted and six people have got life imprisonment. So, there is no question of no action. There is action, action will be complete and we will see that everybody is brought to book through the proper system, the legal system.

2. *Extracts from Lok Sabha Speech*[2]

. . . The people of Punjab – Sikhs, Hindus, Muslims and of all other communities – have stood rock-like together with the country. The fundamentalists have not been able to break their communal amity. The secessionists have not been able to suborn their national loyalty. The terrorists have not been able to terrorise them. The people of Punjab have prevailed. Once more, as so often before, the people of Punjab have saved the country.

But violence continues. There are two reasons – basic and fundamental

One is the succour and support which the Punjab terrorists have been receiving from across the border and from abroad. We have taken a range of action against this. We are hopeful that the change over in Pakistan from a military rule to democratic rule will lead to the complete cessation of all support to terrorists from across the border. Some signs are visible and we are hopeful that this will be fully realised. In Pakistan, those recognising such action could destabilise the region, including their country, are now beginning to assert themselves.

2. Lok Sabha, April 10, 1989.

The second basic reason for our not overcoming it in Punjab has been our inability as a country to present a unified front against terrorism.

The fault does not lie with the people. The people of the country, more especially the people of Punjab, have stood firm against the vilest of terrorism. They have refused to be shaken from centuries of communal amity. They have refused to betray their country. They have refused to be untrue to the message of their Gurus.

The fault lies with some political parties. There are some parties, steadfast in struggle against communalism, terrorism and secession. We welcome their support, we honour their courage, we honour their strength of conviction. Terrorists may be a miniscule minority but they draw comfort from what some politicians and some political parties say and do. They also draw comfort those who stay silent, those who do not denounce the dangerous pronouncements and nefarious actions of others.

During the debate on the President's Address, the Opposition disowned the views of a Member as expressed in a pamphlet, in whose publication he had connived. Yet, he continues to be their honoured and much-vaunted colleague. I do not understand and I cannot understand how they can disown him when he is not in Parliament and then applaud him when he speaks. He has not withdrawn from his position of support to the Anandpur Sahib Resolution. He has affirmed on the floor of Parliament that he still supports the Resolution. He is able to be a Member of Parliament only because one Opposition party inducted him and elected him. What does that party say now? Are they ready now at least to withdraw from him their benevolent patronage

Double standards led to his election. He is widely known to have participated in a United States television programme sponsored by a third country to preach hatred and disaffection against the unity of India. He did not have a word to speak against terrorism even on that programme. Can his party not find anyone more worthy to festoon with their ticket? Or is this what to expect of a party whose two representatives visited a neighbouring country in so critical a time as March, 1984 and there lavished praise on the hospitality of a military dictator but did not uttar a word against the support of their hosts to terrorists, secessionists and traitors? And what of the other Members of the Opposition?

Are they prepared now at least to denounce the Member,

dissociate themselves from his Party, keep aloof from his Front? Are they prepared now at least to tell the country where they stand? Do they stand with this one man and the Anandpur Sahib Resolution or do they stand with the people of this country?

Secularism is the key to the strength of India. The protagonists of Khalistan will be broken only on the rock of secularism. The only hope of the secessionists is to suborn our innate secularism, to suborn the innate secularism of our people. They hope by terror to divide community from community. They want to fan the flames of communal hatred so that India is destroyed in a communal conflagration from the ashes of which their 'Khalistan' will emerge. They are out to destroy centuries of the closest bonds between Hindus and Sikhs. The are out to smash to smithereens our composite Punjab. They want to smash the Punjab that is equally a home for the Sikhs and the Muslims and the Hindus and the Christians and many others. They tried to convert the shrines into fortresses. They failed. They tried to convert the canons of Sikhism into the canons of war. They failed. The people of Punjab and the people of this country refused to let Hindu fight Sikh and Sikh fight Hindu. The people of Punjab and the people of this country remembered the tolerance and compassion that has been preached by all the Gurus. They remembered our composite culture which is our greatness. They remembered our secularism which is inborn in every Indian.

I put the insistent question, therefore, and there is no escaping the question. I ask it again of every member of this House. Are you with those who stand with the core of the Anandpur Sahib Resolutions? Are you with those who stand for communalism? Or, are you ready to stand and fight against communalism, for secularism?...

Prime Minister V.P. Singh's Views, 1989

The agony of Punjab continues. While separatism is no answer to our problems, there is an urgent need for a national endeavour to resolve the problem. A national effort will be made to resolve the complex problems like Punjab.

(Extract from Prime Minister V.P. Singh's First Address to the Nation on December 3, 1989).

Shri Rajiv Gandhi, Leader of the Opposition in the Lok Sabha, 1989[3]

. . . Then there is the question of Punjab. I have raised some points earlier. I will not expand. I will talk very precisely. We have raised a number of points in the joint meeting which the Government has not answered, which we feel the Government should answer. The immediate task is to deal with those that are calling for Khalistan. What has the Government done? Is it just sitting and watching while the Jor Mela is going on and harder and stronger statements are being made? Nothing has happened. They have not been picked up for one reason only. That gentleman would have been in jail today. If it were not for the specific instructions from the Prime Minister's Office to the then Government asking the Governor not to arrest him. That is why they are out today. . . .

We will show you the telexes also. The telexes have come in the newspapers and we can show them. We want to know the Government's stand on those people that are asking for Khalistan. Pick them up, arrest them and show that you have guts!

The Government should clarify its position on the Anandpur Saheb Resolution. Somebody has said in this House that the Congress Government has referred it to the Sarkaria Commission. The Congress Government did not refer it to the Sarkaria Commission. If some Sikh from Punjab referred it, we do not know about it. We want to know the Government's position on the Anandpur Saheb Resolution because very senior members of the National Front are mixed up with the Bharat Mukti Morcha or whatever it is called. I have raised this issue in the Rajya Sabha. It has still not been answered. I have raised it in the Rajya Sabha where your Members of Parliament have categorically upheld the Anandpur Saheb Resolution. The country wants to know. When you were in opposition you need not have told the country. Today, you must tell the country. How can you not tell the country? We want to know what your position in regarding the fundamentalists in Punjab who are throwing Hindus out of hostels, closing down liquor and meat shops. This has been started in these two weeks. What are you doing about it? What are you doing about Pakistan's training? What are you doing about the take over of religious institutions by the

---

3. Extract from the Speech in Lok Sabha, December 28, 1989.

fundamentalists? There are more weapons today going into the Gurdwaras than there were during pre-Blue Star and pre-Black Thunder periods. Why are you not using the Religious Institutions (Prevention of Misuse) Act? When are you going to wake up? Will you wake up when you need another Black Thunder? Are you going to wait so long? Are you not going to act till they are occupied again? For heaven's sake, do something. . . .

Prime Minister Shri Chandra Shekhar's Views, 1990

Unfortunately there is problem in Kashmir, Problem in Punjab. . . . These problems are to be tackled with a sense of reconciliation. Any path of confrontation is going to harm not only to the country but also to the people who resort to this confrontationist path. I appeal to the youngmen, who have taken to violence to eschew violence. If you want to have a solution, you will have to learn the way of Mahatma Gandhi, the path of non-violence, of peace. With the organised will of the people, you can change everything. I think that people will learn that death is gruesome, whether death comes because of a terrorist activity or because of a police action. The government will never like to have any police action unless and until it is coerced, it is forced to that situation. I humbly appeal to all the people that they should give up violence and try to come to the mainstream to contribute for the development of this country.

Extract from the Address to the Nation by Prime Minister Shri Chandra Shekhar reported in *Indian Express*, November 18, 1990.

Prime Minister Shri P.V. Narasimha Rao's Views, 1992

Friends, the election process in Punjab has begun. We have fulfilled our commitment to hold elections in Punjab within February 1992. Even as I am speaking to you, nominations are being filed, both for the Vidhan Sabha of Punjab and also Lok Sabha.

I am leaving on a foreign tour just now. By the time I come back, this part of the election process would be over. I would, therefore, reiterate before leaving the country that my Government is determined to resolve all the outstanding questions regarding Punjab in consultation with the elected State Government of Punjab. This I have said before and I would like to say again.

I would also like to add that this is the only way of resolving problems. I see no other way. We are committed to this process and I would like the people of Punjab to know that this commitment will be fulfilled.

It is not fair to keep the people of any part of the country deprived of the democratic process. So, this opportunity is coming to the people of Punjab to exercise their franchise and see that the democratic process for which they have been waiting for a long time is restored now. I have no doubt that they also desire elections in Punjab. Therefore, I would again expect the people as well as all the political parties in Punjab to participate in the elections. I would also urge that in this respect there should be no hesitation on the part of any party and, therefore, all parties should participate and do their duty by the country and by the State of Punjab.

We have made all arrangements for a free and fair election. I am sure that the election will be smooth and the transition to the democratic set up will be exactly as we intended.

I would like to wish you on this occasion all the best and I also pray that the elections in Punjab will usher in an era of peace, prosperity and harmony. Jai Hind.

(Text of the Prime Minister's Appeal, January 31, 1992)

15

POLITICAL PARTIES ON PUNJAB: Election Manifestoes, 1991 and 1992

1991 Elections

On the eve of every election, major political parties come out with their election manifestoes. These manifestoes, reflect what will be done should the party come in power. Every party makes it a point to say something on everything that may be agitating people's minds. In this context it would be of interest to refer to the views of the major political parties relating to the Punjab crisis.

Bharatiya Janata Party (BJP)

To mend matters in the Punjab we will :

1. Create a kilometre-deep Security Belt all along the Indo-Pak border – as has already been done by Pakistan on its own site – to prevent all movements of terrorists, smugglers and their lethal cargo,
2. Post Army Units in the acutely disturbed border areas to maintain order and restore confidence,
3. Give relief and provide rehabilitation to the widows and orphans of 1984 outrages,
4. Punish the guilty men of the 1984 terror,
5. Have the various grievances of the people of Punjab examined by experts, including social scientists and redress them suitably.

Communist Party of India (CPI)

1. (e) Preservation and strengthening of the secular democratic

set up of the country in the struggle against all types of divisive forces, including Hindutva chauvinists, Khalistani terrorist and Kashmir Muslim secessionists; guarantee of security of life and property for all minorities, effective measures to stop misuse of religious places to fan intolerance and hatred against other communities or to organise communal violence.

2. Immediate multipronged political initiatives at all levels – economic, administrative, psychological, political and mass levels – to solve the Punjab, Jammu and Kashmir and Assam problems.

(Paras refer to paras of the Election Manifesto)

Communist Party of India (Marxist) (CP-M)

4. Immediate solution of Punjab, Kashmir and Assam problems of conceding the genuine demands of the people of these States for protection of their identity within the framework of Indian unity.

(Para refers to para of the Election Manifesto)

Indian National Congress (INC)

Punjab

The Congress will resume with determination and without flinching the struggle against terrorism, secessionism and fanaticism. The Congress will restore law and order, re-establish peace and rebuild democratic processes in Punjab. The Congress believes in negotiated settlements. This was demonstrated in Punjab through the Rajiv-Longowal Accord of July 1985, to which the Congress remains committed. But negotiations are possible only with those who eschew violence and accept the framework of our Constitution. We will continue to strive for a comprehensive settlement on all outstanding issues. The Congress will not hesitate to take whatever new initiatives are required to this end.

Janata Dal (Samajwadi) – J.D.(S)

We emphasise the value of dialogue, mutual understanding and other persuasive methods in resolving social conflicts. It is hoped that the unrest in Punjab, Assam and Jammu and Kashmir will be resolved amicably in the near future. We expect a positive response from the people of Punjab and Assam by getting involved in the democratic process and thus paving the way for the solution of the present crisis.

National Front (NF)

The National Front is convinced that the ultimate solution for violent militancy in parts of the country is restoration of faith in democratic political process within the Federal Constitution. The National Front would want the agony of Punjab and Jammu and Kashmir to end. Only the National Front, with its true commitment to federalism, can find a solution, heal the old wounds, initiate an era of reconciliation and bring the alienated sections back into the national mainstream.

The National Front is committed to economic development of Punjab and Jammu and Kashmir and to finding early solutions for the problem of unemployment in these State, along with the rest of the country.

1992 Elections

BJP Election Manifesto

The BJP released its election manifesto for the Punjab election with the claim that the party took the polls as a part of its sustained struggle against secessionism and the cult of violence in politics.

The manifesto was released by vice-president Baldev Prakash and secretary Madan Lal Khurana, MP, incharge of Punjab affairs. Condemning the Khalistan demand the BJP leaders reiterated their party's commitment to preserve national unity and social harmony at all costs and to fight boldly and determinedly against violence in political life, terrorism and separatism.

The manifesto states that the party will continue its struggle for the interests of Punjab, such as transfer of Chandigarh and Punjabi-speaking areas to Punjab, and more share in the Ravi and Beas waters, and will strive for more power to the State. Centre-State relations should be reviewed to give more powers to the States on a uniform basis to all the States for rapid development.

The party will strive for better civic amenities and rationalisation and reduction in the burden of taxes on citizens and holding early elections to the State Municipal committees.

The party promises to work for employment to all able-bodied youths and start a massive drive to impress upon the Government to find a solution to their problems.

According to the manifesto, the BJP is fully aware of the difficulties and hardships of the Government employees as well as of industrial workers. The party promises to raise its voice for their housing, bonus and other demands.

The BJP is of the view that the unrest in Punjab and the consequent killings of innocent people are a part of the strategy of the discredited Congress and Akali politicians to safeguard their own interest. The BJP pledges that it will exert relentless pressure for a high-level judicial enquiry into the violence in Punjab so that the real culprits behind it are exposed.

The party believes in the glorious future of Punjab and calls upon the people to come forward to fight against power-hungry politicians and take a firm pledge not to repeat the unfortunate happenings of the last 10 years and build a strong and prosperous Punjab on the foundation of communal harmony, unity and integrity.

The party will devote itself to the cause and problems of Scheduled Castes, backward classes and economically weaker sections of society.

The party will demand a fair deal for the hard-working farmers of Punjab. It will strive for early completion of Thein dam and other river water projects besides demanding an economical price for their produce.

The partly feels that disturbed conditions in Punjab for the last 10 years have crippled trade and industry, resulting in huge losses to both. It will make all-out efforts to rehabilitate the economy of the State.

In the concluding remarks, Shri Madan Lal Khurana asserted that his party strongly felt that along with the police officials, such politicians as had been found guilty of involvement in the 1984 riots, should be proceeded against.

(*Hindustan Times*, February 13, 1992)

Congress Manifesto

The Congress, in its manifesto reaffirmed its commitment to values of democracy, secularism and rule of law besides giving top priority to restore normalcy.

It has pledged to strive for the broadest possible consensus and cooperation of all to solve the key issues which have defied solution of Punjab problem so far, through constitutional mechanism and democratic methods of negotiations and persuasion.

The Congress has also promised to establish the office of "Lok Ayukt" to provide a clean, efficient and responsible administration at all levels and root out corruption.

The manifesto also promises to implement the Jawahar Rozgar Yojana and start projects for self-employment. It has emphasised on generating employment opportunities through national rural employment programme, rural landless employment guarantee programme and integrated rural development programme.

The manifesto also assured immediate and adequate relief to migrants who are victims of militancy. It has promised to enhance compensation to Rs. 1 lakh besides providing free education, pension and employment to the affected families.

The manifesto sought the vote and support of Punjabis to translate the vision of what it called "Golden Punjab" into a reality.

It also promised to solve all outstanding issue within the framework of Rajiv-Longowal accord.

(*Times of India*, February 7, 1992)

CPI Election Manifesto

The election manifesto highlighted the plight of Punjab and the Centre's "hamhanded and dishonest approach".

It said, "Punjab is going to poll in very grave circumstances, much worse than at the time of June elections, aggravated by unwise and undemocratic boycott decision of sections of Akalis."

(*Hindustan Times*, February 13, 1992)

Shiromani Jagat Akali Dal (S.J.A.D.)

The party was formed on Jan. 21, 1992 by a senior Akali leader Jiwan Singh Umranangal at Umranangal his native place in Beas. It was a joint venture with Baba Ajit Singh Nihang, the chief of the Taruna Nihang Dal. It may be recalled that Jiwan Singh Umranangal is a former Revenue Minister of Punjab and he has been waging a relentless battle against the militants in which he also lost his son. He was candidate for the Jalandhur parliamentary seat in the aborted June 1991 elections, and he was being supported by the BJP and the

Communist Parties.

Shri Umranangal who is the president said that the purpose of forming this party was to enable all like-minded citizens of the country to join the Akali Dal so as to fight the anti-national forces without any discrimination of caste, colour and religion.

In the traditional Akali Dals, representation is given only to the Sikhs, he said.

Releasing the party manifesto, the president said they had applied to the Election Commission for registration. The symbol given for being registered is either a "cycle" or a "bucket".

The manifesto of the party includes giving priority to national interests, to shun communalism, to eliminate the evil of corruption from the society, to introduce conscription, to give suitable employment to the unemployed, to give free medical care to people, to take steps to increase the quota of Punjabis in the Army, to demand more autonomy for the State, and to get back the Punjabi-speaking areas from the neighbouring States.

The Akali Dal is to contest the elections and president did not rule out the possibility of alignment with like-minded secular parties, to have consensus candidates.

(*Hindustan Times*, January 22, 1992)

16

ELECTION SCENARIO

1. Overview of Assembly Elections

After the reorganisation of Punjab in 1966, the United Front—Akalis, Bharatiya Jan Sangh and Communities Parties, formed the government with justice (Retired) Gurnam Singh (Akali Dal) as the Chief Minister, in March 1967. He was succeeded by Lachman Singh Gill (Akali Dal) in November 1967. President's Rule was imposed in August 1968 and which continued up to February 17, 1969.

In the 1969 Assembly elections, Akali party under the leadership of Sant Fateh Singh won the majority of seats. The ministry was formed by Shri Gurnam Singh with the cooperation of other parties excluding the congress. In March 1970, Shri Parkash Singh Badal of the Akali Dal became the Chief Minister.

In the 1972 Assembly elections, the Congress party won an absolute majority and its ministry was installed under Giani Zail Singh.

In June 1977 elections, Akali party won and Shri Prakash Singh Badal became the Chief Minister. In February 1980, President's Rule was imposed which lasted for about 4 months.

In the 1980 July elections, Congress won and Shri Darbara Singh of the Congress assumed the charge of the Chief Minister.

In the 1985 elections which took place after the assassination of Smt. Indira Gandhi, Prime Minister, Akalis were victorious with 73 seats out of 117 to their credit. In September 1985, Shri Surjit Singh Barnala (Akali Dal) became the Chief Minister. However the Akali Ministry could not stay long. The Union Government first dismissed the Akali Government and later dissolved the Assembly. On May 11, 1985, President's Rule was imposed. This gave Punjab the longest spell of the Central Government's rule. Incidentally this was the third occasion that the Akali Ministry was dismissed by the Centre.

2. Conduct of 1992 Polls

After a long spell of about six years of President's Rule, the State of Punjab went to the polls on February 19 under unprecedented security cover. It may be recalled that the President's rule was imposed in Punjab on May 11, 1985. After much misgivings, the election process was set in motion around midnight of January 24 with the issuance of notification by the President for the 13 Lok Sabha seats. The Governor of Punjab also issued a similar notification for 117 Assembly seats.

Thus these two separate notifications fulfilled the requirements of the Representation of the People Act. These notifications were issued on the recommendations of the Election Commission.

A Government notification was issued in January 19, 1992 which curtailed campaign period to this weeks.

The election to the State Assembly were earlier announced for June 22, 1991 alongwith the general elections, but were postponed after the Congress Government headed by Shri P.V. Narasimha Rao took over at the Centre.

The then Punjab Governor, Gen. O.P. Malhotra resigned in protest over the Centre's decision on the postponement.

The Narasimha Rao Government announced September 25, 1991 as the fresh date for polls but on September 16 Parliament passed a Bill cancelling it and approved extension of President's Rule for the ninth time for another six months.

Prior to the June 22 schedule, the entire State was declared disturbed and "Operation Rakshak-1" was launched to ensure free and fair poll and to restore confidence among the people.

Despite increased deployment of Army and para military forces to ensure peaceful elections, a total of 24 candidates, three for Lok Sabha and 21 for the Assembly, fell to the bullets of militants.

Postponement of polls resulted in a lot of resentment among various Opposition parties too.

Prior to the issuance of the notification reports of Centre working out packages, economic and political, for Punjab evoked different comments from political parties particularly the Akalis.

While those Akalis boycotting the poll stressed the need for "permanent solution first, poll and Government afterwards", those for the poll and the CPI and CPM leaders sought transfer of Union Territory of Chandigarh, joint capital of Punjab and Haryana, to

Punjab under the Rajiv-Longowal Accord before the elections.

The Centre, however, finally felt that all such disputes should be taken up with the new elected Government in Punjab. The Prime Minister made it clear that installation of a popular Government in the State was their first priority.

Lok Sabha elections in the State were held in November 1989 when the United Akali Dal headed by Shri Simranjit Singh Mann won six seats. The Congress won two seats while the Janata Dal and the Bahujan Samaj Party shared one seat each.

Most of the Akali leaders and their factions which had been earlier urging the government to hold elections in the State announced their decision to boycott the poll. Out of about 17 Akali factions, only one of the *Kabul* group, seriously participated in the elections.

A total of 1084 candidates filed their nominations for the 117 Assembly seats as against 2100 candidates in the aborted June 1991 elections. After the withdrawal and scrutiny of nominations, there remained 594 candidates for the Assembly seats. Two candidates namely Captain Amrinder Singh of the Akali Dal (Kabul) and Shri Dilbagh Singh Daleke of the Congress were elected unopposed from Samana and Tarn Taran Assembly constituencies respectively. For the Lok Sabha seats there were only 81 candidates as against, 227.

In all about 90,000 officials were put on poll duty in addition to 10,000 officials kept as reserve. The Election Commission appointed 39 observers.

There were 14,659 polling stations, each headed by a presiding officer assisted by five polling officers. The maximum distance a voter was to cover was two km to cast his vote.

The turnout of the voters was the lowest in all elections held so far in the State. According to the preliminary figures announced by the Election Commission on the night of the polling day the overall polling was between 25 to 30 per cent.

The turnout ranged from 25 per cent in the districts of Sangrur, Gurdaspur, Jalandhar, Kapurthala, Patiala, Ropar and Bhatinda to 40 per cent and above in Ferozepur, Hoshiarpur, Ludhiana and Faridkot. The highest turnout of about 50 per cent was in Hoshiarpur.

According to a Press note issued by the Commission, the difference in poll percentage in the urban and rural areas was marked all through the day. While in the urban areas, polling was higher than 25 per cent, it remained much below that level in the rural areas. The weather continued to be cool all through the day as compared to the last few days, which was one factor affecting the poll percentage, the release claimed.

A striking aspect of the poll exercise, the press note said, was that these were no cases whatsoever of disobedience by the State Government employees drafted for poll duty. This was in contrast to the many reports that the Government employees were likely to flout the orders of the District Election Officers in protest against the requisition of their services for poll work. A total of 90,000 personnel had been deployed on poll duty.

As for violence, the Commission said there had been no major incidents in spite of widespread apprehensions on this score. There was one case of bomb blast in Ludhiana city in which one person was killed and 10 others were injured.

(*Hindustan Times*, February 21, 1992)

The last Assembly elections in 1985, which were conducted under the threat of violence, showed 67.5 per cent voters voting. The 1989 Lok Sabha elections recorded a poll turn out of 62.7 per cent. In the first election in 1967 after the reorganisation of the state, it had recorded on average of polling of 68.2 per cent for the Assembly and 71.1 per cent for the Lok Sabha.

In about 70 per cent of the 115 Assembly constituencies (there were two unopposed returns) the polling was estimated to be as low as 15 per cent. More than 300 villages just did not vote at all. Rural areas recorded from nil to 10 per cent in the Sikh dominated areas.

The districtwise percentage of polling in rural and urban areas as per preliminary estimates was as follows: Amritsar 10 to 30, Bhatinda 5 to 30, Ludhiana 10 to 35, Faridkot overall 25, Ferozepur 35 to 48, Gurdaspur overall 30, Hoshiarpur 20 to 50, Kapurthala 20 to 40, Sangrur 10 to 25, Patiala 10 to 35 and Jalandhar 20 to 40 per cent respectively.

Election was marked by a 48-hour 'Bandh Call' by the main Akali groups.

Allegations regarding use of force by the Administration on voters in some areas to caste their votes were made by leaders of many political parties. They also alleged rigging of polls by the government.

17

STATEMENTS OF POLITICAL LEADERS, 1992

The main political parties in the Punjab are: Shiromani Akali Dal Factions, B.J.P., B.S.P., CPI, CPM, Indian National Congress, Janata Dal and Samajwadi Janata Dal. Of the seventeen Akali factions only two namely Akali Dal (Kabul) and Akali Dal (S) contested the elections. The Samajwadi Dal Janata also did not participate.

To have a comprehensive view of the situation, a resume of statements made immediately after the announcement of election is appended.

Shiromani Akali Dal Factions

1. Akali Dal (Baba-Joginder Singh)
2. Akali Dal (Badal)
3. Akali Dal (Kabul)
4. Akali Dal (Longowal)
5. Akali Dal (Pheruman)
6. Akali Dal (Rajdev)
7. Akali Dal (S)
8. Akali Dal Talwandi)
9. Akali Dal (T-Tara Singh)

Panthic Committees

1. Babbar Group
2. Manochal Group
3. Dr. Sohan Singh Group
4. Usmanwale Group

Student Groups

1. Bittur Group
2. Manjit Group
3. Mehta-Chawla Group

1. Akali Dal (Badal)

Shri Badal's call to International Community link aid to human rights

Akali Dal (Badal) president Parkash Singh Badal called upon the International community to link aid to India with the observance of human rights in this country. Mr Badal said international aid is always given for the welfare of citizens whose basic human rights must be honoured.

Shri Badal called upon the Amnesty International and other human rights organisations all over the world, to make an on-the-spot assessment of the grave violation of all accepted norms of democratic conduct by the Government in Punjab.

In a telegram flashed to the Amnesty, he alleged that a reign of terror had been let loose on the unarmed, peaceful citizens in Punjab against exercising their right to protest in a democratic manner.

He said his party and other Panthic organisations were only exercising their constitutional democratic right to express their view in whichever way they liked. He added that the poll boycott was a forceful rejection of the repressive policies of the Government.

The Akali president said the Government was trying to thwart with the help of bayonet the surge of popular response to the pro-boycott rally. Shri Badal said democracy was being murdered in Punjab and wondered how the Government could become a party to the debate on whether or not the Punjabis should exercise their franchise.

"We are propagating our point through peaceful democratic methods and if the Government had any sense of honour it should leave the debate to be settled peacefully between those canvassing in favour and against the poll". "How is the Government concerned with this debate?", Shri Badal asked.

Shri Badal alleged that Ludhiana and its surrounding areas have been turned virtually into a police and army cantonment and the

Government was trying to brow beat the peace loving Punjabis with the help of deadly weapons. "Is this democracy?", he asked.

The Akali president said one of the reasons why the Panthic organisations had decided to boycott the poll was that they were convinced that the Government would use all the might at its disposal to scuttle the democratic will of the people and to influence the outcome of the poll by resorting to massive rigging. This stand has been fully vindicated by the Government's brutal use of force against the common people in general and the Panthic workers even before campaigning has started. "In sharp contrast to the Government's terrorism, the Panthic organisations were only using democratic and civilised methods of protest", Shri Badal asserted.

Shri Badal appealed to all the national parties, excluding the Congress to join the boycott so that the Government's farce could be totally exposed before National and International community. He asked the national and international human rights organisations to send independent observers to see how the Government was crushing the voice of innocent people in Punjab. He warned the Government of serious consequences if it persisted with its blind confrontationist attitude towards the Sikhs.

(*Hindustan Times*. February 3, 1992)

Badal's Appeal to Punjabis for a Democratic Battle to Boycott Election and Fight the Centre's Nefarious Designs

Shiromani Akali Dal (Badal) president Parkash Singh Badal asked the Punjabis to prepare for a long and decisive battle ahead as the Centre had sensed the doom of its disastrous policies against Sikhs and Punjabis.

In a statement Shri Badal said, "the historic fight had won the first round at Ludhiana on Feb. 2 and the Centre was now in a State of total desperation. All kinds of methods were being adopted to stop the Panthic representatives from meeting the people personally and to break the channels of communication between them", adding that he expected "greater repression against Panthic leaders in the days to come". "But we are prepared for making all kinds of sacrifices. If the Centre thought that it could browbeat us into submission, it was living in a fool's paradise. The Punjabis and the Panth are ready for the decisive democratic battle and we gleefully accept the challenge thrown at us", Shri Badal said.

He also appealed to ensure that the traitors of Punjab, who had defied the will of the people to enter into the poll tamasha, should be prevented from entering the villages. "The iron is hot and the need of the hour is for all Punjabis to strike with united force", he concluded.

He said that the Punjabis were quite capable of fighting the Centre's nefarious designs even if all the leaders were put behind the bars. It is a fight for principles and our strongest weapon is our democratic resolve. Since truth is on our side, it is only a matter of time before the Centre accepts the reality.

Shri Badal said that he was not particularly concerned about the outcome of the election in Punjab because it was a meaningless tamasha and had no relevance to the historic realities of Punjab. One way or the other, it is going to be a non-representative Government since all the proud sons of Punjab had decided to boycott. "We see no difference between the puppets and their masters", he said asking the people to completely expose the hollowness of the Centre's crocodile tears on democracy. "Their pretensions on democracy were fully exposed at Ludhiana where they brought a fully-equipped Army against the peaceful and unarmed innocent people to thwart their totally legitimate and peaceful rally and many of the participating workers were subjected to cruel repression". Shri Badal regretted that when it came to the Sikhs, the Government did not even consider it necessary to keep an appearance of civilised behaviour. It was this attitude of the Government for the past 45 years that has driven the Sikhs to launch the present struggle, he said adding that "the fight will be carried on till a definite and lasting solution was found to the Punjab problem". "At this critical hour, we will not flinch in the face of inhuman repression. We will fight to the finish" the Akali leader declared.

(*Hindustan Times*, February 6, 1992)

2. Akali Dal (Kabul)

On 19th Jan. the Chairman of the parliamentary board of the Akali Dal (Kabul), Captain Amrinder Singh promised a general amnesty to all undertrials and underground Sikh youth in the state if his party came to power after the Assembly elections. He observed, ". . . a general amnesty will provide one such a way to restore peace and give the youth an honourable way out". Further he observed, "I have information that many Sikh youth want to give up their present path of militancy. But they have no faith left in the police. So, only an elected government can provide them an honourable way out through a general amnesty".

(*Times of India*, January 20, 1992)

Akali Dal (K), Formally Announces its Decision to Contest Punjab Poll

The Akali Dal faction led by the former SGPC president, Shri Kabul Singh, formally announced its decision to contest the election despite the poll boycott decision by several rival Akali and AISSF factions.

The Akali Dal (K) will contest the elections on the issue of restoring peace in the strife-torn state and will include general amnesty for all undertrials and underground militants as a means for achieving this end.

The chairman of the party parliamentary board, Capt. Amrinder Singh, said here that the announcement was in accordance with their decision on January 20. "We had decided to participate in the elections but had withheld the announcement till the notification was issued", Capt. Singh said.

Capt. Singh announced the constitution of a seven-member parliamentary board comprising the former Punjab Chief Minister, Shri Surjit Singh Barnala, the former Punjab Home Minister, Capt. Kanwaljit Singh, the Party president, Shri Kabul Singh, the former Assembly Speaker, Shri Ravi Inder Singh, Shri Ranjit Singh Thiara and Raja Narinder Singh. Capt. Singh would be the president of the board.

Capt. Singh announced they would be contesting all the 117 Assembly and all 13 Lok Sabha seats. They would do so with the two left parties with whom a formal electoral adjustment was being thrashed out.

Capt. Singh said they were open to electoral alignments with other democratically minded parties including the Janata Dal and the BSP. He, however, categorically ruled out any poll alliance with the Congress.

While conceding the difficulties posed by the militant's threats and the poll boycott decision by the rival Akali and AISSF factions, Capt. Singh said his party hoped to capitalise on the people's desire for elections and an end to the President's Rule in the State.

(*Times of India*, January 26, 1992)

Akali Dal (Kabul) explains its poll strategy

The chairman of the Akali Dal-K, Capt. Amrinder Singh has totally ruled out any alliance with the Congress or the Bharatiya Janata Party (BJP) to contest the forthcoming State Assembly elections in Punjab and has said that any Akali Dal doing that would be committing suicide.

Expressing this view, Amrinder Singh told the *Hindustan Times* that in Punjab the Sikh view is that it is because of the Congress policies that the State was facing such a grim situation. As many as 16,000 people have been killed during the last eight to nine years and if the Congress hopes to have any alliance or understanding with any of the Akali Dals, it was living in a fool's paradise, he said.

He said that his Dal will have no truck with the Congress under any circumstances although "our rivals had been carrying on a propaganda that we are going to have some understanding with the Congress." It was also untrue that any of the leaders of his Dal including himself had met the Prime Minister in connection with any alliance or understanding of forming a Government after the elections with the support of the Congress.

However, he made it clear that his Dal would have an understanding with the Leftist parties like CPI and the CPM and even Janata Dal and the SJP on seat-sharing basis. His said that the general secretary of Akali Dal-K was holding talks with the Left parties, the Janata Dal and the SJP on seat-sharing basis. A decision in this regard would be taken soon, he said.

Capt. Amrinder Singh expressed himself strongly on the sharing of Ravi-Beas waters about which a controversy has risen again. He said while the Chandigarh issue is a political issue, the water is the life line of Punjab. He said that Union Government was ready to refer the dispute over the sharing of the Ravi-Beas waters to the Supreme Court but the Chief Ministers of Haryana and Rajasthan scuttled the move.

Capt. Amrinder Singh said that the people of Punjab were of the view that the river waters disputes have to be decided on riparian principles. Since Punjab is the riparian State of Ravi and Beas waters, it was in the interest of both Haryana and Rajasthan to make a reference to the Supreme Court to resolve the water dispute. The ratio of water has to be 60:40 between Punjab and Haryana just like all other properties which had been divided on this ratio. But if they do not agree. we will not allow a drop of water to go to this State, he said.

About his party's chances in the elections, Capt. Amrinder Singh said that only two parties are in a position to form a government viz. the Akali Dal-K and the Congress. The Badal and Mann Akali Dals have offered the 13 seats to the Congress on a platter because of the boycott. Actually, they are in league with the Congress and they wanted that Congress should romp home with all the 13 seats so that the party gets majority in the Lok Sabha. He warned the people of Punjab that if they failed to see through this game, the Congress will sweep all the seats and that would lead to a bigger tragedy and those who are boycotting the elections would be the biggest traitors.

He said "we are hoping to pull off our own majority. In the last election we had got 73 seats and we can get these seats again. People in the rural areas are fed up with terrorists and more so with the police atrocities." He however, asked the Centre to ensure that Army stays in Punjab even after the elections for two to three years. That would allay all the fears of the people and they would come forward in large numbers to cast their votes on February 19, Capt. Amrinder Singh said.

(*Hindustan Times*, January 27, 1992)

Akali Dal (K) reiterates its decision to contest poll

An emergency meeting of the Akali Dal (K) reiterated its decision to contest the Punjab poll and to defeat the Congress who was responsible for the troubled situation in the State.

(*Hindustan Times*, January 30)

Akali-K, CPM poll adjustment

Shiromani Akali Dal (Kabul) entered into seat adjustment with *CPI, CPM*. Three seats for Lok Sabha were left for CPM including those of Bhatinda, Sangrur and Phillaur while sixteen seats of Vidhan Sabha left for these parties.

3. **Akali Dal (M)**

Boycott of Elections

Senior Akali Dal leader Parkash Singh Badal reiterated on Jan. 21, his party's stand to boycott the elections in Punjab. He said the decision taken by various Akali Dal factions was final and irrevocable.

Talking to newsmen at Ludhiana after a meeting of the action committee at Gurdwara Akalgarh, Shri Badal made it clear that no efforts by the Government at any level would be permitted to come in the way of the boycott decision. The action committee had set up joint committees at the constituency level to mobilise public opinion in favour of the party decision to stay away from the polls.

Leaders belonging to various Akali Dal factions, including Shri Simranjit Singh Mann, Captain Harcharan Singh Rode, general secretary of the Akali Dal led by Baba Joginder Singh, Shri Kartar Singh Narang of the Akali Dal Babbar, Shri Sukhbir Singh Khalsa of the Sikh Students Federation (Mehta Chawla group) and Shri Sarbjit Singh of the Sikh Students Federation (Manjit group) took part in the meeting.

Shri Badal said the action committee had decided to intensify the struggle if the Government tried to suppress their voice or to check their free movement. He said it would be wrong to compare the Akali boycott with that of the Congress at the time of the last elections. He said the Congress had boycotted the elections with a vested political interest whereas the Akali Dal had taken this decision in the larger interest of the people.

The Akali leader said the action committee would organise district-level rallies at Sangrur on Jan. 29 at Patiala on Jan. 30 and at Jalandhar on Jan. 31 to mobilise public opinion and to motivate the people in support of the boycott decision.

(*Hindustan Times*, January 22, 1992)

Dr. B.L. Wadhera, the Counsel of Shri Simranjit Singh Mann

Akalis may join Poll fray "let the Centre give a creditable assurance that polls will be free and fair". In case it was done, Shri Mann said that his party could reconsider its decision to boycott the polls.

Shri Mann demanded holding of the February 19 elections under the United Nations supervision.

(*Hindustan Times*, January 23, 1992)

Mann denies election offer

Akali leader Simranjit Singh Mann on January 24, denied that he had said that his party could contest elections under certain conditions.

Talking to newspeople, Shri Mann, who was flanked by senior Akali leader Parkash Singh Badal, said, reports that he was reconsidering his earlier stand on the elections were totally false and mischievous.

Shri Mann was quoted by his lawyer friend, Dr. B.L. Wadhera, in Delhi that Shri Mann was prepared to contest the coming Assembly and Lok Sabha polls in Punjab if the Centre gave a credible assurance that the elections would be "fair and free". He was also quoted as having said that the elections could be held under UN auspices.

Shri Mann said he had stated in writing (this was claimed by Dr. Wadhera also) his position regarding elections. It was meant to be shown to human right groups, Amnesty International and other foreign delegations.

Shri Mann, who refused to chide his friend for having made this a public issue and for having compromised his position, said he did not like to react that way.

Shri Badal had rushed this morning after reading the reports and made Shri Mann restate his position.

Shri Mann, who left for Jammu to lead a counter rally at Srinagar, said he stood by the decision taken by the seven-member Akali committee at Ludhiana last week and would campaign for boycotting the elections.

(*Hindustan Times*, January 25, 1991)

Telegrams by Shri Simranjit Singh Mann, President Akali Dal (Mann) to the United Nations Secretary General, *Ambassadors of the USA United Kingdom, Russia, France and China for International intervention*

"Akali Dal leaders and workers were illegally detained by the Punjab police in Bhatinda district. This is tantamount to blatant misuse of authority and clear violation of the Constitution of India. Sikhs, who are struggling to achieve their goal in a peaceful and democratic way to lead an honourable life, are being discriminated against by Hindu fundamentalists. BJP leader Dr. Murli Manohar Joshi was taken to Srinagar by the Government in a Government plane to hoist the national flag there on January 26 last for facilitating BJP propaganda against Muslims of J and K while Simranjit Singh Mann was detained at Punjab and J and K border on January 25 and not allowed to proceed to Srinagar to hold a peaceful rally in support of the minorities of India. Kindly bring this matter to the notice of the United Nations for intervention and prevention of violation of human rights by the Government of India."

(Akali workers were detained on the way on Feb. 8, 1992 and prevented from attending a workers' meeting at Bhatinda).

(*Hindustan Times*, February, 9, 1992)

Punjab Poll a Systematic Fraud – Akali Dal (M)

The Shiromani Akali Dal (Mann) clarified that it was boycotting the elections in Punjab because it is a "systematic fraud" of the Government meant only to install a puppet regime to perpetuate police and army rule.

The Central Government, according to the Dal, is for extra-judicial killings and illegal detention of Sikh youths, religious and political leaders.

The Dal once again appealed to the people of Punjab to be beware of the new Government, if a new Government is formed, which will last as long as it continues to kill Sikh youth. "Therefore let us unitedly defeat the dangerous moves of the Narasimha Rao Government", according to the Dal leaders.

A close associates of Shri S.S. Mann said that the Sikhs of Punjab need to be prudent to realise that the participation of the Congress in elections without addressing the longstanding issues would accentuate fraticidal battle among Sikhs and mar the communal bonds between Hindus and Sikhs.

While appealing to militants groups to sink their differences, the Dal leaders asked the Hindus to demonstrate their kinship and brotherhood with the Sikhs and their keenness to live in Punjab peacefully.

They said that three major opportunities to own the Sikhs and Punjab were frittened away. First in 1961, on the mother-tongue issue. Second in June 1984 during and after "Operation Blue Star"and finally in November 1984 when Sikhs were butchered and burnt alive all over the country. "The present elections have granted the Punjabi Hindus yet another chance to undo the wrongs by siding with Sikhs in their hour of crisis", they pointed out.

"History demands that the Punjabi Hindus visualise the outcome of the present struggle and be wary of the muted welcome in other parts of the country. Punjab is your homeland just as it is of the Sikhs and we implore you to move in unison with the Sikh brethren", the Dal leaders appealed.

The party condemned the killing of innocent men, women and children and acts of kidnapping, assaults, threats and extortion. "We call upon militants to purge their ranks of all those indulging the indiscriminate killing of innocent people", they added.

The Dal appealed the Sikhs in general and the militant Sikh youth in particular to remember that power did not necessarily flow from the barrel of the gun alone but to achieve sovereignty and freedom, a sustained political movement, backed by moral strength, was imperative, "Our character and deeds should bear a reflection of our inner strength. The glorious tradition of the Khalsa has to be relived if we wish to attain our Panthic goal", the Dal members pointed out.

The Dal has cautioned the police, para-military and Army personnel to obey only those orders which were lawful, legal constitutional, morally right and which did not violate any provisions of international law and human rights conventions and convents.

"The party will initiate proceedings against such offenders in Nurenberg like trials for war crimes against humanity including genocide. The party will also revoke the impunity granted to violators of human rights by an amendment to the Cr.PC by the Congress Government", they said.

The Dal also appealed to the International Committee of the Red Cross to send a high-level team to Punjab to monitor the observance by both sides, of all aspects of international law concerning the conduct of hostilities, particularly The Hague conventions of 1907 and the Geneva convention of 1949.

(*Hindustan times*, February 13, 1992)

Shri Badal and Shri Mann Charge the Government with using undemocratic methods

"We have every right to protest and organise the people against elections. The law and the Constitution, about which the Centre is never tired of signing songs, allows us to peacefully take our point of view to the people as it allows those who want to contest," they said.

Shri Badal and Shri Mann lashed out at the Government for "crushing the voice of the Punjabis and the Sikhs".

In a statement they described as "shocking and unbelievable the crackdown on Akali leaders and workers who wee not being allowed even to organise peaceful, democratic meetings. The police had been given "illegitimate powers" to detain any Akali without ascribing any reason.

Describing the Government's action as obscurantist and totally undemocratic, the two leaders said, "This has unmasked the ugly face behind the Government's fake democratic smiles. The Government has forfeited the right to preach to others on democratic norms and values as it has already unleashed an illegal, immoral and undemocratic repression and suppression against the Punjabis in general and Sikhs in particular."

The Akali leaders said even democracy in this country had acquired two different meanings: one for the Sikhs and the other for the rest. While other parties were being allowed to organise their political activities and carry on even their yatras in a provocative fashion in the face of a gave threat to public peace, the Akalis were being denied even the basic right to protest democratically and peacefully This, they said, was reminiscent of the days of the British and the Mughals.

They said the Government was acting out of sheer desperation as it had sensed the mood of the people, which was totally in favour of a boycott of the "poll drama". "The throttling of all democratic channels of protest is bound to lead to very dangerous consequences and the responsibility for this will rest entirely with the Government."

They said the whole Sikh community was virtually being placed under house arrest. "Is this the kind of democracy that the Government believes in?" they asked, adding that the Government had lost the moral right even to talk about democracy. "We are living in the dark age of repressive and totalitarian regime. The Government action has vindicated our stand that the elections here will be merely a state-managed tamasha to mislead national and international opinion."

The Akali leaders said those who had fallen into the trap laid by the Government after betraying their colleagues and the entire Panth must ponder over their actions and their grave implications for the Punjabis in general and Sikhs in particular".

They said all the venues of the meeting by Akali workers were being sealed and even the holy Gurdwaras were being put under siege with the help of the Army.

The Akali leaders appealed to the people to give a befitting reply to the Government's challenge and turn up in large numbers at he Ludhiana rally in order to exhibit the united strength of the Punjabis against the "devious designs" of the Centre.

They warned the Government that in spite of all the "blind repression let loose against the Akalis, the people will never allow the Government to succeed in its nefarious designs of organising a hollow and meaningless defection drama.

(*Hindustan Times*, January 31, 1992)

4. Akali Dal (Pheruman)

Akali Dal (Pheruman) president Mahant Sewa Das Singh today said his party would not contest the elections in Punjab but would support parties which respected the Indian Constitution and fought for the unity and integrity of the country.

The Mahant told reporters the party was not contesting the elections because the Government had not honoured its commitment to include Chandigarh and other Punjabi-speaking areas in Punjab and had not conceded other demands of the State.

The Mahant said his leader, the late Shri Darshan Singh Pheruman, had sacrificed his life for the cause of Chandigarh. "How can we ignore the sacrifice of this great leader who fought till his last breath for the inclusion of Chandigarh into Punjab." the Mahant asked.

The Pheruman Akali Dal president appreciated the stand taken by former Punjab Chief Minister Parkash Singh Badal, who insisted on handling over of Chandigarh to Punjab.

He said that though he had differed politically with Shri Badal in the past, "I must appreciate" his stand on the Chandigarh issue.

He appealed to Shri Badal to participate in the poll if he was concerned about the welfare of the people of Punjab. He should not succumb to the pressure of militants.

He said that it was unfortunate that some Akali leaders were suggesting issuing of a "hukamnama in support of the boycott", of the elections. This would amount to using religion for political purposes, he said.

If a "hukamnama" was issued, the Mahant said, it would also affect the sanctity of the Akal Takht, the highest temporal seat of the Sikhs.

He urged the people of Punjab to ensure that elements fighting for the cause of Khalistan did not get into the Vidhan Sabha by proxy and implement the "evil designs of Pakistan."

(*Hindustan Times*, January 31, 1992)

Punjab Polls no Solution – Mahant Sewa Dass

Akali Dal (Pheruman) president Mahant Sewa Dass Singh said that holding elections in Punjab without first solving the basic problems of the State was not a solution to the vexed problem. He asked the Union Government to make a unilateral announcement granting Chandigarh to the State and solving water dispute.

Addressing a Press conference he impressed upon other Akali leaders not to take law in their own hands to enforce poll boycott. The boycott issue should be pursued in a democratic manner and they should desist from taking any direct action in this regard as it could further malign the Sikhs.

He disagreed with the Government that the heavy deployment of security personnel would ensure free elections. How was free election possible with the deployment of over three lakh army and para-military forces? he asked.

In reply to a question, he said the basic problems of the people should be solved to assuage their feelings. Once their confidence was restored, they were strong enough to teach Pakistan a lesson on their own. On the part of the Government, the Prime Minister should take immediate decision to launch a direct action against Pakistan as the diplomatic efforts would not convince the leadership of that country to solve bilateral issues and desist from interfering in the internal affairs of India.

The Mahant said the onus of maintaining peace in Punjab during elections lies on the Akalis. Any wrong move on their part could give an excuse to the Union Government to further discredit the Sikhs. He also appealed to the Akalis to prevent use of religious places for any political activity lest a Operation Blue Star was repeated by the Government.

(*Hindustan Times*, February 7, 1992)

5. Akali Dal (S)

Shri Sukhjinder Singh, a senior member of the Badal Group, formed a new party to contest elections. While forming the new party Shri

Sukhjinder Singh said, "I have viewed round to the view after deliberations that the recent decision of the poll boycott by various Akali factions is impolitic, illogical and erroneous and showed a negative approach". The poll boycott would facilitate anti-Sikh forces to continue their repressive policies with greater vigour. Over the year, the Government had grown sceptical of the Sikhs and instead of removing their grievances, let loose a reign of suppression resulting in their alienation and militancy, he said.

(*Indian Express*, January 26, 1992)

Boycott of election, no solution — Shri Sukhjinder Singh

Stating that his decision to contest the forthcoming Assembly elections in the state was "irrevocable", the leader of the Akali Dal (S), Shri Sukhjinder Singh, expressed his admiration for the militants whom he described as "freedom fighters struggling for the Sikh community".

Shri Singh, a retired DSP, recently broke away from the Akali Dal (Badal) as senior vice-president to form his own party to contest the forthcoming elections. He has announced his party's decision to contest 90 assembly and 10 Lok Sabha seats. But he did not announce the names of any party office-bearers stating that he was withholding their names "owing to security reasons".

Making it clear that he had broken away since he differed with the Akali Dal (B) leadership's poll boycott decision, Shri Singh stated that he was in favour of a separate Sikh state through the ballot. The Akali leader, who figures high on the terrorists' hit list, has simultaneously accepted heavy security from the Punjab police.

Expressing his sympathies with the slain self styled "Lt. Gen." and panthic committee member Sukhjinder Singh Alias Gora who was killed in an encounter in Batala district, Shri Singh called upon the people to observe a bandh in protest against the killing.

Appealing to the Akali factions to reconsider their boycott decision in the interests of Punjab and the Sikhs, Shri Singh said the response to elections in the rural areas had been lukewarm mainly owing to threats from terrorists. The people of the state were living in terror perpetuated both by the terrorists and the police, he added.

Shri Singh alleged that by boycotting the elections, the Akali and AISSF factions were virtually offering a Congress government to Punjab. "I fail to understand what programme these boycotting parties hope to adopt after the polling is over, except staging dharnas, which would serve little.

(*Times of India*, January 29, 1992)

Extracts from an interview of Sukhjinder Singh

* * * *

If given the required majority, I can offer an honourable and acceptable solution, only a Akali ministry can do this.

* * * *

I, as leader of the party, have a clear vision and genuine perception of the situation. I would appeal to the voters to enable me to secure a comfortable majority.

* * * *

What I have been saying in the past, has vindicated my position. What I stated 10 years ago (he had raised the slogan of Khalistan), was undervalued at that time, but now, reality had dawned on the masses. When one speaks the truth, one is described as a hard-liner. Values become one's enemy, I am a victim of this misconception.

* * * *

Those who want the people to boycott the Punjab poll want to perpetuate a reign of suppression and torture in the state which is the handiwork of the Congress(I).

* * * *

I with to usher in an era of hope, faith, tranquillity and an atmosphere helpful for the solution of the Punjab problem to the satisfaction of the Sikhs. My endeavour would be to establish the rule of law

* * * *

I would very humbly and earnestly appeal to the militants belonging to all organisations to facilitate a smooth and peaceful conduct of the elections as this would go a long way in helping them, they should declare a truce during the elections and if the results of the ballot cannot satisfy them, they can revert to the bullet. I assure them from the core of my heart that they will not meet with many opposition from us.

(*Indian Express*, February 2, 1992)

Kabul faction rebels to boycott poll

The pro-election Akali Dal (Kabul) faction suffered a major setback, with seven of its party leaders announcing a poll boycott. Although the rebels said they were not leaving the party, sources said they were likely to join the Badal faction of the Akali Dal.

Announcing the decision, the former Punjab minister and general secretary of the erstwhile Akali Dal (L), Shri Natha Singh Dalam, said the forthcoming elections were was no solution to the Punjab problem.

The rebels comprise seven middle-rank leaders and members of the working committee of the erstwhile Akali Dal (L), many of whom are former MLAs and ministers.

The Press conference in which all the seven rebels were present was attended by several senior leaders of the Badal group, including the SGPC president, Mr. Gurcharan Singh Tohra.

(*Times of India*, January 28, 1992)

6. AISSF urges Sikh leaders to boycott Punjab polls

All-India Sikh Students Federation (AISSF) chief Bhai Manjit Singh urged Sikhs belonging to the Congress and Communist Parties to refuse to contest the elections under the prevailing conditions in Punjab. They should join the mainstream of Sikhs and boycott the elections, he added.

Talking to reporters, he said that the boycott decision of the various Akali factions and the Federation was final. The independent candidates would not get any backdoor support from any Akali faction, he added.

Bhai Manjit Singh was confident that the factions led by Shri Kabul Singh, president of United Akali Dal Longowal and Capt.

Amrinder Singh would also boycott the elections.

(*Hindustan Times*, January 29, 1992)

7. Khalistan Commando Force (KCF) on support to Shri Sukhjinder Singh

Khalistan Commando Force (KCF) has said that it does not own leaders like Shri Sukhjinder Singh. A Press note said that a meeting of the top leaders was held near Batala and it was decided that the Panthic Committee Zaffarwal, whose support Shri Sukhjinder Singh has been claiming should have nothing to do with him. He cannot be trusted as he is a power-hungry politician.

One-page statement in Punjabi bearing the names of Shri Wassan Singh Zaffarwal, Shri Kewal Singh Sukhadhira, Chota Raju, Aulukh Beri and Shri Jarnail Singh Hoshiarpuri said that Shri Zaffarwal had never met Sukhjinder Singh and never extended any support to him.

(*Hindustan Times*, January 30, 1992)

8. Akali Dal (T)

Shri Jagdev Singh Talwandi forms a new Akali Dal

Shri Jagdev Singh Talwandi, patron Akali Dal (Badal), announced the formation of a new Akali faction to be known as Akali Dal-T.

Shri Talwandi, who was elected chairman of the new party, said his party would not participate in the current Punjab elections and follow the policy of militants.

The decision to form a new party was taken at a meeting of Akali leaders and workers from all over the State with Shri Talwandi in the chair.

Briefing newsmen Shri Talwandi said the meeting through a resolution expressed the view that Shri P.S. Badal and Shri S.S. Mann, presidents of Akali Dal-Badal and Akali Dal-Mann respectively were the stooges for the Centre and had boycotted the February 19 polls at the instructions of the Centre.

Shri Talwandi was authorised to nominate office-bearers and working committee of the new party. Those who were present at the meeting included Shri Randhir Singh Cheema and Shri Jaswinder Singh Brar, former Ministers, and Shri S.S. Dhullar district president Akali Dal-B, Ferozepur.

(*Hindustan Times*, January 31, 1992)

7. **Panthic Panel may sponsor candidates: Shri Gurcharan Singh Manochal**

The panthic committee headed by Gurbachan Singh Manochahal may sponsor candidates in the forthcoming Punjab elections as it is averse to leaving the field wide open for "anti-panthic forces and traitors to the Sikh cause".

An emergency meeting of the panthic committee and its militant outfits resolved to take this decision only after a formal notification is issued by the Centre.

The panthic committee maintained that it had little faith in the Constitution and was committed to the goal of "Khalistan". However, it said "traitors" and "puppets of the Central Government" could not be permitted to assume office and weaken the Sikh struggle. It feared that traditional Akali leaders would "axe" the Sikhs once they came to power.

The Bhindranwale Tiger Force of Khalistan supreme. Shri Manochahal, said that if they contested the elections, it would be only to show to the world that the Sikhs stood for a sovereign, independent state.

Shri Manochahal asked his supporters to step up political activities immediately as a strategy to meet the electoral challenge, if required.

(*Times of India*, January 23, 1992)

10. **Panthetic Committee decides to contest elections**

The apex body of militants – the Panthic Committee led by Baba Gurbachan Singh Manochahal announced its decision to enter the election fray in Punjab, while the Akali Dal (Badal) patron, Shri Jagdev Singh Talwandi, launched a new party.

The Panthic Committee released its first list for seven Lok Sabha and 16 Vidhan Sabha candidates, and declared that it would contest 10 Lok Sabha and at least 70 Assembly seats, according to Bhai Balwinder Singh Shahpur, chief of the 'Deshmesh Regiment of Khalistan'.

Baba Manochahal, releasing the first list asked all other aspirants for the ticket to file their nomination papers on time and contact the committee for clearance of their names.

Giving reasons for contesting the polls. Baba Manochahal said the committee did not want to leave the "arena open to traitors."

"This is to show the world that Sikhs did not want to remain slaves but wanted to become nationals of a sovereign state, he added.

Bhai Shahpur said the Panthic Committee chief issued his statement after an important meeting held somewhere in the Tarn Taran area.

Bhai Manochahal said the militants would like to make it clear to the Sikh Panth that they had no faith in the Indian Constitution. They aimed at 'Khalistan' and would continue the struggle for its achievement.

(*Times of India*, 31 January 1992)

Baba Manochahal said that the candidates should necessarily belong to militant families or having link with the present on-going Sikh struggle.

(*Hindustan Times*, January 31, 1991)

Panthic Committee not to contest

The Panthic committee member and Bhindranwale Tiger Force of Khalistan chief, Shri Gurbachan Singh Manochahal, has denied the report published in a section of the Press that he had asked his men to contest elections and issued a list of prospective candidates.

In a statement released to the Press he alleged the news items circulated by a news agency was actually planted by the government agencies to defame the Panthic panel and to serve vested interests.

According to the Press release, Shri Manochahal said he had not authorised anybody to issue such a statement and that he stood by his decision to boycott the ensuing elections. He said the Akalis had boycotted the elections for ulterior motives while he had taken the decision as he was convinced that it would strengthen the movement for attainment of Khalistan.

(*Times of India*, February 1, 1991)

11. All India Sikh Conference (Babbar) for Contesting elections

The All India Sikh Conference (Babbar), appealed to the Akali Dal (Mann) and the Akali Dal (Badal) to participate in the forthcoming Punjab elections

The AISC general secretary, Shri Gurcharan Singh Babbar, said all Akalis should participate in the elections and put their viewpoint before the people.

He said that the Badal and Mann factions of the Akali Dal should not approach the Akal Takht for issuing an appeal to the people of Punjab to boycott the February 19 elections.

"It will result in a serious rift among the Sikh community," he said.

Shri Babbar said major parties such as the BJP, the SJP, the Janata Dal, and the CPM should prevail upon the Akalis to participate in the elections.

(*Times of India*, January 29, 1992)

12. All India Youth Akali Dal for postponing elections

The All India Youth Akali Dal urged President R. Venkataraman to direct the Central Government and the Chief Election Commissioner to postpone the elections in Punjab and try to solve the Punjab problems prior to holding of the elections.

The Dal delegation led by All-India Youth Akali Dal (Doomchheri) general secretary Balwinder Singh Talwandi presented a memorandum to the President on February 4, 1992.

They said in the memorandum that it is a considered view of the Dal as well as other political leaders of the various parties, excluding Congress and BJP, that the elections will prove "useless" exercise if they are held without solving the Punjab problems.

The Akali Dal delegation said a Government formed after the forthcoming elections would be of those parties and elements which have not waged any struggle for solving the problems of the people of the State. The Congress has never voiced the problems of Punjab.

(*Hindustan Times*, February 5, 1992)

13. Delhi Sikh Gurdwara Management Committee (DSGMC) Appeals to political parties to boycott elections

The Delhi Sikh Gurdwara Management Committee (DSGMC) appealed to the political parties, including the Bharatiya Janata Party, CPI, CPI-M and others to boycott the Punjab elections.

The DSGMC president, Shri Rajinder Singh Monga, told newsmen that the atmosphere in the State was not conducive to hold elections.

He said elections in the present situation would not be fair. He criticised the Government for holding elections in Punjab in the prevailing situation. The Government should have held talks with the Punjab Akali Dals and others before announcing the elections.

Shri Monga appealed to the BJP to reconsider its stand about contesting the elections. He said prominent Sikh leaders met the Janata Dal leaders, including Shri V.P. Singh and Shri S.R. Bommai to appeal to them not to participate in the elections.

(*Hindustan Times*, February 8, 1992)

14. Sikh Council Condemns the boycott call

Sikh Council president Rajinder Singh Dolly and general secretary Ajab Singh Daler condemned the decision of various Akali factions to boycott the Punjab elections. They said that in the larger interest of peace, stability and integrity of the country these so-called patriotic leaders should have taken part in elections. Instead, for their own selfish ends they were sacrificing the interest of the Punjabis, they added.

(*Hindustan times*, February 8, 1992)

15. B.J.P. — Party to go alone in Punjab elections

The BJP decided to go it alone in the Punjab elections. At a meeting of the party's working committee on January 27, it was decided that the BJP would contest 60 to 70 Assembly seats and six to seven Lok Sabha seats.

The meeting was chaired by Dr. Murli Manohar Joshi, Party president, and attended by Shri L.K. Advani, Shri A.B. Vajpayee, Mrs. Vijayaraje Scindia and Shri J.P. Mathur.

(*Times of India*, January 28, 1992)

The BJP announces the number of Candidates

The BJP formally announced to contest nine Lok Sabha and 70 Assembly seats.

(*Times of India*, January 29, 1992)

BJP leader Shri Atal Behari Vajpayee moots the idea of mobile booths

The BJP leader, Shri Atal Behari Vajpayee, mooted the idea of mobile polling booths in sensitive villages of Punjab to assuage the fear psychosis among voters and to counter the militants threat.

Addressing a Press conference Shri Vajpayee hoped people would participate in the elections in a big way to defeat secessionist and anti-national forces. Later, Shri Vajpayee addressed a public meeting which was held at the local Hindu College Hall (Amritsar) because of bad weather.

Attacking the Akalis for boycotting the elections. Shri Vajpayee said they could have told their supporters to go to the polling booths, but leave their ballot papers blank as a mark of protest. But since this would have exposed how little support the Akalis had among the masses, they had opted for confrontation and coercion.

The BJP leader said the Akalis would have boycotted the elections even if the Union Government had announced a pre-poll package. Both Shri Parkash Singh Badal and Shri Simranjit Singh Mann had insisted on a package but gave no firm assurance of participating in the poll.

Shri Vajpayee denied a report, published in this paper (*Times of India*), that the BJP had established links with the militants. He pointed out that 200 BJP activists, including the state party chief, had sacrificed their lives at the hands of the militants.

The BJP leader said senior politicians like Shri Parkash Singh Badal should have seen through the gameplan of Pakistan, which was to keep India weak. Not only the misguided youth, but also seasoned politicians of the state would have to correct their approach, he said. A handful of gun-wielding "young boys" could not be permitted to run the state and decide the destiny of the nation, he added.

(*Times of India*, February 19, 1992)

16. Congress Party

Shri Beant Singh, Punjab State Congress President: Chandigarh to be given to Punjab

If Congress came to power in Punjab after the elections next month, it would ensure that Chandigarh was transferred to the state and Punjabi-speaking areas of neighbouring states were ceded to Punjab, the state PCC president, Shri Beant Singh, said.

Speaking to newsmen after the two-day meeting of the party's state parliamentary board, Shri Beant Singh said restoration of the democratic set-up in Punjab was a necessity for the people were fed up with militant-sponsored violence. There was a feeling that an elected government would be able to deal with terrorists more effectively, he added.

The Punjab Congress leader said the Centre should announce a package of concessions for the state before the elections. This should include a sufficient share of the Yamuna waters for the state. The concessions would go a long way in assuaging the feelings of the people who felt neglected by the government on the one hand and harassed by terrorists on the other.

(*Times of India*, January 23, 1992)

Congress committed to Polls — Shri C. P. Thakur

"The Congress party is committed for holding elections in Punjab after generating political consensus", said Shri C.P. Thakur, the official spokesman of the Congress, during a discussion on Punjab elections organised by The Indian Society.

He said apart from generating political consensus for holding elections another precondition is creating an atmosphere in Punjab for holding free and fair polls. The silent majority who has no political axe to grind and are only looking for a breathing space should have a sense of security when they exercise their franchise, he added. Another important precondition to the elections is that those who do not want the elections to be held for their personal political gains should be isolated, he said.

Justifying the decision for holding the elections, Shri Thakur said the political scenario in Punjab is in a total chaos. The places vacated by the political parties are now occupied by certain undesirable elements and by those who might be having some genuine grievances. He said to get the people of Punjab back into the national mainstream it is necessary to hold elections.

Shri Thakur said violence in Punjab has to come to an end as today the youth of the State is totally confused as to his identity and thus easy to be misled. One has to admit that the history long emotional bond between the two major communities has developed cracks and it is high time that political process in the State is initiated for the interest of the country, he said.

(*Hindustan Times*, January 24, 1992)

Union Home Minister S.B. Chavan on Punjab poll

Union Home Minister S.B. Chavan said that he was hopeful of eventual participation in the polls by "most" Akali groups, "under whatever name they call themselves".

Even though some of them may seek the militants help in the polls, or claim to represent their viewpoint, "there is no reason for apprehension that they could work for Punjab's session from India."

Whatever their views for support base, the candidates will be swearing by the Indian Constitution and if elected, will have to take oath under the same statute book, Shri Chavan pointed out.

He said in the course of an interview that the spurt of violence that has accompanied the beginning of the poll processes should not surprise anybody. This was obviously being done at the instance of the Pakistan Government in order to prevent the holding of elections and scare the people away from the hustings.

Shri Chavan said he had directed the Punjab Governor to provide adequate security to all candidates, and those campaigners who are under threat from the militants, on the basis of the lists to be provided by the political parties.

Punjab would get adequate support of the security forces, an assessment of which was being made at present. No effort would be spared on this score, he assured.

He said: "My determination is to go ahead with the polls, no matter where the pressures come from. They will be free and fair. I mean what I say."

Reacting to a report that Shri Simranjit Singh Mann, leading one of the Akali Dal factions, had sought "credible assurance" on this score from him, Shri Chavan said that his words should be taken for what they are.

The Government was "convinced" that the people of Punjab want election". They want peace and economic development denied to them by years of turmoil. He hoped that political leaders of Punjab would also "realise their responsibility to the people of Punjab".

The Home Minister hoped that the political parties would keep in view the suggestion made by the Prime Minister that the political parties should come to some understanding with regard to fielding of candidates, which would be better than every party contesting every seat.

The Home Minister said the political package that many parties had sought and some Akali groups had sought to make a precondition to participation in the polls could not be given because of its "Wide implications". Handing over of Chandigarh to Punjab, for instance, had its "linkages" with other States. The Congress leadership of Haryana had "reacted violently" to any unilateral action by the Centre. On the question of river waters and territorial disputes, the neighbouring States had also argued against any package.

"A package should be one that all parties must accept. First of all, Punjab must accept. Then the question is who in Punjab would accept it an what is the guarantee that this would be honoured after the polls," Shri Chavan observed.

(*Hindustan Times*, January 30, 1992)

Minister of State for Home M.M. Jacob's Statement calling upon Akalis not to boycott elections, February 10, 1992

Calling upon Akali Dal factions not to boycott elections in Punjab, Minister of State for Home M.M. Jacob said the key to solving the State's problems lay in holding elections.

"It is unfortunate if the President's Rule is imposed again and again in the State. It is a shame to ask members of Parliament to enforce President's Rule because we cannot rule the State ourselves."

"This is the only opportunity in a parliamentary democracy to select a government which can solve the problems of the State," Shri Jacob said during a panel discussion on Punjab.

A duly elected government can protect the cultural identity of the State as well as tackle administrative problems like that of making Gurmukhi the second official language in the neighbouring State of Haryana.

"There should be someone responsible for attending to issues like water etc. "We don't believe in dictating to others," the Home Minister said while emphasising the importance of holding elections in Punjab.

He said his government was committed to hold elections in Punjab and to implement the Rajiv-Longowal accord.

Accusing Pakistan of attempting to thwart Punjab elections, he said Pak want to show India in a poor light to the world. There may be fears, he said, about the election process being disrupted by militants trained across the border "but if people of Punjab want elections, a handful of militants cannot stop them. Fear is not an important factor in these elections."

(*Hindustan Times*, February 11, 1992)

17. Punjab Election a Farce : CPI

CPI leadership described the present elections in Punjab "as a crude joke on the hapless people of the State". These elections, without any political initiative, first the boycott by the Akalis, then police excesses in the holding back candidates, arresting the boycotting leaders and not allowing them to propagate, would inevitably lead to urban-rural divide and communal polarisation", CPI State secretary Piara Singh Deosi said. He said, "this election is going to be a farce. The people have undergone untold suffering during the last several years. What kind of election is this? First, the candidates were stopped by the police from filling their nominations, then they were detained and later forced to withdraw and finally those who could still succeed are prisoners of the police. No campaign from 6 p.m. to 8 a.m."

Earlier, BSP leader Kanshi Ram, MP, had alleged that 35 of his candidates were being detained in police stations and not allowed to canvass. Similar allegations had come from Congress candidate Ms. Santosh Chaudhry from Phillaur seat.

Shri Deosi said that the Government was adopting rough methods to meet the challenge of the boycotting Akalis by arresting them under TADA, by banning their rallies and marches. The Government should take along the contesting parties and people to meet this challenge. These leaders, who in his view ran away from their duty, still had the right to preach their boycott. How can the boycott of the Akalis is anti national and that of the Congress in June was democratic?" he asked.

Shri Deosi saw a big conspiracy behind the polls. "The Congress had cleverly designed to keep the Akalis away from the polls by offering them a political package and later scuttling all efforts towards that. Once these Akalis were out, the game is to win a good number of Lok Sabha seats and then install some Government for a brief period. Later the Centre could impose its own rule. This is very tragic for Punjab", he lamented.

The CPI leader had serious apprehensions about free elections in Punjab. Why is the staff being inducted from outside? Why not trust the Punjab employees? he asked.

Shri Deosi also demanded the release of all Akali leaders. The demand has also been voiced by the BJP leaders.

(*Hindustan Times*, February 13, 1992)

18. CPM Criticises Prime Minister P.V. Narasimha Rao on Punjab Policy

The general secretary of the CPM Shri Harkishan Singh Surjeet, accused the Prime Minister, Mr. P.V. Narasimha Rao, of putting "narrow" political interests of the Congress party before those of the country in tackling the Punjab problem.

The veteran Communist leader said by postponing the announcement of a political package for Punjab to a post-election date the Prime Minister had failed to involve moderate Akalis in the forthcoming elections and make the exercise meaningful.

Shri Surjeet told the press that he had held discussions with various Akali leaders before they announced their decision to boycott the elections on January 17, and his impression was that they were waiting for the government to declare the package so that they could come out in favour of taking part in the elections.

Shri Surjeet released to the press a letter which he sent to the Prime Minister on January 19 expressing anguish over the handling of the situation in Punjab.

The general secretary said during his discussions with the Prime Minister in the recent past, he got the impression that the government was sincerely thinking of announcing a political package for the beleaguered state before it goes to poll.

(*Times of India*, January 26, 1992)

CPI Candidate shot dead

On January 26, militants killed CPI state council member Harpal Singh, the joint nominee of the two left parties.

(*Times of India*, Jan. 27, 1992)

Shri Harkishan Singh Surjeet, CPM General Secretary criticises the Government for withholding package

Shri Harkishan Singh Surjeet, CPM general secretary, expressed the view that an assurance on Chandigarh, putting on trial those involved in the 1984 riots and an assurance that Article 356 (imposition of President's Rule) would not be used in Punjab, could have been the political package for Punjab that would have involved the moderate Akalis in the February 19 elections.

Claiming that political package initially had the approval in principle of the Prime Minister, Shri P.V. Narasimha Rao, Shri Surjeet said in a debate *Eyewitness*, HTV's video magazine of this month, that even though he knew that the CCPA members had agreed on that package, he heard on the midnight of January 24 that the notification for the election was issued without the package.

The Prime Minister's failure to produce a package had "contributed to the situation which has become more complicated and difficult perhaps they feel that if everyone boycotts, like Assam, they can have some seats. Perhaps they only want with force, with the paramilitary forces, to get some 13 seats in Parliament. Now I have come to this conclusion: the narrow outlook of the Congress has barred the way."

According to Shri Surjeet: "I discussed with Shri Vajpayee and he told the Prime Minister that if you hand over Chandigarh I have no objection. Then Shri V.P. Singh told them "I would like an immediate political package so that moderate Akalis are involved.

(*Times of India*, February 5, 1992)

Shri Harkishan Singh Surjeet,general secretary, CPM, appeals the Akali Dal leadership to stop misusing Gurdwaras

Addressing an election rally at Ahmedgarh, Shri Surjeet asked the Akali leaders to instead issue an appeal and pass resolutions from the gurdwaras urging the militants to surrender their weapons and join the national mainstream.

Shri Surjeet pointed out that more than 12,000 innocent people had been killed in Punjab by militants. These included 200 CPM workers. Nevertheless, the party would continue its fight against separatists and militants who were acting on the diktats of Pakistan.

Shri Surjeet alleged that the Centre was not keen on solving the Punjab problem. He said he had written seven letters to the Prime Minister since July, seeking certain measures for the solution of the problem. He said he had suggested that Chandigarh should be transferred to Punjab, the river waters issue be referred to the Supreme Court and the guilty of the 1984 riots be punished. The last letter he wrote was on January 24 in which he had warned that the Centre would be responsible for the worsening of the situation. "Today, we are living under fear and threats. If the Centre had taken the steps, the elections in Punjab would have been held without any fear," he asked.

(*Times of India*, February 14, 1992)

19. Samajwadi Janata Party (SJP)

Shri Om Prakash Chautala: Party to contest election

The Secretary General of the Samajwadi Janata Party's national executive, Shri Om Prakash Chautala said in January 20, that his party would contest the Punjab elections. He reiterated that his party would not accept any package other than the Indira Gandhi Award of 1970 whereby Chandigarh was to go to Punjab and 107 Hindi-speaking villages of Abohar and Fazilka would be given to Haryana. He further stated that Haryana should be given enough money to build its own capital.

(*Times of India*, January 21, 1991)

Shri Chandra Shekhar : Party not be contest elections

The Samajwadi Janata Party (SJP) decided not to "participate" in the elections in Punjab as the government had failed to make adequate preparation for the polls in the state, the party leader, Shri Chandra Shekhar, announced.

Talking to newsmen, the former Prime Minister said the government had also aggravated the "sense of frustration and despair" among the people and in the process it had lost the credibility to hold free and fair poll.

"The SJP in no way wants to be a party to this inept handling of a very critical and sensitive situation in the state," Shri Chandra Shekhar said, clarifying that it was not boycotting the polls.

"Boycott and non-participation are two different things," he said.

In June last when he was the Prime Minister, a political climate was created in which various Akali parties and all other parties were ready to participate in the electoral process and there was a hope for future.

However, no sooner the Congress returned to power, the

scheduled June elections in Punjab were "inexplicably postponed and later cancelled, which further deepened the profound sense of alienation of the Punjab masses." he said.

Shri Chandra Shekhar said that the Punjab governor and the bureaucrats in the Centre as well as the state were opposed to postponement of June elections. Even the Chief Election Commissioner was opposed but he was "coerced" by the government to issue orders, he said.

(*Times of India*, February, 1992)

20. Shiv Sena to boycott Punjab poll

The All India Hindu Shiv Sena will boycott the elections to Parliament and the Assembly in Punjab to be held on Feb. 19. Citing the reason for the boycott, Sena president Surinder Kumar Billa said the minority community felt unsafe and insecure there.

Addressing newsmen Shri Billa said about five lakh members belonging to approximately one lakh families had migrated from the villages and cities of Punjab to other parts of the country due to killings of innocent persons, kidnapping and deteriorating law and order situation there.

Shri Billa said the Government should first try to bring these people back to Punjab and arrange to rehabilitate them and their names should be entered in the voters list. The Sena chief also demanded that Hindi language should be recognised as the second language after Punjabi in Punjab and a security belt along the borders of Pakistan should be activated.

(*Hindustan Times*, February 5, 1992)

21. Punjab Peoples Party (PPP) floated

The newly-floated Punjab Peoples Party (PPP) said that its door was open to electoral adjustment with like-minded secular parties and is of the view that any political party which talks of boycotting the forthcoming elections in Punjab would be doing immense harm to Punjab where the people wanted the restoration of democracy.

Air Marshal (retired) M.S. Bawa, PPP president, and Col. (retired) H.S. Attari told media persons at a Press conference that the party wished to give a direction to peace, progress and prosperity in Punjab and had no illusions of forming the government.

They said they would launch a mass-movement against terrorism by mobilising right-thinking people. Peace could return to Punjab only if terrorism was eliminated. However, to eliminate terrorism, it would also be necessary to study the root causes of this phenomenon and formulate plans to remove those causes.

"It is not the psyche of the Sikhs alone that needs to be understood. There is also the psyche of Hindus, the Muslims, the Christians and other communities that live together in Punjab," Air Marshal Bawa said.

They said the only way to stop terrorism was for the government to take bold action on the strength of intelligence reports available to it. If it made a beginning results would follow.

Even more important than a package for Punjab was the need to curb terrorism, they said. Once there was peace, there would also be progress and prosperity.

They said a good beginning had been made with the Union Home Minister, Shri S.B. Chavan, observing a two-minutes silence in honour of those who lost their lives in the 1984 riots. This was at a meeting they organised on December 12.

Col. Attari said the Army and para-military forces deployed in Punjab could be withdrawn through a carefully planned exercise. He did not think that terrorists would feel more free to operate if the security forces were withdrawn.

Replying to a question, Air Marshal Bawa said that the PPP would depend on the large number of ex-servicemen in Punjab. He said they could be relied upon to do the grassroot level work.

They were opposed to Punjab having been split up into Haryana and Himachal Pradesh and said they would like this process to be reversed eventually. At this point of time, it was necessary that Punjab was "rescued" from further disaster.

(Air Marshal Bawa shot into prominence during the 1971 conflict with Pakistan when he commanded a base in the western sector and created history in the "Battle of Longowal" and was awarded the Ati Vishisht Seva Medal. In January 1989, he was awarded the Param Vishisht Seva Medal. He retired on December 31, 1990, after a career of 38 years in the Indian Air Force.)

(Based on *Times of India*, January 28, 1992)

22. Diverse Statements

Lt. General Jagjit Singh Aurora Akalis decision to boycott the elections in justified.

Countering this, prominent Sikh leader, Lt. Gen. Jagjit Singh Aurora, said it is a well-known fact that the Congress at that time did not want the elections on grounds that the situation in the State was not conducive. "The Congress was responsible for not letting the elections take place earlier and now when the situation is worse than before the Government is going ahead with the polls only because they had promised to do so", he said.

He said the best possible time for holding the elections was during the Janata Dal regime as the Government had credibility with the Sikh masses – a fact which the present Government lacks. He said the Congress had a chance to improve its credibility but did nothing. The people of Punjab want to know what will happen after the elections. They feel cheated as the earlier promises made by the Congress Government were never kept. He was referring to the Rajiv-Longowal accord.

Justifying the decision of Akalis boycotting the elections, Shri Aurora said why anyone would risk his life when there is no earnest effort from the Government for solving the Punjab problem. He said it is widely accepted that elections would be like the previous elections where the State Government was eventually dismissed by the Centre.

Emphasising the point that no effort has been made by the Congress Government for "healing the wounds of the Sikhs Shri Aurora questioned why the people who were responsible for the 1984 riots have not been punished so far. He said not even a resolution sympathising with the families of those who were killed in riots was passed in Parliament despite the fact that such a resolution was passed for the victims of the Bhopal gas tragedy.

(*Hindustan Times*, January 24, 1992)

Shri Ram Jethmalani, an eminent lawyer for Punjab package to ensure peaceful polls

The forthcoming elections in Punjab would be much more violent than ever before if the Akali factions and the militant groups were not wooed to participate. He said the primary objective should be to end violence and bring those back to the political mainstream who were derailed for the past some years.

Speaking in a public meeting on 'Future of Punjab' organised by the Indian Society for Public Awareness he said it was unfortunate that no effort had so far been made in this direction. The sole motive of holding elections under the prevailing circumstances without offering any package was to keep the Akalis out of the electoral process, he alleged.

Shri Jethmalani said that as a first step towards bringing normalcy in Punjab and ensuring participation of all sections in the elections, the Government should immediately implement the Rajiv-Longowal accord. This would give a moral support to the Akalis and help in nursing the Sikh psyche.

He said the Akalis were reluctant to contest elections due to their past experience with the Government. A growing feeling among the Akali leaders was that even during the last elections which were abruptly called off, they got a number of their candidates killed without any consequence. "Give us something so that we could reason out with the militants for participating in the elections", was the view point of the Akali leaders whom Shri Jethmalani claimed to have met during his just concluded tour of Punjab.

(*Hindustan Times*, January 26, 1992)

'The Punjab Group' urges transfer of Chandigarh to Punjab

"The Punjab Group" urged the Government to transfer Chandigarh to Punjab, as also the contiguous Punjabi-speaking areas. The dispute over river waters should be referred to the Supreme Court and those guilty of crimes during the 1984 riots should be brought to book.

In a statement issued, it has urged all political parties to make these demands a part of their electoral campaign.

The group has welcomed the announcement of elections in Punjab, and appealed to all political parties to respond with courage to this opportunity for winning back for the people of Punjab the right to have a Government of their choice. Punjab has been denied this right longer than any other State. It is the duty of all political parties to help in ending this injustice.

"The Punjab Group believes that the people are eager, even

anxious, to resume their democratic rights and responsibilities. As they search for ways of doing so, they deserve the guidance and assistance of their leaders. In this respect a place of special mention belongs to Akali leaders. The whole of Punjab, and indeed the whole country, looks up to them for restoring peace and democracy to Punjab. They must come forward, assume their full share of responsibility and authority, and thus guide the people in serving the cause of Punjab," the statement said.

Recalling the dismissal of earlier Governments in Punjab by the Union Government for partisan ends, the group has noted that this has caused a severe erosion of the people's faith in the democratic process. The group, therefore, urges the Union Government and all parties to commit themselves to renunciation of such dangerous practices and designs. Only a democratically elected Government, chosen through a process in which all the people of the State have duly played their full part, can bring peace to the State.

"The Punjab Group appeals to all Punjabis as well as the administration of the State to help in preserving the fair name of Punjab by ensuring that the elections are, and are seen to be, free of violence, free of unfair practices, free of any pressures and coercion which may interfere with the democratic right of the people to elect a Government according to their own independent judgement."

The signatories are Shri I.K. Gujral, ACM Arjan Singh (retd), Shri Amrik Singh, Shri Kuldip Nayar, Shri B.G. Verghese, Shri Rajinder Sachar, Ambassador Gurbachan Singh, Shri S.S. Gill, Shri Tirlochan Singh, M. Maheep Singh, Shri Pran Chopra and Lt. Gen. J.S. Aurora (retd.).

(*Hindustan Times*, January 23, 1992)

A New Formula on Chandigarh Mooted

A new formula has been mooted to resolve the deadlock over Chandigarh.

Well-placed sources here assert that both Punjab and Haryana could build new capitals for themselves in their State with Central Assistance.

Punjab could also choose Amritsar as the new capital as suggested by some Congress leaders. Similarly, Haryana could have its own capital anywhere in the State.

The new idea was being placed before the people of the State and a Government elected after the elections could take a stand on this, the sources said. This would not adversely affect the right of Punjab over Chandigarh while Haryana could continue to lay claim on Abohar and Fazilka.

The sources said that Amritsar would be declared a holy city after the elections. Also Haryana and Himachal have been asked to give Punjabi a second language status in their respective areas. He was hopeful about an early announcement soon in this connection.

It seems Home Minister Shri S.B. Chavan has been talking to the Chief Ministers of these State to do the needful.

Haryana Chief Minister Shri Bhajan Lal held an emergency Cabinet meeting to consider giving Punjabi the second language status. But no decision seems to have yet been taken.

(*Hindustan Times*, January 25, 1992)

Move to make Amritsar Capital hailed by Chief Khalsa Diwan

The move to make Amritsar the Capital of Punjab has been welcomed by the Chief Khalsa Diwan.

Commenting on the news item, Shri Dilbir Singh, Secretary of this organisation hoped that the people of Punjab would join him in accepting the offer, without of course their claim on Chandigarh. He asked the Government to pump in sufficient funds so as to raise the required infrastructure for the Capital.

Recalling the importance of the city he said it was the summer capital of Maharaja Ranjit Singh and that it was also the commercial capital of Punjab in the pre-partition days.

Shri Singh said if Amritsar is made the capital, it would give a boost to its trade.

(*Hindustan Times*, January 26, 1992)

Move on Amritsar as the capital of Punjab

The reported offer by the Central Government to declare this holy city as the capital of Punjab was widely welcomed by the local political, social and religious leaders.

Even a section of the militants, owing allegiance to the Panthic Committee member Gurbachan Singh Manochahal, have shown a positive reaction towards this offer. In a recent statement, Manochahal said the move to declare "Guru Ram Dass ke Nagri" as the capital would enhance its status the world over. However, he also wanted the retention of Chandigarh in Punjab as "it is an integral part of this State."

A number of leaders who were interviewed by UNI, however, expressed the fear that the move would not materialise and was just a pre-election gimmick by the Centre.

Former AICC general secretary, Shri R.L. Bhatia, who has in the past represented the Amritsar constituency in the Lok Sabha, had recently demanded at a party rally at Tarn Taran, in the presence of Union Communications Minister of State Shri Rajesh Pilot, that the Centre should declare Amritsar as the capital of the State before the February 19 polls.

Though BJP vice-president Baldev Parkash was not available for comments, junior party leaders in the city, while welcoming the move, have doubted the Centre's sincerity. BJP councillor Harish Taneja pointed to the non-implementation of the Rajiv-Longowal accord.

Veteran CPI leader Satya Pal Dang was of the view that in today's world, the proximity of capital to an international border did not matter. He also favoured the transfer of Chandigarh to Punjab.

Local industrialist and Chief Khalsa Dewan secretary Dalbir Singh said the location of the capital in this historic city was the cherished dream of every Punjabi. Khalsa College principal H. S. Souch recently dwelled upon the importance of the city and said that during Maharaja Ranjit Singh's time the city occupied a place of importance. It was commercial capital of undivided Punjab.

Veteran freedom fighter Shamsher Singh Verka, too welcomed the move, stating that the importance of the city, where the historic Golden Temple and the Jallianwala Bagh was located, should now be enhanced. Leaders of various trade organisations also welcomed the move as it would attract entrepreneurs and improve the economic status of this border region.

All-India Sikh Students Federation (AISSF) president Manjit Singh and the Akali Dal (Mann) general secretary Ram Singh said the city should have been declared the capital just after partition. However, even now such a move would be welcome as it would not only raise the importance of the city but would also benefit the Majha belt, where unemployment was increasing.

(*Hindustan Times*, January 29, 1992)

Shri Khushwant Singh

Appoint Minister for Punjab

So much has been happening in the Punjab at the same time that it looks like a modern impressionistic painting: No one can be sure what it represents. One thing is sure it will have elections in a few days. How many people will vote (or be allowed to vote without fear), how many parties will put up candidates openly and how many will do so surreptitiously no one really knows. The decision ultimately rests with militants who continue to call the shots. Their main targets will be the Akalis who despite their bluster and bravado have proved themselves not only to be muddle-headed but chicken-hearted as well. Will they leave the field wide open to the Congress and the BJP? That will be a great pity. I am sure what the Punjab needs is an Akali Government committed to the Constitution led by Amrinder, Barnala, Badal or Sukhjinder. It will be in the best position to contain terrorism.

What about the terrorists? Haven't they had enough of killing and being killed? My information for whatever it is worth is that they have and would be happy to make an honourable settlement. Rajesh Pilot, the only Minister from the Centre to visit the most terrorist-infested areas of Tarn Taran, was given a tumultuous welcome. He dispensed with his security and had long talks with their leaders. It transpired that what they asked for was release of their comrades held in custody without trial, cessation of police and army activities against them, implementation of the Rajiv-Longowal accord and setting up of a major industry in every district. No one spoke of Khalistan. None of this seems unreasonable or impracticable. All it needs is courage to go ahead. No more consultations with Chief Ministers or political parties. No more commissions to go into this or that. Make whatever decisions you deem fair to Punjab, Haryana, Himachal and Rajasthan regarding Chandigarh, boundary adjustments, distribution of river waters and present them to the States concerned as final. Appoint one minister who has no other job except to see they are implemented within a few months. Seeing that at the moment the man most acceptable to the Central Government as well as the parties concerned is Rajesh Pilot – let him Pilot this package deal to bring it to a happy conclusion. There will be a lot of mischief-makers raising all kinds of frivolous objections: there will be carping and criticism within the Cabinet. Ignore it. Let dogs bark but get the caravan of peace resume its march.

(*Hindustan Times*, February 1, 1992)

Earlier views of Shri Khushwant Singh on Punjab Problem (1974)

Firstly, wherever Sikhs are scattered among other people, the attachment to tradition declines and the rate of apostasy rises. This is most evident in the Sikh communities in foreign lands. In the United States, Canada, and England the number of *kesādhārī* Sikhs is extremely small and ever-diminishing. On the other hand, in countries such as Malaya or in East Africa, where Sikhs live in compact groups, incidence of apostasy is lower. The same phenomenon can be observed in India. In the Sikh districts of East Punjab, the Khalsa traditions flourish; among smaller Sikh communities in other parts of India, they are on the decline.

Secondly, the abolition of communal considerations by the Indian Government, e.g. separate electorates, weightage in services, and above all the non-enforcement of rules regarding *pahul* in the armed forces, have taken a heavy toll of the Khalsa. This was amply proven by the attitude of the untouchable castes of Sikhs. By the Scheduled Castes Order, 1950-1951, while all Hindu untouchable castes were given special privileges, only four sub-castes of untouchable Sikhs were included in the list. The sub-castes excluded from the schedule showed little reluctance in abandoning the Khalsa tradition and declaring themselves Hindus in order to claim the benefits. It proved more than even that religious sentiment is a poor argument against economic benefit.

Thirdly, there is close connection between the Punjabi language and Sikhism. In families where Punjabi has been replaced by other languages – English among the rich and the anglicised. Hindi amongst those desirous of getting the best in a Hindu-dominated India – the study of the *Granth*, the observance of Sikh ritual and Khalsa traditions have had a short lease of life.

Fourthly, with the resurgence of Hinduism, the official commitment to secularism is being reduced to a meaningless clause in the constitution. The emphasis on Sanskrit and Hindi, study of the Aryan classics, insertion of cow-protection as a directive clause of the constitution, the increase in the number of cow-protection societies, the growth of Hindu political groups such as the Bharatiya Jan Sangh and the militant R.S.S.S., and the suspicion with which other minorities have come to be regarded are but some indications of the way the wind is blowing. Hindus, who form 80 per cent of the population, will in due course make Hinduism the state religion of India.

The four conclusions listed above lead to the fifth: the only chance of survival of the Sikhs as a separate community is to create a state in which they form an compact group, where the teaching of Gurmukhi and the Sikh religion is compulsory, and where there is an atmosphere of respect for the traditions of their Khalsa forefathers.

(Khushwant Singh, *A History of the Sikhs*, Volume 2: *1839-1974*, 1978)

Shri Gurcharan Singh Tohra's Statement, February 11, 1992

Extracts

. . . It may be recapitulated that since 1947, the Sikhs have been betrayed by the ruling elite of India.

We cannot be party to this nefarious game (election). We appeal to all people and leaders of J.D., the BJP and the CPI to boycott and stoutly oppose the elections.

We have won a moral victory by defying the Government's fascist measures to stop the members of the SGPC from attending this emergency meeting. Police had searched every nook and corner to locate the members and hold them back. But we can see them sitting here.

(A resolution was adopted at the meeting of the SGPC denouncing the Government which was trying to foist a puppet Government in Punjab. Many leaders including Gurcharan Singh Tohra were arrested. However boycott march could not take place as the security forces blocked the way).

(*Hindustan Times*, February 12, 1992)

18

1992 ELECTION ANALYSIS

The counting of votes began on February 20 at 115 centres for the 115 Assembly constituencies and 13 Parliamentary constituencies. Sixty officers worked as returning officers, many handling more than one constituency.

The votes from various polling booths were mixed to be later put into bundles of 100 each. This exercise was undertaken to maintain the secrecy of the ballots so as to obliterate the identification of the voters with a particular party or group. Ballot papers from 14,659 polling stations were brought to the sub-divisional headquarters under tight-security for counting late at night.

The Congress swept to power with a thumping mandate from the voters.

TABLE 18.1: Party-wise Position in 1992 Assembly Elections

(*No of Seats : 117*)

Party	Number of seats contested	Number of seats won
1. INC	117	86
2. BSP (Bahujan Samaj Party)	106	9
3. BJP	67	6
4. CPI	20	4
5. CPM	17	1
6. S. Akali Dal (Kabul)	61	3
7. Janata Dal	37	1
8. Others and Independents	169	7

The lowest victory margin was recorded at Mansa where the Congress candidate Shri Sher Singh Gagowal defeated his nearest rival Shri Buta Singh of the CPI by 36 votes.

Punjab Assembly — Seats and winners

The following is the district-wise list of winners for the 117-member Punjab Assembly:

Gurdaspur district: 1. Fatehgarh: Sukhwinder Singh (Cong-I). 2. Batala: Jagdish (BJP). 3. Qadian: Rajinder Singh (Cong-I). 4. Sri Hargobindpur: Gurnam Singh (CPI). 5. Kahnuwan: Partap Singh (Cong-I). 6. Dhariwal: Ms. Sushma Mahajan (Cong-I). 7. Behal (Cong-I). 8. Dina Nagar (SC): Krishna Kumar (Cong-I). 9. Narot Mehra (SC): Kishan Chand (Cong-I). 10. Pathankot: Raman Kumar (Cong-I). 11. Sujanpur: Raghunath Sahais (Cong-I).

Amritsar district: 12. Beas: Birpawan Kumar (Cong-I). 13. Majitha: Ranjit Singh (Ind). 14. Verka (SC): Gurmej Singh (Cong-I). 15. Jandiala (SC): Sadul Singh (Cong-I). 16. Amritsar (North): Faquir Chand (Cong-I). 17. Amritsar (West): Mrs. Bimla Dang (CPI). 18. Amritsar (Central): Mrs. Lakshmi K. Chawla (BJP). 19. Amritsar (South): Maninderjit Singh Bitta (Cong-I). 20. Ajnala: Harcharan Singh (Cong-I). 21. Rajasansi: Parminder Singh (Cong-I). 22. Attari (SC): Sukhdev Singh (Cong-I). 23. Tarn Taran: Dilbagh Singh Daleke (Cong-I). 24. Khadoor Sahib (SC): Ranjit Singh Chagalwadi (Sad-K). 25. Naushehra Pannuwan: Jagir Singh (Cong-I). 26. Patti-Sukhwinder Singh (Cong-I). 27. Valtoha-Gurjit Singh (Cong-I).

Jalandhar district: 28. Adampur: Rajinder Kumar (BSP). 29. Jalandhar Cantt: Beant Singh (Cong-I). 30. Jalandhar (North): Avtar Singh Henry (Cong-I). 31. Jalandhar (Central): Jaikishan Saini (Cong-I). 32. Jalandhar (South-SC): Mohinder Singh Kaypee (Cong-I). 33. Kartarpur (SC): Jagjit Singh (Cong-I). 34. Lohian: Brij Mohinder Singh (Cong-I). 35. Nakodar: Rao Singh (Cong-I). 36. Nurmahal: Gurvinder Singh (Cong-I). 37. Banga: Satnam Singh (BSP). 38. Nawan Shahar: Dilbagh Singh (Cong-I). 39. Phillaur (SC): Santokh Singh (Cong-I).

Kapurthala district: 40. Bholath: Jagtar Singh (Cong-I). 41. Kapurthala: Gulzar Singh (Cong-I). 42. Sultanpur: Gurmel Singh (Cong-I). 43. Phagwara (SC): Joginder Singh (Cong-I).

Hoshiarpur district: 44. Balachaur: Hargopal Singh (BSP). 45. Garh Shankar: Shangara Ram (BSP). 46. Mahalpur (SC): Avtar Singh

(BSP). 47. Hoshiarpur: Naresh (Cong-I). 48. Sham Chaurasi: Gurpal Chand (BSP). 49. Tanda: Mrs. Surjit Kaur (Cong-I). 50. Garhdiwala (SC): Dharampal Sabharwal (Cong-I). 51. Dasuya: Ramesh Chander (Cong-I). 52. Mukerian: Kewal Krishan (Cong-I).

Ludhiana district: 53. Jagraon: Darshan Singh (Cong-I). 54. Raikot: Nirmal Singh (Cong-I). 55. Dakha (SC): Malkiat Singh (Cong-I). 56. Qila Raipur: Tarsem Lal (CPI). 57. Ludhiana (North): Rakesh Kumar (Cong-I). 58. Ludhiana (West): Harnam Dass (Cong-I). 59. Ludhiana (East): Satpal Gosain (BJP). 60. Ludhiana (Rural): Malkiat Singh (Cong-I). 61. Payal: Harnek Singh (Cong-I). 62. Kum Kalan (SC): Ishar Singh (Cong-I). 63. Samrala: Karam Singh (Cong-I). 64. Khanna (SC): Shasher Singh (Cong-I).

Ropar district: 65. Nangal: Madan Mohan Mittal (BJP). 66. Anandpur Sahib: Ramesh Dutt (BJP). 67. Chamkaur Sahib (SC): Shamsher Singh (Cong-I). 68. Morinda: Jagmohan Singh (Cong-I). 69. Kharar: Harnek Singh (Cong-I).

Patiala district: 70. Banur: Mohinder Singh (Cong-I). 71. Rajpura: Ashbal Singh (Cong-I). 72. Ghanaur: Jasjeet Singh (Cong-I). 73. Dakala: Lal Singh (Cong-I). 74. Shutrana (SC): Hamir Singh (Cong-I). 75. Samana: Capt. Amrinder Singh (SAD-K): 76. Patiala (Town): Brahm Mohindra (Cong-I). 77. Nabha: Rajkumar (Cong-I). 78. Amloh (SC): Sadhu Singh (Cong-I). 79. Sirhind: Harbans Lal (BJP).

Sangrur district: 80. Dhuri: Dhanwant Singh (Cong-I). 81. Malerkotla: Abdul Guffar (Cong-I). 82. Sherpur (SC): Raj Singh (BSP). 83. Barnala: Som Dutt (Cong-I). 84. Bhadaur (SC): Nirmal Singh (BSP). 85. Dhanaula: Manjit Singh (Cong-I). 86. Sangrur: Jasbir Singh (Cong-I). 87. Dibra: Gurcharan Singh (Cong-I). 88. Sunam: Bhagwan Dass (Cong-I). 89. Lehra: Om Parkash (Cong-I).

Ferozepur district: 90. Balluana (SC): Babu Ram (Cong-I). 91. Abohar: Sajjan Kumar (Cong-I). 92. Fazilka: Ms. Prabha Devi (Cong-I). 93. Jalalabad: Hans Raj (Cong-I). 94. Guruharsahai: Sajwar Singh (Cong-I). 95. Ferozepur: Bal Mukand (Cong-I). 96. Ferozepur (Cantt): Ravinder Singh (Ind.)). 97. Zira: Inderjit Singh (SAD-K). 98. Dharamkot (SC): Baldev Singh (BSP).

Faridkot district: 99. Moga: Mrs. Malti (Cong-I). 100. Bagha Purana: Vijay Kumar (JD). 101. Nihal Singhwala: Ajaib Singh (CPI). 102. Panj Grain (SC): Gurcharan Singh (Cong-I). 103. Kot Kapura: Upinder Kumar (Cong-I). 104. Faridkot: Avtar Singh (Cong-I). 105. Muktsar: Harcharan Singh Brar (Cong-I). 106. Giddarbaha : 107. Malout: Baldev Singh (CPI). 108. Lambi: Gurnam Singh (Cong-I).

Bhatinda district: 109. Talwandi Sabo: Harminder Singh (Cong-I). 110. Pakka Kalan (SC): Baldev Singh (Cong-I). 111. Bathinda: Surinder Kapoor (Cong-I). 112. Nathana: Gulzar Singh (Cong-I). 113. Rampura Phul: Harbans Singh Sidhu (Cong-I). 114. Joga: Surjan Singh Joga (Indian People's Front). 115. Mansa: Sher Singh (Cong-I). 116. Budhlada: Hardev Singh (CPI). 117. Sardulgarh: Kirpal Singh Makha (Cong-I).

(*Hindu*, February 22, 1992)

Party Position in Lok Sabha

Total Seats	13
Congress	12
BSP	1

As many as 54 candidates out of a total 81 who contested for the 13 Lok Sabha seats in Punjab lost their security deposits in the polls.

They included seven Bahujan Samaj Party candidates followed by five each of BJP and Janata Dal, two Akali Dal (Kabul) and 34 independents and others.

In three of the constituencies, Jalandhar, Patiala and Ludhiana, which returned Congress candidates, all other candidates lost their security deposits.

A record low of 21.58 per cent turnout was recorded in the state, only 28,42,480 voters turned out to exercise their franchise out of a total of 1,31,69,795, nearly 1,26,230 votes were rejected.

The Congress got the maximum of 13,81,975 votes (50.88 per cent) while the Lok Dal got the minimum 1,070 votes (0.04 per cent).

The Bahujan Samaj Party and the Bharatiya Janata Party secured 5,07,794 and 4,50,574 votes (18.69 per cent and 16.59 per cent) respectively.

The Shiromani Akali Dal (Kabul) which fielded three candidates for the Lok Sabha constituencies got 77,970 (2.87 per cent) votes and two of its candidates in Patiala and Ferozepur constituencies lost their deposits.

TABLE 18.2: Lok Sabha Turn Out, 1989 and 1992

Constituencies	Turnout 1992	Turnout 1989	Invalid votes (92)	Hindu population *all per cent*
Amritsar	24.3	59.1	4.5	22.5
Tarn Taran	8.8	63.6	6.2	22.5
Bhatinda	13.9	61.8	5.0	23.0
Faridkot	25.8	64.3	4.4	20.6
Ferozepur	43.7	64.9	4.6	44.3
Gurdaspur	36.4	58.8	3.7	48.1
Hoshiarpur	35.5	59.3	4.2	59.4
Jalandhar	30.9	59.1	3.2	55.9
Kapurthala	25.2	60.1	4.1	38.8
Phillaur Ludhiana	16.8	59.8	3.9	32.2
Patiala	23.7	63.6	5.4	42.3
Ropar	14.4	68.5	5.8	41.8
Sangrur	10.9	71.7	5.0	23.7

Note: Figure in the last column, taken from the 1981 Census, relate to districts, not Lok Sabha constituencies.

TABLE 18.3: Rural Urban Turn Out in Assembly Elections, 1985 and 1992

Number of Constituencies	% of Turnout 1985	% of Turnout 1992
Urban (12)	57.7%	38.3%
Semi-urban (11)	67.8%	26.5%
Semi-rural (24)	68.4%	25.3%
Rural (70)	68.8%	15.1%

TABLE 18.4: District-wise Voter Turn Out in 1992 Elections

District	% of Turnout
Amritsar	16.1%
Bhatinda	13.9%
Faridkot	24.3%
Ferozepur	13.1%
Gurdaspur	21.5%
Hoshiarpur	36.9
Jalandhar	30.4
Kapurthala	25.8
Ludhiana	16.6
Patiala	22.9
Ropar	19.8
Sangrur	13.3

Prime Minister P.V. Narasimha Rao on Election Results

The orderly completion of the election process in Punjab has vindicated the ideals of democracy, secularism and tolerance that form the Indian way of life.

. . . ideals of democracy, secularism and tolerance have drawn strength from the qualities of courage, compassion and patriotism that have so distinguished the valiant sons and daughters of Punjab through history.

I bow to the verdict in all humility and reiterate our resolve to fulfil our pledge with the involvement of all.

(*Times of India*, February 22, 1992)

Observations made by other Leaders

1. Dr. Murli Manohar Joshi, B.J.P. President—Results distorted and lopsided since most of the voters stayed away.
2. Mufti Mohammad Sayeed, Janata Dal Leader—Punjab poll manipulated.
3. Harkrishan Singh Surjeet, General Secretary, CPM — Outcome of poll not in the general interest of the country —communal divide.
4. CPI—A good beginning.
5. Akali Dal (Mann)—Congress government a representative of the Hindu fundamentalist aspirations.
6. G.S. Tohra, SGPC President—Sikhs have rejected the Centre.
7. Captain Amrinder Singh—Akali Dal (K). Militants responsible for rout.

Analysis of Election Results

There is not much for analysis. Results were on expected lines. The victory for the Congress was a foregone conclusion. Equally obvious was the effect of the boycott of election by almost all Akali factions. The Congress won with the support of mainly Hindu votes. The Akalis sway over the rural voters was almost complete which was evident from the poor voting in the rural areas on their boycott call. The only new characteristics was the emergence of the B.S.P. as the second largest party after the Congress.

19

ELECTION RESULTS, 1952 TO 1992

TABLE 19.1: Total Electorates, Vote Polled, Invalid Votes and Turnout

(In Lakhs)

Year	Electorates	Votes Polled	Invalid Votes	Turn Out (%)
1952	67.2	49.9	N.A.	55.3
1957	92.1	71.8	1.7	55.0
1962	107.5	67.9	2.4	65.4
1967	63.1	42.9	2.0	71.1
1971	69.5	40.8	0.9	59.9
1977	81.6	56.1	1.1	70.1
1980	97.4	59.7	1.3	62.7
1984	107.0	69.3	3.0	67.6
1989	129.5	79.4	1.7	62.7
1992	131.7	28.4 (Estimated)	1.26	21.58 (Estimated)

Note: Approximately 33 lakh voters cast their votes.

TABLE 19.2: Party-wise Lok Sabha Seats Contested and Won 1951 to 1992

	BJP/RJS	Cong (I)	JD	SAD	SAD(M)	Others
First Lok Sabha (1952)	00/09	16/18	—	02/8	—	—
Second Lok Sabha (1957)	00/16	21/22	—	—	—	1/11[1]
Third Lok Sabha (1962)	03/17	14/22	—	03/7	01/01	01/01[2]
Fourth Lok Sabha (1967)	01/8	9/13	03/08	—	—	—
Fifth Lok Sabha (1971)	00/05	10/11	—	01/12	—	02/02[1]
Sixth Lok Sabha (1977)	—	0/13	—	09/09	—	01/01[1] 03/03[3]
Seventh Lok Sabha (1980)	—	12/13	—	01/07	—	—
Eighth Lok Sabha (1984)	00/03	02/12	—	07/11	—	—
Ninth Lok Sabha (1989)	00/03	02/13	01/04	00/04	06	04[4]
Tenth Lok Sabha (1991 but in Punjab in 1992)	00	13	—	—	—	1[5]

Note: 1. Communist Party of India (CPI).
2. Akali Dal Master Tara Singh.
3. Janata Party.
4. Independents 03, B.S.P. 01.
5. B.S.P. 1.

TABLE 19.3: Party-wise Percentage of Votes Polled, 1952 to 1992

Year	BJP	INC	J.D.	SAD	CPI	CPM	Others
1952	5.6	42.8	—	11.4	5.0	—	—
1957	16.0	51.3	—	—	16.8	—	—
1962	15.2	41.3	—	12.5	4.7	—	—
1967	12.5	37.3	22.6	—	4.3	1.9	—
1971	4.5	46.0	—	30.9	6.2	2.2	—
1977	—	34.9	12.5 (J.P.)	42.3	1.7	4.9	—
1980	—	52.5	10.0 (J.P.)	23.4	1.3	2.5	—
1984	3.4	37.6	2.27	37.2	3.8	3.0	—
1989	4.2	26.5	0.1 (J.D.)	1.3	2.1	3.9	+
1992	16.59	50.88	0.04 (L.D.) (L.D.)	2.87 (KABUL)	—	—	18.69 (BSP)

\+ 1989 — SAD(M) = 29.2, BSP = 18.6, Independents = 12.7.

TABLE 19.4: Constituency and Party-wise Lok Sabha Members and % of Votes, 1952 to 1992

Constituency	Name	Party	% of Votes polled
1	2	3	4
First Lok Sabha (1952)			
1. Amritsar	Gurmukh Singh Musafir	INC	47.9
2. Bhatinda (Kapurthala-Bhatinda)	Hukam Singh	AP	24.3
3. Faridkot	Hukam Singh		
4. Ferozepur	Lal Singh	SAD	19.5
5. Gurdaspur	Teja S. Akarpuri	INC	47.2
6. Hoshiarpur	Diwan Chand Sharma	INC	24.8
7. Jalandhar	A.N. Vidyalankar	INC	50.2
8. Ludhiana	Lal Singh	SAD	19.5
9. Patiala	Ram Pratap Garg	INC	47.2
10. Phillaur (SC) (Jullundur)	A.N. Vidyalankar	INC	50.2
11. Ropar	Diwan Chand Sharma	INC	24.8
12. Tarn Taran	S.S. Majithia	INC	36.8

Contd.

TABLE 19.4 *Contd.*

1	2	3	4
Second Lok Sabha (1957)			
1. Amritsar	Gurmukh Singh Musafir	INC	43.9
2. Bhatinda (Kapurthala-Bhatinda)	Hukam Singh	INC	28.1
3. Faridkot	Iqbal Singh	INC	43.2
4. Ferozepur (Ferozepur-Ludhiana)	Iqbal Singh	INC	43.2
5. Gurdaspur	Diwan Chand Sharma	INC	40.3
6. Hoshiarpur	Baldev Singh	INC	61.4
7. Jalandhar	Swaran Singh	INC	25.3
8. Ludhiana	Bahadur Singh	INC	26.6
9. Patiala	Achint Ram	INC	47.2
10. Phillaur (Jalandhar)	Swaran Singh	INC	25.3
11. Ropar (Hoshiarpur)	Baldev Singh	INC	61.4
12. Tarn Taran	S.S. Majithia	INC	36.8
Third Lok Sabha (1962)			
1. Amritsar	Gurmukh Singh	INC	39.8
2. Bhatinda (SC)	Dhanna Singh Gulshan	SAD	23.8
3. Faridkot	Iqbal Singh	INC	36.2
4. Ferozepur	Iqbal Singh	INC	36.2
5. Gurdaspur	Diwan Chand Sharma	INC	48.1
6. Hoshiarpur	A.N. Vidyalankar	INC	41.8
7. Jalandhar	Swaran Singh	INC	51.5
8. Ludhiana	Kapur Singh	SAD	34.6
9. Patiala	Hukam Singh	INC	46.6
10. Phillaur (SC)	Sadhu Singh	INC	48.2
11. Ropar (Hoshiarpur)	A.N. Vidyalankar	INC	39.4
12. Sangrur	Ranjit Singh	—	—
13. Tarn Taran	S.S. Majithia	INC	50.3
Fourth Lok Sabha (1967)			
1. Amritsar	Yagya Datt Sharma	BJS	31.8
2. Bhatinda (SC)	Kikar Singh	SAD	47.1
3. Faridkot	Iqbal Singh	INC	36.2
4. Ferozepur	Sohan Singh Basi	SAD	49.7
5. Gurdaspur	Diwan Chand Sharma	INC	31.7
6. Hoshiarpur	Ram Kishan	INC	29.3
7. Jalandhar	Swaran Singh	INC	39.2
8. Ludhiana	Davinder Singh	INC	36.6
9. Patiala	Mohinder Kaur (W)	INC	60.1
10. Phillaur (SC)	Sadhu Ram	INC	38.1
11. Ropar (SC)	Buta Singh	INC	38.1
12. Sangrur	Nirbpur Kaur (W)	SAD	54.7
13. Tarn Taran	G.S. Dhillon	INC	46.7

Contd.

TABLE 19.4 *Contd.*

1	2	3	4
Fifth Lok Sabha (1971)			
1. Amritsar	Durgadas Bhatia	INC	53.4
2. Bhatinda (SC)	Dhan Singh Bhaura	CPI	51.5
3. Faridkot	Gurdas Singh Badal	INC	44.3
4. Ferozepur	Mohinder Singh Gill	INC	56.4
5. Gurdaspur	Prabodh Chandra	INC	62.6
6. Hoshiarpur	Darbara Singh	INC	53.9
7. Jalandhar	Swaran Singh	INC	53.6
8. Ludhiana	D.S. Garcha	INC	54.8
9. Patiala	Sat Pal Kapur	INC	47.9
10. Phillaur (SC)	Sadhu Ram	INC	59.8
11. Ropar (SC)	Buta Singh	INC	52.8
12. Sangrur	Teja Singh Swatantra	CPI	38.0
13. Tarn Taran	G.S. Dhillon	CPI	46.7
Sixth Lok Sabha (1977)			
1. Amritsar	Baldev Prakash	BLD	49.9
2. Bhatinda (SC)	Dhanna Singh Gulshan	SAD	61.8
3. Faridkot	Prakash Singh Badal	SAD	59.2
4. Ferozepur	M.S. Sayanwal	SAD	87.8
5. Gurdaspur	Yagya Datt Sharma	BLD	50.9
6. Hoshiarpur	Balbir Singh	BLD	61.9
7. Jalandhar	Iqbal Singh Dhillon	SAD	62.1
8. Ludhiana	Jagdev Singh Talwandi	SAD	59.9
9. Patiala	Gurcharan Singh Tohra	SAD	56.1
10. Phillaur (SC)	Bhagat Ram	CPM	61.6
11. Ropar (SC)	Basant S. Khalsa	SAD	57.3
12. Sangrur	Surjit Singh Barnala	SAD	64.5
13. Tarn Taran	Mohan Singh Tur	SAD	56.9
Seventh Lok Sabha (1980)			
1. Amritsar	R.L. Bhatia	INC	59.5
2. Bhatinda (SC)	Hakim Singh	INC	40.9
3. Faridkot	G.K. Brar (W)	INC	50.4
4. Ferozepur	Balram Jakhar	INC	68.7
5. Gurdaspur	Sukhbans Kaur (W)	INC	58.5
6. Hoshiarpur	Zail Singh	INC	48.7
7. Jalandhar	R.S. Sparrow	INC	50.4
8. Ludhiana	D.S. Garcha	INC	54.5
9. Patiala	Amrinder Singh	INC	56.1
10. Phillaur (SC)	S.S. Chaudhary	INC	47.0
11. Ropar (SC)	Buta Singh	INC	52.3
12. Sangrur	Gurucharan Singh	INC	48.7
13. Tarn Taran	Lehna Singh Tur	SAD	46.0

Contd.

TABLE 19.4 *Contd.*

1	2	3	4
Eighth Lok Sabha (1985)			
1. Amritsar	R.L. Bhatia	INC	49.0
2. Bhatinda (SC)	Teja Singh Dardi	SAD	46.0
3. Faridkot	Shaminder Singh	SAD	51.1
4. Ferozepur	Gurdial Singh Dhillon	INC	38.0
5. Gurdaspur	Sukhbans Kaur (W)	INC	38.0
6. Hoshiarpur	K. Chaudhary	INC	47.9
7. Jalandhar	R.S. Sparrow	INC	50.8
8. Ludhiana	Mewa Singh	SAD	48.2
9. Patiala	Charanjit Walia	SAD	45.0
10. Phillaur (SC)	Sunder Singh	BSP	29.3
11. Ropar (SC)	Charanjit Singh	SAD	54.0
12. Sangrur	B.S. Ramuwalia	SAD	36.7
13. Tarn Taran	Tarlochan Singh Tur	SAD	55.3
Ninth Lok Sabha (1989)			
1. Amritsar	K. Singh	IND	47.0
2. Bhatinda (SC)	S. Singh	SADM	53.2
3. Faridkot	J. Singh	SADM	48.6
4. Ferozepur	D. Singh	IND	30.9
5. Gurdaspur	Sukhbans Kaur (W)	INC	40.5
6. Hoshiarpur	K. Chaudhary	INC	32.2
7. Jalandhar	I.K. Gujral	JD	48.1
8. Ludhiana	R.K. Bularal (W)	SADM	53.5
9. Patiala	A. Singh	IND	46.6
10. Phillaur (SC)	H. Lakha	BSP	29.3
11. Ropar (SC)	Bimal Kaur (W)	SADM	60.4
12. Sangrur	R. Singh	SADM	36.7
13. Tarn Taran	S.S. Mann	SADM	89.2
Tenth Lok Sabha (1991) *(1992 in the Case of Punjab)*			
1. Amritsar	R.L. Bhatia	INC	*
2. Bhatinda (SC)	Kewal Singh	INC	*
3. Faridkot	Jagmit Singh Brar	INC	*
4. Ferozepur	Mohan Singh	BSP	*
5. Gurdaspur	Sukhbans Kaur (W)	INC	*
6. Hoshiarpur	Kamal Chaudhary	INC	*
7. Jalandhar	Yash Pal	INC	*
8. Ludhiana	Gurcharan Singh	INC	*
9. Patiala	Sant Ram Single	INC	*
10. Phillaur (SC)	Santosh Chaudhary (W)	INC	*
11. Ropar (SC)	Harchand Singh	INC	*
12. Sangrur	Gurcharan Singh	INC	*
13. Tarn Taran	Surinder Singh Kairon	INC	*

* Percentage not available at the time of compilation.

TABLE 19.5: Party-wise Position in Vidhan Sabha Election, 1952 to 1992

Year	Seats	BJP	INC	CPI	CPM	JP	SAD	Other	Indepen-dents	BSP
1952	126	—	96	4	—	—	13	4	9	
1957	154	9	120	6	—	—	—	6	13	
1962	154	8	91	9	—	—	19	11	16	
1967	104	9	48	5	3	—	—	30	9	
1969	104	8	38	4	2	—	43	5	4	
1972	104	—	66	10	1	—	24	—	3	
1977	117	—	17	7	8	25	58	—	2	
1980	117	1	63	9	5	—	37	—	2	
1985	117	6	32	1	—	1	73	—	4	
1992	117	6	86	4	1	—	3 Akali Dal (Kabul)	—	8*	9

* Janata Dal 1, Independents and Others 7.

20

PROMINENT AKALI LEADERS

Master Tara Singh (June 1885-November 1967)

Master Tara Singh, a giant among the Akali leaders of the Punjab, was born at village Harial, District Rawalpindi (now in Pakistan) on 24 June, 1885. His father, Bakshi Gopi Chand was a village Patwari. Tara Singh's original name was Nanak Chand and he got his present name at the age of 17 on embracing Sikhism. He received his early education at his native village. In 1907, he graduated from the Khalsa College Amritsar. During his academic career he won many of distinction and prizes. In the field of sports he distinguished himself by attaining captainship of football and hockey teams.

In 1908, he was appointed Headmaster of the Khalsa High School Lyallpur (now in Pakistan).

He joined the Akali movement in its very start in 1921. Soon he became one of its prominent members. He was elected member of the Shiromani Gurdwara Prabandhak Committee (S.G.P.C.). He took an active part in all the 'morchas' of the Akali movement. He was also charged with sedition and tried for three years. He outrightly rejected the offer of release on condition after the passage of the Gurdwara Act, 1925. He was released unconditionally after sometime.

Master Tara Singh took a prominent part during the twenties in the boycott of the Simon Commission. He completely identified himself with the 1930 Civil Disobedience Movement launched by Mahatma Gandhi. He was elected President SCPC while in jail. He remained the President of the Akali Dal for a member of years. He broke with the Congress during the Second World War for he wanted to safeguard the future of his community against the Muslim League's demand for Pakistan inclusive of Punjab. He vigorously opposed the Cripps Mission and the Cabinet Mission Plan as they failed to do justice to the legitimate demands of the Sikhs. His struggle did not end with independence in 1947. He continued his struggle for the protection of Punjabi language and the formation of Punjabi Suba. He achieved his aim to a large extent in 1966 when the Punjab was reorganised and trifurcated into Punjab, Himachal Pradesh and Haryana. He died in November 1967.

Gyani Kartar Singh (1905-NA)

He was born in village Nagoke in Amritsar but settled at Chak 40 (Lyallpur). He joined the Akali movement at the age of 19. In 1937, he was elected to the Punjab Assembly. He became the President of the Akali Dal in 1946. He was considered the brain behind the Akali party and is said to be the propounder of the Akali concept of the Sikh state. He was a close collaborator of Master Tara Singh and later on parted company with him. After independence, he was often a member of the Punjab Cabinet. At a meeting on August 20, 1944 at Amritsar attended by leaders of Sikh parties, he said, "Let us give up now the practice of looking up to Mr. Gandhi (Mahatma Gandhi) for the protection of over interests." He further said, "It Pakistan is foisted upon the Sikhs with the help of British bayonets, we will tear it into shreds as Guru Gobind Singh tore up the Mughal Empire." (*'Civil and Military Gazette'*, August 21, 1944).

Sant Fateh Singh (Oct. 1911 to Oct. 3 1972)

He was a religious leader who in due course became on Akali leader and rival of Master Tara Singh. He spent most of his early years in meditation. His main area of activity was Ganganagar in Rajasthan. He was instrumental in building gurdwara, orphanage and several educational institutions. He took part in Quite India movement. He was jailed during PEPSU agitation (1949). He courted arrest during Punjabi Suba agitation (1955). He come into prominence in 1960 in the Punjabi Suba agitation. He went on fast and ended it after 23 days. He parted company with Master Tara Singh and formed a rival Akali Dal in 1962. He let the Akali party to success in Punjab elections held in 1970 and installed the Gurnam Singh Ministry in Punjab. He announced retirement from active politics in March 1972.

Baldev Singh (1902-1961)

He was the son of a wealthy steel magnate of district Amritsar. He joined Sikh politics in 1937, when he was elected to the Punjab Assembly. He financed many programmes of the Akali party. He also donated liberally to the Sikh National College at Lahore. In June 1942, he entered into an agreement known as the 'Sikander-Baldev Pact' with the Unionist party which despite its championing the cause of the agriculturists, though found favour in the eyes of Sikh agriculturists also had its primary interest in the welfare of the Muslim Jats. One of the terms of the agreement was providing his replacing Dasaunda Singh is the Punjab Cabinet. In 1954 he was one of the two arbitrators appointed to resolve the dispute between the Akali Dal and SGPC over control of Delhi Gurdwaras. Baldev Singh was the Sikh representative in the negotiations for the transfer of power and became the Defence Minister of Nehru Government. (1947-52). He remained at the helm of Sikh affairs till 1957.

Sant Harchand Singh Longowal (1932-1985)

Sant Harchand was born in village Gidariani in District Sangrur. He was humble by nature. His soft spokeness and religious devotion earned him the little of a 'Sant'. On every religious festival he devoted himself to 'Shabad Kirtan'. In 1953, he was invited by the Sikh Sangat of Longowal to hold a 'Kirtan Darbar' in their village. Harchand Singh held his 'Kirtan Darbars' and money began to flow for the construction of the Gurdwara which was subsequently constructed. Thereafter his association with the Longowal village became very intimate. Ultimately Sant Harchand Singh Longowal settled there and his continued stay at Longowal gave him the suffix 'Longowal'.

On the Baisakhi Day of 13 April, 1963, when Damdama Sahib (Talwandi Saho) became the 5th Akal Takhat, Sant Longowal became its first 'jathedar' and held this position for about a year.

In 1975, Sant Longowal acquired the status of an important Sikh leader. In 1980 and 1981, he was elected the President of the Akali Dal. Sant Longowal was considered as a liberal Sikh leader. In 1985, Rajiv Gandhi-Longowal Accord was arrived at. Unfortunately a militant group of Sikhs was opposed to this accord and this led to his assassination on 20th August, 1985.

Sant Jarnail Singh Bhindranwale (1947 to 1984)

He received very little formal education and left school in class fifth or sixth. Under the influence of Sant Gurbachan Singh, he decided to serve God. In 1966, under family pressure he married and had two sons Ishwar Singh and Inderjit. In 1977, he acceded to the 'gaddi' of Sant Gurbachan Singh at Bhudwali who had passed away in 1971. After his accession to the 'gaddi' Jarnail Singh added the suffix Bhindrawale to his name and started a militant programme 'to cleanse the Sikhs of the impurities which had entered in their hearts and manifest in their actions'. He came to limelight when he attacked a Nirankari congregation in Amritsar on 13 April, 1978. In the words of Chand Joshi, "it is this incident which brought him to the notice of Sanjay Gandhi and Giani Zail Singh fighting with their back-to-the-wall' against the Janata government and looking for a "Sant to tackle the Akalis". Giani Zail Singh himself was facing a judicial enquiry instituted by the ruling Akali party in the state and he assiduously propped up Bhindranwale. He ordered his protege, the then, SSP of Faridkot, to issue as many gun licences as possible to Sant Bhindranwale. There is enough evidence of monetary support to Sant Bhindranwale from the Congress (I).

To say, however, that Bhindranwale was only a creation of the Congress (I) would be an error of history, since in the wider perspective, he became the articulator of the new class of the increasing Sikh middle peasantry. His appeal transcended the narrow Jat-Sikh base to include the *mazhabis* (scheduled caste Sikhs) essentially because his insistence on purity psychologically appealed to the new aspirants in the social structure.

Through 1978 and 1979 Bhindranwale acted as the front paw of the Congress (I) and his religious sermons were laced with references to "the unSikh Sikhs dominating the Akali Dal and the SGPC". His most vitriolic attacks were reserved for Prakash Singh Badal, the former Chief Minister who was known as the moderate among moderates.

With the elections in 1980, Jarnail Singh Bhindranwale, who had built up a sizeable following among women in the Moga-Faridkot region, became an essential ingredient of both Giani Zail Singh and Mrs. Sukhjinder Kaur, both candidates for Parliament. Bhindranwale openly campaigned for the Congress(I) candidates and it was his armed men who were polling agents in most of the booths.

With the Congress victory in 1980, Bhindranwale assumed a new role: that of Home Minister Giani Zail Singh's hatchet man against Akalis. Jarnail Singh Bhindranwale's religious discourses were now laced with criticism of the State government." (*Bhindranwale: Myth and Reality*, 1984, Vikas).

The turning point in Bhindranwale's 'psyche' came after his arrest in 1981 for the murder of Lala Jagat Narain—a veteran leader of Punjab. In 1982, in the first week of June, he went to Pakistan clandestinely on a 'pilgrimage to the Nankana Sahib.' He moved into the Guru Nanak Niwas at the Golden Temple in 1983. He organised a militant movement against the government. During the Operation Blue Star of June 5, 1984, he was killed (became a martyr according to his followers) in the premises of the Temple complex at Amritsar.

Surjit Singh Barnala (Oct. 21, 1925)

Sardar Surjit Singh Barnala was born at Ateli Begpur in Haryana. His father Sardar Nar Singh served in the judicial service in the erstwhile state of Nabha. Surjit Singh passed his matriculation in the year 1940 from Nabha. He later shifted to Lucknow and did his graduation in the year 1944. He passed his law from Lucknow University in 1946 and started his legal practice in 1946 at Dhanaula in Nabha and later shifted his venue of practice to Bhatinda. In 1950, he joined as a public prosecutor but soon resigned and restarted his practice. He was a Member of Punjab Assembly in 1966-67, Minister of Education 1969-71 and Chief Minister in 1985 for about one year and a half.

Member Lok Sabha 1977-79, Minister of Irrigation, Government of India 1977-79, Governor Tamil Nadu during National Front Government and resigned soon after the formation of Congress Government at the Centre in 1991.

Parkash Singh Badal (8 Dec. 1927)

He entered politics as a member of Akali Dal. He was a member of S.G.P.C. for a number of years. He was first elected to the Punjab Assembly in 1957, became the Chief Minister of Punjab 1970-71; elected to the Lok Sabha in 1977; Minister for Agriculture at the Centre, again Chief Minister of Punjab in 1977 after resigning from the Lok Sabha. He became leader of the opposition in Punjab in 1980.

Shri Badal was imprisoned during the Emergency. Shri Badal has been the president of the Shiromani Akali Dal (Badal). He along with five other Panthic groups decided to boycott the February 19 Punjab elections. His views are reflected in the interview given to Kulvinder Kaur and published in the *'Indian Express'*, Jan 26, 1992. His replies to various questions are given below.

The poll boycott decision is the highest form of protest planned by us against the continued apathy of the Centre toward the genuine demands of Punjab and the Sikhs, which we have been amplifying for the past 40 years. All democratic political parties lodge protests off and on. We too have been staging dharnas, holding demonstrations, organising rallies and bandhs to register our protests in the past. We have taken this extreme step because our earlier protests failed to move the Government to redress our grievances.

****

We have decided to hold district-level rallies throughout Punjab to mobilise public opinion in favour of the boycott and to oppose police repression.

****

Under ordinary circumstances, elections are a must for a political party. But now Punjab is passing through abnormal conditions where elections have become secondary. Our first priority at the moment is Punjab and the Sikh problem and we would prefer to fight for its solution rather than contest the elections. However, this does not mean we do not believe in democracy or that we are running away from the democratic set-up and elections. We have always championed democracy and entered the poll fray last June. But by annulling that election process at the last moment, the Centre itself committed a highly undemocratic act at the time.

****

The people should not pay much attention to the temporary relief that would accrue to them if they elect their own representatives on February 19. Any government that is formed would be a transitory, puppet government. Punjab has a long history of such governments, which lasted less than two years because the Centre chose to dismiss them on political and communal considerations. We are striving for a permanent solution to the people's ills and hope that the people will join hands with us.

* * * *

This is the time when other Punjab parties should cooperate with us to force the Government to give Punjab and the Sikhs their due.

Now full surgery is required to pacify Punjab because the wounds are too deep to be healed by the application of an ointment. The Centre must take hold steps.

I cannot elaborate on them steps. One thing is clear that the Punjab problem calls for a political solution. Unfortunately, the Government has always considered Punjab from the point of view of law and order and treated it as such by sending in para-military forces and the Army.

The chances of Akali unity after the common boycott decision are very bright. The six organisations have been able to come on one platform and achieve unity of thinking and action as regards an important issue. In pursuance of the poll boycott decision, we would be appearing together on public platforms to mobilise public opinion of our cause. We are now nearer our goal of Panthic unity and are hopeful that the way will also be cleared for a common organisational set-up.

(*Indian Express*, January 26, 1991)

Captain Amrinder Singh

He belongs to the royal family of Patiala. A product of Doon School, he is said to have been a close friend of the Late Rajiv Gandhi and admirer of late Sanjay Gandhi. He was selected for the NDA in July 1959 and was subsequently commissioned into 2 Sikh Regiment in June 1963. In 1966, he sought to be discharged to look after their land and vast property. He made his debut in politics in 1969 when he contested the Dakala Assembly seat and lost. He joined the Congress and won the Patiala Lok Sabha seat in 1980 only to region four years later in 1984 in protest against Operation Blue Star. Thereafter he joined the Akali Dal. He worked as an Agriculture Minister in Shri Surjit Singh Barnala's government for about six months. He became a prominent member of the Akali Dal (Kabul) and vigorously pleaded for taking part in 1992 Punjab elections. He became the

Chairman of the Parliamentary Board of Akali Dal.

He contested Assembly seats from two constituencies. He was returned unopposed from Samana but lost at Kharar.

Extracts from interview are given below:

The poll is going to make a major contribution to the solution of the problem as it would end the era of confrontation between the militants and the security forces and lead to a general amnesty for our youngsters.

****

Punjab is smeared with the blood of the youth, whether militants, civilians, or men of the security forces and some one has to come forward to try and stop this gory drama. And then, there is the question of economic reconstruction of the state including tackling of unemployment.

****

The problem of militancy is going to exist for a long time to come. Militants are being indoctrinated by Pakistan and the mischief has been going on for the past six years. But we have to take the plunge, without waiting for any watershed situation which could be a very distant goal.

****

Who are the quislings, he (Parkash Singh Badal) or we who are fighting the Congress(I) to preserve the Akali roots in Punjab? They (Badal and his followers) have an understanding with the Congress(I). If the Akalis do not contest the elections, the Congress(I) is sure to come to power in Punjab, it is clear that Prime Minister P.V. Narasimha Rao wants every Lok Sabha seat in Punjab to establish a majority at the Centre. Those boycotting the polls should also realise that 70 per cent of the people being killed in the Punjab violence are the Sikhs.

****

I am hundred per cent sure that we will win the elections and form our government.

(*Indian Express*, February 1, 1992)

Simranjit Singh Mann

Shri Mann, an Ex-police officer—turned politician is said to stand for an independent and sovereign Sikh state. He identifies himself with the cause taken up by the militants. He contested Lok Sabha election from the Tarn Taran Parliamentary Constituency in 1989 election and won with a comfortable majority on the Shiromani Akali Dal—SAD (Mann) ticket. Extracts from his interview are given below, to illustrate his view on the Punjab situation:

The boycott decision is a strategic one, but the party has got to be strengthened. Six lakh membership forms have already been distributed for this purpose.

* * * *

A boycott is a democratic way of protest. The Centre has failed to fulfil any of the promises made to the Sikhs. The Government entered into an accord with the elected government (Rajiv-Longowal Accord) but it was never implemented. The Government reiterates that talks will be held with the elected government, but its credibility is eroded and any Sikh organisation which now negotiates with the Government would be discredited.

We are not even sure that the Government will complete the electoral process. The Government postponed the June 1991 elections at the eleventh hour. Narasimha Rao was not even a member of the Parliament when he advised President R. Venkataraman to cancel the election. Then, on what criteria did the President accept his advice? All the three persons (Rao, Venkataraman and Seshan) who murdered democracy in June are still on the scene.

* * * *

Even if we form the government, the spectre of Article 356 will loom large over our heads.

Essentially it is (Punjab Problem) political in nature. For a permanent solution, the Akali Dal (Mann) and Akali Dal (Badal) are in favour of associating the militants in the political process. Otherwise any Akali government formed in the state would be at odds with the militants.

* * * *

The Government must come out with a political package and associate the militants in the political process. There must be a guarantee by some international body that the government will carry through the elections.

* * * *

It is past experience which has influenced our decision. We lost candidates but we were still in the field. It is the Centre which failed us. Now there has to be a guarantee that elections will be held and the government will not resort to Article 356.

* * * *

There is strong apprehension that the government would rig the poll in favour of Congress(I) or its puppet with the help of Army.

* * * *

Militants are an essential component and the Akalis will have to take them along.

* * * *

It is for the Akalis to take them along. It is the militants who are making sacrifices for a cause. It is incumbent on every Akali leader to realise that. Otherwise the Akalis will form a Barnala-type government which would lead to civil war with our own people.

* * * *

I don't have state protection. I go to the masses and am one with them. At mass gatherings, I speak out against the killing of innocents, looting and extortion. I have a voice which is heard, which would be lost if I go in for political power.

* * * *

Our party's goal is also the establishment of a sovereign and independent Sikh State. Where we differ with the militant is the method to adopt to achieve this goal.

* * * *

The militants are already making sacrifices and the people are supporting them. We do not want to burden the masses by launching a mass movement at the moment.

* * * *

We are in harmony with Sikh thought and the process to achieve the political goal to free ourselves.

* * * *

The Government is driving a wedge between the Sikhs and India. We will end up launching a mass struggle to free ourselves from the shackles of Delhi.

It (transfer of Chandigarh to Punjab) will at least re-establish the *bona fides* of the Government.

(*Indian Express*, January 26, 1992)

21

CHRONOLOGY OF MAIN EVENTS, 1809 TO 1992

A. Before February 1992 Elections

1809 – Maharaja Ranjit Singh establishes a strong Sikh Empire. Friendly relations with the British and Treaty of Amritsar with them.

1839 – Death of Maharaja Ranjit Singh.

1845-1846 – First Sikh War – Victory of the British.

1846 March 9 – Treaty between the British Government and the Lahore Darbar Favourable for the British.

1846 March 11 – Articles of Agreement concluded between the British government and the Lahore Durbar — Conditions imposed on the Lahore Durbar.

1849 March 29 – Annexation of the Punjab by the British — Maharaja Dalip Singh step down from the throne of his illustrious father Maharaja Ranjit Singh. Hands over the Koh-i-noor diamond to the British.

1919 April 13 – Jallianwala Bagh Massacre.

1928 Feb. – Sikhs Representation before Nehru Committee.

1928 May – Presentation of Memorandum on Sikh Representation.

1932 April 16 – Ramsay MacDonald Award on communal representation.

1936-37 – First elections under the 1935 Act and the Khalsa Nationalist Party winning 15-20 seats out of the total 175 seats in Punjab.

1942 March 31 – Master Tara Singh's note to Stafford Cripps.

1942 June – Sikander Baldev Pact.

1943 June – Statement of Master Tara Singh regarding Azad Punjab.

1944 August 20 – Gyani Kartar Singh's speech.

1944 September 3 – Protest Day by the Sikhs.

1945-46 – General Election: Formation of the Panthic Party in Punjab to contest elections and its securing 22 seats of total seats of 175 (Muslim League 79, The Congress 51, Unionists and Independents 10 each).

1946

March 22 – Shiromani Akali Dal passing a resolution stating Khalistan to be its political objective.

April – Meeting of a Sikh delegation with the Cabinet Mission. Memorandum by the Central Akali Dal (Baba Kharak Singh's Group) to the Cabinet Mission.

May 25 – Master Tara's Singh letter to the Secretary of State for India for the protection of rights of Sikhs.

June 11 – Reply of the Secretary of State assuring Master Tara Singh regarding safeguarding of their interests.

June 10 – A Council of Action formed by the Sikh political parties to direct Sikh opposition to the Cabinet Mission Proposals.

July 18 – Sir Stafferd Cripps' statement in the British Parliament regarding Sikhs.

August 16 – Direct Action Day by the Muslim League under Shri Jinnah.

1947

Jan. 5 – Congress repeats its assurances of its support to minorities, particularly the Sikhs.

April 12 – Shri Bhim Sen Sachar and Swarn Singh ask for a division of the Punjab with two separate ministries — one for Muslim and the other for non-Muslim zones.

April 13 – Baisakhi Day: Master Tara Singh and 280 'jathedars' vow at the Akal Takht to sacrifice their lives for the community.

June 2 – Akali Dal working committee meeting demands Chenab as the boundary for the partition of Punjab.

June 3 – Viceroy's statement regarding careful consideration to the Sikhs.

July 15 – R.A. Butler's concern for the Sikhs in British Parliament.

Sep. 2 – Congress's assurance to the Sikhs and Sardar Baldev Singh join the Nehru Cabinet.

Sep. 21 – Master Tara's statement.

1948

– Dar Commission.

– Master Tara Singh's statement.

– Rejection of demand.

Nov. 4 – Many Sikh members of the East Punjab Assembly submit a 13-point memorandum to the Constituent Assembly asking for adequate representation to the Sikhs.

Nov. 12 – Rejection of the Demand by Minority Committee. Formation of the PEPSU with the merger of the Sikh states and Maharaja Yadvendra Singh becoming the 'rajpramukh' — Governor.

1949

Oct. – Punjab Cabinet under Shri Gopi Chand Bhargava.

1951

June – President's Rule.

1952

April – General Elections — Shri Bhim Sen Sachar becomes the Chief Minister of the Punjab.

1955

States Reorganisation Commission

1956

Jan. – Sardar Pratap Singh Kairon replaces Shri Bhim Sen Sachar as Chief Minister of Punjab.

– Merger of PEPSU with the Punjab.

1957

– General Elections — Sardar Pratap Singh Kairon as Chief Minister till June 1964.

– Regional Formula.

1961

Dar Commission.

1964

July – Shri Ram Kishan as the Chief Minister.

1965

Sep. 1 – Akali leaders declare their support to the government when Pakistani forces cross the international border.

1966

March 10 – The Congress Working Committee passes a resolution for the creation out of the existing state of Punjab a state with the Punjabi as the state language.

July – President's Rule.

Nov. 1 – Reorganisation of Punjab and creation of three States of Punjab, Himachal Pradesh and Haryana.
– Shri Gurmukh Singh Musafir as the Chief Minister of Punjab.

1967

March-Nov. – A United Front of the Akalis, the Jan Sangh and the Communists wins an overall majority. Shri Gurnam Singh (Akali) becomes the Chief Minister (March 8, 1967 to November 25, 1967).

Nov. 22 – Death of Master Tara Singh.

1968

Nov., 1967-August, 1968 – Shri Lachhman Singh Gill of Master Tara Singh group becomes the Chief Minister (November 27, 1967 to August 23, 1968).

August 13 – President's Rule. Governor Shri D.C. Pavate.

1969

February – Akali Party of the Sant Fateh Singh group comes into power. Formation of Ministry by Shri Gurnam Singh.

August 15 – Shri Darshan Singh Pheruman of the Swatantra Party goes on fast to death in the Central Jail, Amritsar.

October 27 – Death of Shri Darshan Singh Pheruman.

1970

Jan. 26 – Sant Fateh Singh's fast for the restoration of Chandigarh to the Punjab.

Jan. 29 – Smt. Indira Gandhi Award: A part of Fazilka Tehsil and Abohar to Haryana, besides a grant of Rs. 10 crore for building a new Capital.

March 25 – Fall of the Gurnam Singh Ministry.

March 27 – Parkash Singh Badal becomes the Chief Minister with the support of Jan Sangh.

1971

March 1 – Badal group gets only one seat out of 13 Lok Sabha seats.
June 13 – Shri Badal resigns. President's Rule in Punjab.

1972

August – Sant Fateh Singh's agitation and his arrest with several thousand Akalis.
March 17 – Defeat of Akalis in General Elections. Giani Zail Singh of the Congress takes office of Chief Minister.

1977

– Anandpur Sahib Resolution passed at the Akali conference.
– Akali-Janata Government comes into power with Shri Parkash Singh Badal, Chief Minister.

1980

Feb. – President's Rule imposed.
July – Formation of Congress Government with Shri Darbara Singh, Chief Minister.

1983

Oct. – Shri Darbara Singh resigns and President Rule imposed.

1984

– Rise of Sant Bhindranwale as leader of Sikhs.
June 6 – Operation Blue Star at Golden Temple Amritsar.
– Death of Sant Bhindranwale and hundreds of Sikhs in the Golden Temple Complex.
– White Paper on Punjab by the Central Government.
– Assassination of Smt. Indira Gandhi, Prime Minister.
– Shri Rajiv Gandhi becomes Prime Minister.

1985

– Rajiv-Longowal Accord.
– General Elections and Shri Surjit Singh Barnala forms the Akali Ministry.
May 13 – Rajiv-Longolwal Accord.

May 13 – Rajiv Gandhi's statement in Lok Sabha.

1986

Jan. 25 – The Mathew Commission on transfer of territory between Punjab and Haryana submits its report.

Jan. 26 – Damdami Taksal and AISSF militants hold a 'Sarbat Khalsa' at Amritsar.

Jan. 30 – Jathedar Kirpal Singh, head priest of the Akal Takht calls for 'Sarbat Khalsa' at the Akal Takht on February 16.

Feb. 16 – Shri G.S. Tohra resigns as SGPC President after the 'Sarbat Khalsa' at Anandpur Sahib.

April 1 – Shri Siddhartha Shankar Ray appointed Governor of Punjab.

April 3 – A Commission headed by Supreme Court Judge E.S. Venkataramiah is appointed to determine and specify the Hindi-speaking areas of Punjab to be given to Haryana in lieu of Chandigarh.

April 29 – The five-member Panthic Committee declares in Amritsar. The Sikh's battle for the creation of Khalistan.

April 30 – Punjab Police, paramilitary forces and commandos enter the Golden Temple Complex to flush out terrorists and secessionists hiding in the shrine.

May 1 – Ban on National Council of Khalistan and Dal Khalsa extended for further two years.

May 31 – The term of the Venkataramiah Commission on transfer of territory between Haryana and Punjab extended till June 10, 1986.

June 7 – Justice Venkataramiah Commission submits its report on the Punjab-Haryana territorial issue and recommends transfer of 70,000 acres of land from Punjab to Haryana in lieu of Chandigarh.

July 6 – Baba Amte visits Golden Temple in Amritsar on a peace mission.

August 10 – The militants shot dead General A.S. Vaidya, the former Chief of the Army Staff, at Pune (General Vaidya was associated with the Operation Blue Star in 1984).

Dec. 2 – Akali Dal leaders Parkash Singh Badal, G.S. Tohra and Kuldip Singh detained.

Dec. 3 – Death sentence confirmed to assassins of Smt. Indira Gandhi by Delhi High Court.

1987

May 11 – President's Rule is imposed in Punjab.

Oct. 21 – Security forces raid the Golden Temple in Amritsar.

1988

March 6 – The Punjab Assembly, kept under suspended animation is dissolved.

March 9 – Bhai Jasbir Singh Rode takes over as the Akal Takht Jathedar.

May 4 – National Council of Khalistan and Dal Khalsa are declared unlawful associations.

May 15 – Operation Black Thunder: one hundred and forty six persons, many of them terrorists surrender to the security forces in the Golden Temple Complex, Amritsar.

May 18 – All the terrorists in the Golden Temple Complex in Amritsar, surrender to the security forces.

August 9 – The Supreme Court acquits the Sub-inspector Balbir Singh in the Indira Gandhi assassination case and confirms the death sentence on Satwant Singh and Kehar Singh.

Sep. 21 – One hundred and thirty-eight detenus of the Operation Blue Star are released from Jodhpur Fort.

1989

Jan. 6 – Satwant Singh and Kehar Singh, convicted in Indira Gandhi murder case, hanged inside Tihar Jail in New Delhi.

March 3 – Prime Minister Rajiv Gandhi announces in Parliament a package of measures including government's decision to release all the remaining Jodhpur detainees, except those facing serious charges, for resolving Punjab tangle.

March 27 – Thakkar Commission report in two parts laid on the table of both Houses of Parliament.

April 7 – Special Investigation Team (SIT), files its second charge sheet in New Delhi Court, implicating five persons for waging war against the state and plotting to kill Indira Gandhi. This includes former IPS Officer Simranjit Singh Mann already in police custody.

May 7 Jasmer Singh, president of Unified Akali Dal (UAD) is killed by terrorists.

May 9 – Parliament approves extension of President's Rule in Punjab by six months from May 11.

July 17 – Surjit Singh Barnala reassumes presidentship of Akali Dal.

Oct. 12 – President's Rule is extended for six more months in Punjab.

Nov. 22, 24, 26 – Shiromani Akali Dal (Mann) gets 6 out of 13 Lok Sabha seats in Punjab. Shri S.S. Mann contests from jail and is elected.

Dec. 1 – Punjab Governor S.S. Ray orders immediate release of four Akali leaders including former Chief Minister, Parkash Singh Badal.

Dec. 2 – Simranjit Singh Mann, president of Akali Dal (Mann) and his four associates released from Bhagalpur jail after withdrawal of all cases pending against them.

1989

March 3 – Discussion in Rajya and Lok Sabha and Prime Minister Rajiv Gandhi's speeches.

April 10 – Prime Minister Rajiv Gandhi's speech in Lok Sabha on the Thakkar Commission Report.

Dec. 28 – Discussion in the Lok Sabha.

1991

April 24 – Poll dates for Punjab announced.

June 21 – Punjab elections postponed.

June 22 – Punjab Governor General O.P. Malhotra resigns on postponing Punjab elections.

August 5 – Shri Surendra Nath appointed Punjab Governor.

September 18 – Parliament approves extension of President's Rule in Punjab saying polls must be held before 15 Feb, 1992.

B. Chronology of Election, Jan.-Feb. 1992

January

Jan. 6 – Punjab poll soon: Election Commissioner T.N. Seshan.

15 – Election Commissioner announces Punjab poll schedule for 13 Lok Sabha and 117 Assembly seats. Fixes Feb. 19 as the polling date.

17 – 4 Akali groups decide to boycott Punjab polls.

21 – Shri Jiwan Singh Umranangal forms a new party called the Shiromani Jagat Akali Dal and decides to contest elections under the banner of the newly formed party.

22 – The Punjab group welcomes the announcement of elections.

23 – Chandigarh to be given to Punjab, in case the Congress comes to power, states the Punjab PCC president.

24 – Panthetic group headed by Gurbachan states that it may sponsor candidates.

25 – Kabul faction to contest Punjab elections. Shri Sukhjinder Singh, a senior leader of the Badal group forms a new party to contest elections.

– Three nominations filed on the first day.

26 – CPI candidate Shri Harpal Singh shot dead by militants.

27 – No. agreement on elections with BJP and Congress – Captain Amrinder Singh, Chairman of the Akali Dal (K).

28 – A new party named 'Punjab People's Party' launched; the party to contest Punjab elections. BJP to go alone in Punjab elections. Kabul (Akali) faction rebels to boycott Punjab poll.

29 – All India Sikh Students Federation urges Akali leaders to boycott elections.

– All India Sikh Conference (AISC) asks Mann and Badal group to contest elections. Akali Dal (S) defends decision to contest elections.

– Chief of the Bhindranwale Tiger Force of Khalistan to boycott elections.

– By boycotting the elections, the Akalis have fallen into Congress trap — Shri V.P. Singh.

30 – Panthic Committee led by Baba Gurbachan Singh Manochahal decides to contest elections.

– Prime Minister P.V. Narasimha Rao urges all political parties to take part in the Punjab elections.

– The Punjab Naxalites group decides to contest four Lok Sabha and nine Assembly seats.

– CPI (ML) for boycotting the elections.

– The BJP president, Dr. Murli Manohar Joshi, CPM general secretary Shri Harkishan Singh Surjeet and CPI general secretary Shri Chaturanan Mishra ask Akali leaders not to ask the Akal Takht to issue dictates banning Akali groups from contesting the poll.

– Shri S.S. Mann, Akali Dal president (Mann) opposes issuance of any edict from the Akal Takht.

31 – The Panthic Committee member and Bhindranwale Tiger Force of Khalistan Chief Baba Gurbachan Singh Manochahal states that they will not contest elections.

- Shri Chandra Shekhar announces that SJP would not contest elections.
- Akali Dal (K) releases list.
- JD to contest Lok Sabha seats.
- The Govt. of Punjab makes elaborate arrangements to prevent the Akali leaders reach the venue of meeting at Jullundur and detain workers and leaders including Shri Simranjit Singh Mann, president of Akali Dal (M) and Bhai Manjit Singh, president of the AISSF.
- Filing of nomination papers comes to end.

February

2 – Anti-poll rally organised by various Akali groups lathicharged at Ludhiana and several hundred activitists arrested.
- Akali Dal (Mann) president Simranjit Singh Mann urges the Government to call off the Feb. 19 polls in Punjab as he said there could be post-poll "communal tension and bloodshed". (*H.T.*, February 3, 1992).
- Akali Dal (Panth Khalsa) headed by former member of Parliament Shri Rajender Singh decides to boycott Punjab elections.

3 – Chief Election Commission Shri T.N. Seshan orders inquiry into the allegations made by Akali and other leaders regarding preventing some of their candidates to file their nominations to make the contest easy for the Congress.
- 33 nominations (29 for Vidhan Sabha and 4 for Lok Sabha) rejected and 39 candidates officially withdraw.

4 – Sukhjinder Singh faction of Akalis to boycott election.
- Captain Chanan Singh Sidhu of the Sukhjinder Singh group decides not to withdraw his papers.
- Shiv Sena to boycott Punjab poll.
- BJP for probe into allegations regarding preventing candidates from filing nominations.
- Shri Bir Devinder Singh, a Congress leader of Punjab flays Shri Simranjit Singh's remarks made on February 2.
- Delhi teachers protest against the election duty in Punjab.
- Orders issued by the Delhi Administration to its employees for performing election duty in Punjab contain packages of incentives as well as warnings.

– Punjab Government declares holiday in Punjab on February 19 i.e. election day.

– Shri Harkishan Singh Surjeet CPM general secretary criticises the government for withholding package of measures on Punjab.

– All India Youth Akali Dal urges the President R. Venkataraman to direct the Chief Election Commission to postpone the election in Punjab.

5 – Captain Amrinder Singh, Chairman of the Parliamentary Board of the Akali Dal (Kabul) and Shri Dilbagh Singh Daleke of the Congress elected unopposed from Samana and Tarn Taran Assembly constituency's respectively.

– Delhi teachers demand not to do poll duty in Punjab rejected.

– Parkash Singh Badal, president Akali Dal (Badal) asks Punjabis to be ready for the struggle and also boycott elections.

– 675 candidates (594 for Assembly and 81 for Parliament) left in the field to contest elections — lowest record number of contesting candidates.

6 – Election Commission rejects some of the reports sent by the Punjab Government in respect of a few complaints made by political parties or their candidates that they had been detained by the State police and thus denied the opportunity to file their nomination papers.

– Punjab polls no solution, says Mahant Sewa Dass, president Akali Dal (Pheruman).

– Congress manifesto promises normalcy.

– BJP apprehends rigging.

7 – JD giving second thoughts on contesting Punjab poll.

– CEC briefs Punjab poll observers.

– Six Party Akali plan to organise boycott march from Feb. 11 from Anandpur Sahib.

– BJP stops poll campaign.

– Delhi Sikh Gurdwara Management Committee's appeal to political parties to boycott Punjab election.

8 – BJP for fair polls and resumes campaign.

– Akalis bid to hold meeting at Bhatinda failed and many Akali leaders including Parakash Singh Badal and Simranjit Singh Mann detained.

– Shri Mann sends telegrams to the United Nations Secretary General, Ambassadors of the USA, Russia, United Kingdom, France and China for International intervention.

9 – Delhi State Civil Supplies Corporation employees file a writ petition in Delhi High Court against the posting of its members on poll duty in Punjab.

– 170 Government school teachers of Delhi court assert at Raj Niwas protesting against being sent forcibly for pooling duty in Punjab.

10 – Top Akali leaders held under the Terrorist and Disruptive Activities Act (TADA) on the eve of the proposed poll boycott march from the historic Anandpur Sahib.

– Terrorists kill a headmaster and eight teachers of Government scholars in an apparent bid to score away Goverment employes from election duties.

– Schools closed in Punjab till February 24 in view of the Lok Sabha and Assembly elections.

– Minister of State for Home, M.M. Jacob asks Akalis to fight polls.

– Presidium of the All India Sikh Students Federation (AISSF) and President of the Akali Dal (Baba) give a call for Punjab bandh's on February 18 and 19.

11 – Election boycott march by the Akalis foiled by the security forces backed by Army. Many Akali leaders arrested.

– Resolution passed by the SGPC denouncing the Centre as treacherous which was trying to foist a puppet government on Punjab.

– Four BJP campaigners shot dead at Amritsar.

– Delhi High Court restrains DDA poll order.

– Representatives of delhi Panthic parties organise rally in Delhi against Punjab poll.

– Delhi teachers on fast against poll duty.

– Punjab colleges closed for security reasons.

– Teachers killed to whip up fear — S.B. Chavan.

– Home Minister S.B. Chavan assures fair poll.

– Gurcharan Singh Tohra criticises government.

– CPI alleges that election campaign is hampered.

– Akali Dal (Kabul) pledges to restore peace if comes to power in the Punjab election.

12 – Various Government Employees Union in Punjab and Haryana reiterate their decision to boycott poll duties in the wake of the killing of a teachers who were assigned poll duties.
– 3 Congress campaigners in Phillaur Parliamentary Constituency shot dead by militants.
– Delhi Sikh Gurdwara Management Committee (DSGMC) for poll boycott.
– J.D. seeks release of Akali leaders.
– BJP releases election manifesto.
– Akali factions call for 48 hour Punjab bandh from February 18.
– Punjab election a farce — CPI.
13 – Poll officer killed in Punjab.
– Punjab poll picking up — S.B. Chavan, Union Home Minister.
– Punjab Congress expels 18 rebels.
– The BJP leader Shri Atal Behari Vajpayee moots the idea of mobile polling booths in sensitive villages to assuage the fear psychosis among voters and to countract the militant's thread.
– Shri Harkishan Singh Surjeet, general secretary of the CPM calls upon the Akali Dal leadership to stop misusing gurdwaras and issuing edicts on poll boycott from them.
14 – Home Minister S.B. Chavan sees Akalis — Pakistan nexus.
– Shri Chavan reviews security arrangements for the elections.
– Congress responsible for mess — BJP president M.M. Joshi.
– Hindi and Punjabi Ballot papers for Punjab.
– Akali Dal (Mann) flays government for arrests.
15 – A special Police Officer (SPO) killed and about 20 Congress supporters injured in a blast in the residential compound of a Congress candidate at Ludhiana.
– Some Punjab candidates censored.
– Poll boycott to help Pakistan — BJP leader L.K. Advani.
16 – Five poll campaigners killed in Punjab.
– A portion of rail track blown up near Amritsar.
– The State Government makes all arrangements to ensure free and peaceful polls — State Chief Secretary-cum-Chief Electoral Officer.
17 – Election campaign ends in Punjab.
– Delhi High Court directs that all Central Government and Delhi Administration employees, could be asked to report for Election duty in Punjab, but employees of the Delhi

Development Authority, the New Delhi Municipal Committee, the Municipal Corporation Delhi, Government Companies and Societies based in Delhi do not come under this.

– The Editors' Guild of India condemns censorship by the Punjab Government.

– Blasts at many places.

18 – Near bandh in Punjab on the call by some militant outfits and six Akali factions to protest against elections in the state.

– Shri Rajinder Sachar president Peoples Union for Civil Liberties flays press censorship in Punjab.

19 – Low turnout in Punjab poll — 10 to 15 per cent in villages and 20 to 50 per cent in towns.

– Elections rigged – says Akalis – elections a force.

20 – Congress gets two-thirds majority in the Assembly elections.

– Massive rigging — Opposition.

21 – All results declared. Congress get 86 Assembly seats and 12 Parliament seats.

22 – Congress Ministry formed with Shri Beant Singh as Chief Minister.

22

TOWARDS A PEACEFUL PUNJAB

The Hindus and Sikhs have lived very amicably, brotherly and peacefully for several centuries.

A joint Gurdwara-cum-Mandir was got built up at Goindhowal (Hoshiarpur, Punjab) by Ahluwalia, Sikh origin saint Shri Hari Baba who was later almost worshipped as incarnation of Lord Gaurang by both Hindus and Sikhs.

There was a practice in many Hindu families that the eldest son used to be brought up on Sikh tenets and others as Hindus.

Marriages among the Hindu and Sikh families have been common.

This bears enough testimony of brotherhood and solidarity even in the face of danger.

The Punjab problem is not tractable but is certainly within easy reach as everything is not lost as yet.

The Punjab problem brooks no further delay.

Terrorism of all forms must be condemned but terrorists should be handled with care and caution.

Here, it is not proposed to present a philosophical treatise on the solution of the problem. Already reams of paper have been used and hundreds of speeches made.

It was very unfortunate that on three occasions Akali Ministry was dismissed, naturally leading to many misapprehensions among the Akalis with the result that they did not contest 1992 elections. The Union Government should be sensitive to such issues.

The guiding principle of a welfare state is to examine each demand of its citizens very carefully and if found genuine, accept it without any reservation.

Accords are normally between a State and a State or among States but not between a State and a certain section of people.

As a first step, to assuage the feelings of the Sikhs, Chandigarh should be handed over to Punjab or entire expenditure for establishing a Capital of Punjab should be borne by the Union Government.

All other problems should be handed over to a Commission comprising not less than three High Court Judges, not serving in or belonging to Punjab (on account of obvious reasons).

The Government should announce the reforms immediately.

There are more important issues to be tackled and we can only hope and pray that the saner elements will rise equal to the occasion and find an amicable solution that ensures for all of us an India in which all communities live in peace.

APPENDIX

Terrorism in Punjab

TABLE A1: Persons Killed in Punjab, 1981 to 1991

	1981	1982	1983	1984	1985	1986	1987	1988	1989	1990	1991
Persons killed by terrorists											
Hindus	10	8	35	237	45	324	425	858	442	743	744
Sikhs	3	5	40	122	17	193	478	1,044	734	1,694	1,874
Total	13	13	75	359	63	520	910	1,949	1,188	2,467	2,591
Cops killed by terrorists	2	2	20	20	8	42	95	110	152	493	496
Terrorists killed	14	7	13	77	2	78	328	373	699	1,321	2,177
Terrorists arrested	84	178	296	1,630	491	1,581	3,750	3,882	2,466	1,759	1,949

Source: Times of India, February 9, 1992.

TABLE A2: Training Camps in Pakistan

Pakistan	Opposite Indian Location
Chungi Point	Ajnala (Amritsar distt.)
Dera Sahib	Ajnala (Amritsar distt.)
Hazura	Ferozepur
Jalalabad	Gurdaspur
Kartar Singh Gujranwala	Dera Baba Nanak (Gurdaspur distt.)
Kasur	Khem Karan (Amritsar distt.)
Lahore	Amritsar
Narowal	Dera Baba Nanak (Gurdaspur distt.)
Purana Kahana	Khalra (Amritsar distt.)
Shekhupura	Ajnala (Amritsar distt.)
Sialkot	Gurdaspur
Zaffarwal	Dera Baba Nanak (Gurdaspur distt.)

Source: Times of India, February 9, 1992.

TABLE A3: Strength of Terrorists

	Range			
	Patiala	Jalandhar	Ferozepur	Border
Hardcore terrorists	206	106	140	964
Non-hardcore terrorists	50	20	38	103
No. of Gangs				
Khalistan Commando Force	10	9	16	28
Bhindranwale Tiger Force of Khalistan	8	4	1	17
Khalistan Liberation Force	10	2	5	8
Babbars	8	3	4	12
Other gangs	1	1	3	17

Note: Patiala range: Ludhiana, Patiala, Ropar and Sangrur districts.
Jalandhar range: Hoshiarpur, Jullundhur and Kapurthala districts.
Ferozepur range: Bhatinda, Faridkot and Ferozepur districts.

Source: Times of India, February 9, 1992.

TABLE A4: Terrorists' Arsenal

Type of Arms	Quantity
AK 47	1,700
Self Loading rifle	50
GP machine guns	130
Medium machine guns	20
Rocket launchers	120
Rockets	1,350
Grenade launchers	5
Grenades	30
Explosives	2,600
Night vision devices	3
Light machine guns	13
Dragnov sniper rifles	4
Two inch mortars	1

Source: Times of India, February 9, 1992.

PART II

BIBLIOGRAPHY

BIBLIOGRAPHY

Published Sources

Abraham, A.S., 1983, The Politics of Terror: Implications of Punjab Extremism, *Times of India*, October 21, p 8, col 3-5.

Abraham, A.S., 1984, The Politics of Violence; Varieties of Terrorism, *Times of India*, May 18, p 6, col 3-5.

Abraham, A.S., 1985, Pressures on the System: Coping with Trauma of Punjab, *Times of India*, August 23, p 8, col 3-5.

Adhikari, G., 1945, *Sikh Homeland through Hindu-Muslim-Sikh Unity*, People's Publishing House, Bombay.

Adhikari, G., 1944, *Pakistan and National Unity*, People's Publishing House, Bombay.

Adhikari, Gautam, 1983, Orthodoxy vs Modernisation: Punjab Highlight the Larger Tussle, *Times of India*, October 19, p 8, col 3-5.

Adhikari, Gautam, 1984, The Liberty-Equality Utopia: A Detective Framework, *Times of India*, May 23, p 8, col 3-5.

Advani, L.K., 1985, Rajiv Longowal Accord: Volte Face: An Interview with . . ., *Organiser* 37(12) August 4, p 1+.

Aggarwal, J.C. and Chowdhry, N.K., 1992, *Election in India (From 1952 to Bye Election 1991): Analysis and Overviews*, Shipra, New Delhi.

Aggarwal, K.P., 1980, the Tragic Destruction of a Valiant Army, *Sikh Review* 28(317) May, p 46-50.

Agrawal, S.P. and Aggarwal, J.C., 1992, *Information India: Global View, 1991-92*, Concept Publishing Company, New Delhi.

Agrawal, S.P. and Aggarwal, J.C., 1991, *History of Rise and Fall of Non-Congress Government of India*, Shipra, New Delhi.

Agrawal, S.P. and Aggarwal, J.C., 1991, *Lok Sabha and Vidhan Sabha Elections in India 1989-1990*, Concept Publishing Company, New Delhi.

Agnivesh (Swami), 1984, Arya Samaj's Close Links with Sikhs, *Times of India*, April 13, p 8, col 7-8; April 14, p 8, col 7-8.

Ahluwalia, Jasbir Singh, 1984, Article 25 of the Constitution of India and the Sikhs, *Sikh Review* 32(324) April, p 62-65.

Ahluwalia, M.L., Relations of the Lahore Durbar with China; Mai Chand Kaur's Rule in the Punjab; Sher Singh and the First War of Succession; Some Facts behind the Second Anglo-Sikh War; Ladakh's Relations with India, *Proceedings of the Indian Historical Records Commission*, vols XXX–XXXIII.

Ahluwalia, M.L. and Kirpal Singh, 1964, *The Punjab's Pioneer Freedom Fighters*, Orient Longmans, Calcutta.

Ahluwalia, M.M., 1965, *Kukas: The Freedom Fighters of the Punjab*, Allied Publishers, Bombay.

Ahuja, Charanjit, 1985, Punjab: The Unresolved Issues, *Indian Express* (Magazine Section) December 8, p 3, col 1-8.

Aitchison, Charles (Sir), 1892, *Lord Lawrence*, Clarendon Press, Oxford.

Aiyar, Swaminathan S., 1985, Punjab: And Miles to Go, *Indian Express* (Magazine Section) August 11, p 1, col 5-8+.

Aiyar, Swaminathan S,, 1985, The Hindu Factor, *Mainstream* 23(37) March 11, p 11-12.

Akbar, M.J., 1985, The Siege Within, Penguin Books Ltd., Middlesex.

Amarjit Kaur, et al., 1984, The Punjab Story, Rolibooks International, New Delhi, 199p.

Amar Nath, 1929, *The Development of Local Self-Government in the Punjab 1849-1900*, P.G.R.O., Lahore.

Amar Singh, 1946, *Memorandum of the Central Akali Dal*, West End Press, Lahore.

Ambedkar, B.R., 1946, *Pakistan or the Partition of India*, Thacker and Co., Bombay.

Amrik Singh, ed., 1985, Punjab in Indian Politics: Issues and Trends, Ajanta Publications, Delhi, 479p.

Amte (Baba), 1986, Observations, *Seminar*, 326, October, p 17-19.

Ananda Prakash, 1981, Economic Cost of Passion Politics, *Commerce* 143(367) October 17, p 686.

Ananda Prakash, 1983, Anatomy of Akali Agitation, *Commerce* 146(3741) February 12, p 254-258, map.

Ananda Prakash, 1985, It's Defeat for Secessionists, *Commerce* 151(3880) October 5, p 648-651.

Ananda Prakash, 1985, Punjab Settlement: Universal Feeling of Relief, *Commerce* 151(3871) August 3, p 200-201+.

Ananda Prakash, 1986, Punjab: Terrorism Eroding Industrial Base, *Commerce* 152(3926) August 16, p 328-330.

Anon, n.d., *9th Lok Sabha*: Who is Who? Lok Sabha Secretariat, New Delhi.

Anon, n.d., *Imperial Gazetteer of India*, Provincial Series, Punjab, vol I, Superintendent of Government Printing Press, Calcutta.

Anon, n.d., *Parliamentary Papers Relating to the Punjab: 1847-1949*, Harrison and Son, London.

Anon, n.d., *Lahore Political Diaries 1846-1849*, Punjab Government Records.

Anon, n.d., *Mutiny Reports*, vol III, parts I-II; vol VIII, parts I-II, Punjab Government Records.

Anon, n.d., *Settlement Reports of the Punjab*, Civil And Military Gazette Press, Lahore.

Anon, *Sikhs in Action*, Government Printing Press, Lahore.

Anon, n.d., *Sikhs War Records: The Great War 1914-1918*, Privately Published.

Anon, 1842, *Letters on Recent Transactions in India*, by Officer of the Bengal Army, Smith Elder and Co., London .

Anon, 1846, *History of the Campaign of the Sutlej and War in the Punjab: Memoirs of Many Distinguished Officers*, Charles Edmonds, London.

Anon, 1855, *Census Reports: Punjab,* Government Printing Press, Calcutta, 1855 Onward.

Anon, 1878, *Old Punjabee: The Punjab and North West Frontier of India*, Kegan Paul and Co., London

Anon, 1884, *The Maharaja Duleep Singh and the Government*, W.S. Orr and Co., London.

Anon, 1872, *Kukas: Papers Relating to the Kuka Sect* (selection from the Records of the Government of the Punjab), Lahore .

Anon, 1872, *Kukas: Parliamentary Paper No, 356 on the Kuka Outbreak* (Reply to an Address in the House of Commons, July 22).

Anon, 1888, *Punjab Cavalry: History of Second Punjab Cavalry, 1849-1886*, Kegan Paul and Co., London.

Anon, 1893-1912, *Selection from State Papers Preserved in the Military Department*, ed., by George W. Forrest, Government Printing Press, Calcutta.

Anon, 1895, *Proceedings on the Trial of Bahadur Shah*, Superintendent of Government Printing Press, Calcutta.

Anon, 1897, *Punjab Legislative Council Debates* Punjab Government Press, Lahore, 1897 Onward, Later Called the *Punjab Legislative Assembly Debates*.

Anon, 1914, *Komagata Maru Commission of Enquiry Report*, Government Printing Press, Calcutta.

Anon, 1920, *Congress Punjab Inquiry Report 1919-1920*, Karnatak Printing Press, Bombay .

Anon, 1921, *Indian Reforms Scheme: Report of the Working of the Sikh Deputation to England, 1920*, Mufid-I-Am Press, Lahore.

Anon, 1922, *Government Allegations against the Sikhs*, Hyderabad.

Anon, 1923, *Patiala and the Great War*, Medici Society, London.

Anon, 1923, *35th Sikhs Regimental Records, 1887-1922*, Sham Lall & Sons, Peshawar .

Anon, 1924, *Army in India and Its Evolution*, 1924, Government Printing Press, Calcutta.

Anon, 1924, *Truth about Nabha*, S.G.P.C., Amritsar.

Anon, 1925, *Voice of India on the Sikh Settlement*, Director, Information Bureau, Punjab .

Anon, 1930, *Memorandum on Sikh Representation (Presented to the Indian Statutory Commission)*, Superintendent of Printing, Calcutta .

Anon, 1941, *Sikh Invasion and British Victories on the Sutlej*, Blackwood and Page, London.

Anon, 1945, *A Short History of 14th Punjab Regiment: 1939-1945*, Lund Humphries, London.

Anon, 1947, *Congress and the Problem of Minorities*, All India Congress Committee; Shankar Rao Deo, Allahabad .

Anon, 1947, *Sikh Memorandum to the Boundary Commission*, Mercantile Press, London.

Anon, 1948, *Note on the Sikh Plan*, Government Printing Press, Lahore .

Anon, 1948, *R.S.S. in the Punjab*, Government Printing Press, Lahore

Anon, 1949, *Punjab Administration Reports*, Punjab Government Press, Lahore, 1849 onward.

Anon, 1950, *Partition Proceedings*, vol VI, (1950) Alipore, Calcutta.

Anon, 1979, (Book Review), *Punjab Past and Present* 13(1) April, p 243-246.

Review of the Book: Mohinder Singh, 1978, *The Akali Movement*, Macmillan Co. Publishers, New Delhi, xiv, 245p.

Anon, 1979, (Book Review) *Social Science Research Journal* 4(1) March, p 150-155.

Review of the Book: Pettigrew, Joyce, 1978, *Robber Nobleman* Ambika Publications, New Delhi.

Anon, 1980, (Book Review) *Punjab Past and Present* 14(1) April, p 228-229.

Review of the Book: Mittal, S.C., 1977, *Freedom Movement in Punjab, 1905-1929*, Concept Publishing Co., New Delhi, 256p.

Anon, 1980-1981, (Book Review) *Indian History Review* 7(1-2) June-July, p 326-328.

Review of the Book: Mohinder Singh, 1978, *The Akali Movement*, Macmillan Co., Publishers, New Delhi, xiv, 245p.

Anon, 1981, 2, 109 Akalis Court arrest in Delhi, *Times of India*, September 8, p 1, col 6-8+.

Anon, 1981, Against Communalism: CPI(M) in Punjab to Hold Convention, *New Age* 29(24) June 14, p 7.

Anon, 1981, Akali Dal (L) Stance Causes Apprehension, *New Age*, 29(31) August 2, p 15.

Anon, 1981, Akali Plea for UN Membership, *Times of India*, August 5, p 1, col 1-8+.

Anon, 1981, (Book Review) *Calcutta Journal of Political Studies* 2(1) Winter, p 121-124.

Review of the Book: Wallace, Paul and Chopra, Surendra, eds. 1981, *Political Dynamics of Punjab*, Guru Nanak Dev University, Amritsar, 381p.

Anon, 1981, (Book Review) *Hindustan Times* (Magazine) December 13, p iv, col 7-8.

Review of the Book: Uprety, Prem Raman, 1980, *Religion and Politics in Punjab in the 1920's*, Sterling Publishing Pvt. Ltd., New Delhi, p vii, 222p.

Anon, 1981, (Book Review) *Indian Journal of Training and Development* 11(1-2) January-June, p 89-90.

Review of the Book: Tandon, Prakash, 1981, *Return of Punjab*, Vikas Publications, New Delhi, 277p.

Anon, 1981, (Book Review) *Journal of Sikh Studies* 8(1-2) February-August, p 156-158.

Review of the Book: Gandhi, Surjeet Singh, 1980, *Struggle of the Sikhs for Sovereignty*, Gurdas Kapur and Sons (P) Ltd., Delhi, xxii 551p.

Anon, 1981, (Book Review) *Punjab Journal of Politics* 5(2) July-December, p 196-200.
Review of the Book: Dalip Singh, 1981, *Dynamics of Punjab Politics*, Macmillan Co. Publishers, New Delhi, vii, 295p.

Anon, 1981, (Book Review) *Teaching Politics* 7(3-4) p 71-77.
Review of the Book: Wallace, Paul and Chopra, Surinder, eds., 1981, *Political Dynamics Punjab*, Guru Nanak Dev University, Amritsar.

Anon, 1981, CPI Draws Multiple Campaign Plan in Punjab, *New Age* 29(30) July 26, p 13.

Anon, 1981, CPI Punjab Secretariat on Critical Situation, *New Age* 29(48) November 29, p 11.

Anon, 1981, CPI State Council Says Government Responsible for Explosive Situation in Punjab, *New Age* 29(40) October 4, p 15.

Anon, 1981, Conflicting Claims as Punjab Stir Begins, *Times of India*, January 3, p 1, col 7-8.

Anon, 1981, Dangerous Drift in Akali Politics, *Link* 23(49) July 19, p 23-24.

Anon, 1981, Darbara Singh Camp Crestfallen, *Times of India* July 26, p 5, col 1-2.

Anon, 1981, Darbara Singh on the way out, *Organiser* 33(12) August 9, p 10.

Anon, 1981, Diversionary Move, *Economic and Political Weekly* 16(16) April 18, p 687.

Anon, 1981, Drifting from Bad to Worse, *Link* 24(17) December, p 25.

Anon, 1981, Genesis of the Demand for Khalistan, *Sikh Review* 29(336) December, p 18-25.

Anon, 1981, Government 'Interference' Main Cause of Conflict, *Time of India* October 16, p 7, col 1-2.

Anon, 1981, Government May Agree to Study Akali Demands, *Times of India*, November 24, p 1, col 2-3+.

Anon, 1981, IA Boeing Aircraft Hijacked to Lahore: Demand for Release of Bhindranwale: 45 Passengers Freed, *Times of India*, September 30, p 1, col 1-41.

Anon, 1981, The Joint Movement in Punjab: A Survey, *People's Democracy* 5(7) February 15, p 6-8.

Anon, 1981, Khalistan Drama on Akali Stage, *Link* 23(51) August 2, p 31-33.

Anon, 1981, 'Khalistan' Leaders Claim Support in U.S., *Times of India*, October 3, p 1, col 1-4.

Anon, 1981, Khalistan Stir: Origin and Aims, *Times of India*, October 2, p 1, col 2-4+.

Anon, 1981, Move for President Rule in Punjab Denied, *Times of India*, November 26, p 1, col 4-5+.

Anon, 1981, Noisy Scenes in Punjab Assembly, *Times of India*, January 24, p 1, col 2-4.

Anon, 1981, On Development in Punjab, *People's Democracy* 5(45) November 8, p 6-7.

Anon, 1981, Over a Lakh Court Arrest in Punjab, *New Age* 29(2) January 11, p 9.

Anon, 1981, PM Lashes Out at Foreign Press on Khalistan Issue, *Times of India*, October 10, p 13.

Anon, 1981, People Warned Against Destabilising Punjab, *Times of India*, October 10, p 6, col 4-5.

Anon, 1981, Police Fails to Prevent Punjab Assembly Gherao: Two Killed at Bhatinda, *New Age*, 29(4) January 25, p 1-2.

Anon, 1981, Punjab: CPI Campaigns for Communal Harmony, *New Age*, 29(46)November 15, p 7+.

Anon, 1981, Punjab: Cashing on Indira Image, *Link* 23(29) May 10, p 14-15.

Anon, 1981, Punjab: Left Base Expanding, *Link* 23(21) January 4, p 13.

Anon, 1981, Punjab: Opposition Outwitted, *Link* 23(41) May 24, p 33-34.

Anon, 1981, Punjab: Pernicious Slogans of Khalistan and Sikhs-a-nation; *New Age* 29(19) May 10, p 9.

Anon, 1981, Punjab: Some Improvement but Danger Persists: CPI's Campaign against Secessionist, *New Age* 29(51) December 20, p 15.

Anon, 1981, Punjab: Who is Afraid of Indira? *Link* 23(31) March 15, p 29-30.

Anon, 1981, Punjab Conference of CPI(M), *People's Democracy* 5(50) December 13, p 1+.

Anon, 1981, Punjab Hotting Up, *Link* 24(9) October 11, p 8-13.

Anon, 1981, Punjab Politics: Dangerous Game, *Mainstream* 20(14) December 5, p 4-6.

Anon, 1981, September: An Omnious Month, *Link* 24(9) October 11, p 15-16.

Anon, 1981, A Sikh Nation, *Hindustan Times* (Magazine) October 4, p 1, col 6-8.

Anon, 1981, The Sikh Stand Point: Punjab Crisis, *Sikh Review* 29(336) December, p 7-17.

Anon, 1981, They Play Politics as Punjab Suffers, *Times of India* October 10, p 1, col 4-5+.

Anon, 1982, Akalis: Centre May Evolve Package Deal, *Times of India*, October 30, p 1, col 2-3+.

Anon, 1982, Akali Agitation: The Morcha Politics, *Link* 25(10) October 17, p 30-31.

Anon, 1982, Akali Dal Morcha to Continue: Longowal, *Times of India*, October 21, p 1, col 2-4+.

Anon, 1982, The Akali Dilemma, *Link* 24(51) August 1, p 25-27.

Anon, 1982, Akali MLAs and MPs Directed to Resign, *Times of India*, November 19, p 1, col 1-2+.

Anon, 1982, Akali Morcha will be Harmful, *People's Democracy* 6(32) August 8, p 3.

Anon, 1982, Akalis Want Demands Accepted First, *Times of India*, October 24, p 1, col 2-4+.

Anon, 1982, Alarming Situation in Punjab, *People's Democracy* 6(26) June 27, p 5+.

Anon, 1982, Badal Cautions Moves, *Link* 25(10) December 26, p 15-16.

Anon, 1982, (Book Review), *India Quarterly* 38(3-4) July-December, p 419-420.

Review of the Book: **Prabha, K.**, 1979, *A Structural Analysis: A Case Study of Punjab*, Inter-India Publications, New Delhi, 214 p.

Anon, 1982, (Book Review) *Social Action* 32(1) January-March, p 102-104.

Review of the Book: **Uprety, Prem Raman**, 1980, *Religion and Politics in Punjab in the 1920's*, Sterling Publishers Pvt, Ltd., New Delhi, vii, 222p.

Anon, 1982, (Book Review) *Tribune* April 17, p 4, col 4-6.

Review of the Book: **Satinder Singh**, 1982, *Khalistan: An Academic Analysis* Amar Prakashan, New Delhi, 184p.

Anon, 1982, CPI(M) Stand on Akali Demands, *People's Democracy* 6(37) September 12, p 2+.

Anon, 1982, Centre Akali Dialogue: When Talks Fail...., *Link* 25(18) December 12, p 7-9.

Anon, 1982, Centre May Accept Some Akali Demands, *Times of India*, November 2, p 1, col 5-6.

Anon, 1982, Centre's Stand Reiterated: No Unilateral Decision on Akali Demands, *Times of India*, December 9, p 1, col 2-3+.

Anon, 1982, The Chandigarh Question, *Link* 25(14) November 14, p 17-18.

Anon, 1982, Communal Clouds over Punjab, *Secular Democracy* 15(5) May, p 8-15.

Anon, 1982, Conciliatory Gesture to Akalis by PM., *Times of India*, November 10, p 1, col 5-6+.

Anon, 1982, The Controversial Resolution, *Link* 25(16) November 28, p 11-12.

Anon, 1982, Delhi Steps to Prevent Akalis Entry, *Times of India*, November 13, p 1, col 4-5+.

Anon, 1982, Dharamyudh Politics Evades Solution, *Link* 25(14), November 14, p 14.

Anon, 1982, Dismissal of Zail Urged: BJP for Presidents Rule in Punjab, *Times of India*, June 4, p 1, col 7-8+.

Anon, 1982, Efforts to Defuse Tension in Punjab, *Times of India*, September 19, p 1, col 2-5.

Anon, 1982, Extremists in Punjab Step Up Activities, *Times of India* October 28, p 1, col 2-3+.

Anon, 1982, Fresh Government Move on Akali Demands Likely, *Time of India* November 17, p 1, col 7-8+.

Anon, 1982, Fresh Punjab Formula Being Worked Out, *Times of India* November 21, p 1, col 2-3+.

Anon, 1982, The Glorious Past, *Link* 25(18) December 12, p 11-12.

Anon, 1982, Government Ready to Discuss All Issues with Akalis, *Times of India*, October 13, p 1, col 2-4+.

Anon, 1982, Growth of Sikh Separatism: A Historical Review of Communal Sikh Politics, *Secular Democracy* 15(5) May, p 16-22.

Anon, 1982, A Healthy Development, *Link* 24(29) February 28, p 25.

Anon, 1982, Hectic talks in Delhi on Akali Demands, *Times of India* November 3, p 1, col 7-8+.

Anon, 1982, Index and Abstracts of News of Communal Tensions, *Man and Development* 4(3) September, p 131-163.

Anon, 1982, Janata Chief for Consensus on Akali Demands, *Times of India*, October, p 5, col 1-4.

Anon, 1982, Last-Minute Bid to Solve Punjab Tangle, *Times of India*, November 18, p 1, col 2-4+.

Anon, 1982, Longowal May Call Meeting of Minorities, *Times of India*, December 7, p 1, col 7-8.

Anon, 1982, Mrs. Gandhi Likely to Meet Akali Leaders, *Times of India*, November 1, p 1, col 7-8.

Anon, 1982, Mediators to Meet Longowal with New Plan, *Times of India*, November 22, p 1, col 2-3+.

Anon, 1982, New Akali Stir to be Announced on January 26, *Times of India*, December 12, p 1, col 6-7+.

Anon, 1982, New Phases of Agitation Announced: Massive Akali Morcha in Delhi on November 19, *Times of India*, November 5, p 1, col 2-4+.

Anon, 1982, New Phase of Morcha Today: Akali Talks with Centre Bog Down, *Times of India*, November 4, p 1, col 2-3+.

Anon, 1982, No Early Move likely to End Punjab Crisis, *Times of India*, November 23, p 1, col 7-8+.

Anon, 1982, Opposition Uncertainties, *Link* 24(33) March 28, p 30.

Anon, 1982, PM to Unfold New Plan on Punjab Today, *Times of India*, November 11, p 1, col 7-8+.

Anon, 1982, Poised for the Worst, *Link* 25(3) August 29, p 28-29.

Anon, 1982, President's Rule Not Likely in Punjab, *Times of India*, October 17, p 1, col 1-2.

Anon, 1982, Punjab: CPI Proposals to Meet Extremist Menace, *New Age* 30(25) June 20, p 11.

Anon, 1982, Punjab: United Campaign for Communal Harmony, *New Age* 30(20) January 10, p 6.

Anon, 1982, Punjab Crisis: A Pakistani Viewpoint, *Mainstream* 21(11) November 13, p 4.

Anon, 1982, Punjab Swoop on Akalis: 270 Held, *Times of India*, August 28, p 1, col 5-7+.

Anon, 1982, Punjab Talks Begin: Akalis Want Release of Extremists, *Times of India*, October 29, p 1, col 2-3+.

Anon, 1982, Sant, Granthi and Political Power, *Link* 25(2) August 22, p 29.

Anon, 1982, The Sinister Anandpur Saheb Resolution of Akali Dal, *Organiser* 34(12) August 8, p 2.

Anon, 1982, A State of Confusion, *Sikh Review* 30(347) November, p 44-46.

Anon, 1982, Swaran may Again Meet Dal Leaders, *Times of India* November 24, p 1, col 2-3+.

Anon, 1982, Talks on Akali Demands Fail, *Times of India*, November 20, p 1, col 7-8.

Anon, 1982, Tohra's Opportunist Ways, *Link* 24(21) January 3, 34-35.

Anon, 1983, 45 Hurt in Violence in 2 Punjab Towns, *Times of India*, August 30, p 1, col 2-4+.

Anon, 1983, 600 Akali Leaders Held in Punjab Swoop, *Times of India*, April 3, p 1, col 2-4+.

Anon, 1983, Akali Arrests Cross 1, 200 Mark: Punjab Steps to Meet 'Rasta Roko' Stir, *Times of India*, April 4, p 1, col 2-4+.

Anon, 1983, Akali Camp: Many Pulls, *Link* 25(44) June 12, p 6-7.

Anon, 1983, Akali Centre Dialogue: Fresh New Moves, *Link* 25(40) May 15, p 6-8.

Anon, 1983, Akali Dal Suspends 'Rail Roko' Stir, *Times of India*, June 18, p 1, col 2-4+.

Anon, 19833, Akali Dilemma, *Janata* 38(6) March 20, p 13-14.

Anon, 1983, Akali Leaders Urged to Suspend Stir, *Times of India* October 18, p 1, col 1-2+.

Anon, 1983, Akali Politics: Moderation and Militancy, *Link* 26(18) December 11, p 10.

Anon, 1983, Akalis Announce Plan for Prolonged Stir, *Times of India*, August 16, p 1, col 1-2+.

Anon, 1983, Akalis Plan Volunteer Force of 100,000, *Times of India*, April 9, p 1, col 7-8+.

Anon, 1983, Akalis 'Rail Roko' Stir on June 17, *Times of India*, June 13, p 1, col 6-8.

Anon, 1983, Akalis Reject Sethi's Invitation for Talks, *Times of India*, June 22, p 1, col 2-4+.

Anon, 1983, Akalis Set January 26 as Deadline, *Times of India*, November 30, p 1, col 2-5+.

Anon, 1983, Amritsar Killing: Murder of Sanctity, *Link* 25(38) May 1, p 7-8.

Anon, 1983, Badal and 35 Others Detained, *Times of India*, December 22, p 1, col 8+.

Anon, 1983, Beant Singh in Vidhan Sabha, *Link* 26(6) February 18, p 9-10.

Anon, 1983, (Book Review) *Indian Journal of Political Studies* 6-7 July, p 105-107; *Indian Political Science Review* 17(1) January, p 114-115.

Review of the Book: **Dalip Singh**, 1981, *Dynamics of Punjab Politics*, Macmillan Company Publishers, New Delhi, 301p.

Anon, 1983, CPI(M)'s Appeal to People of Punjab, *People's Democracy* 7(28) July 10, p 1+.

Anon, 1983, Centre to Invite Akalis for Talks, *Times of India*, October 25, p 1, col 2-4+.

Anon, 1983, Centre's Dilemma, *Link* 25(41) May 22, p 7-8.

Anon, 1983, Chaturvedi Darbara Discuss Situation, *Times of India* June 24, p 1, col 6-7+.

Anon, 1983, Checking the Rot, *Link* 26(10) October 16, p 9-10.

Anon, 1983, Congress (I) and Akalis Play Havoc with Punjab, *Organiser* 35(11) July 31, p 1+.

Anon, 1983, Delhi Akali Leaders Denounce Extremism, *Link* 25(39) May 8, p 10.

Anon, 1983, Dialogue with Akalis to Continue, *Times of India* May 19, p 1, col 1-2+.

Anon, 1983, Explosive Situation Develops in Punjab, *New Age* 31(19) May 8, p 5.

Anon, 1983, Extremists Slay Eight Bus, Train Passengers, *Times of India* October 7, p 1, col 1-2+.

Anon, 1983, Eyes on Election, *Economic and Political Weekly* 18(36-37) September 3-10, p 1543.

Anon, 1983, Foreign Hand Behind Punjab Trouble: PM, *Times of India* November 17, p 1, col 1-2+.

Anon, Fresh Government, Initiative on Punjab Likely, *Times of India* April 10, p 1, col 7-8.

Anon, 1983, Government Not to Yield to Khalistan Demand, *Times of India*, May 5, p 1, col 4-5+.

Anon, 1983, Government Ready for Talks with Akalis in Delhi, *Times of India*, April 13, p 1, col 2-4+.

Anon, 1983, Grenade Thrown at CRPF Picket: Punjab Alert as Arms Stolen from Armoury, *Times of India*, April 8, p 1, col 2-4+.

Anon, 1983, In Punjab an Amicable Solution is Necessary, *Janata* 38(16) June 12, p 7-9.

Anon, 1983, In Sheer Helplessness, He Raised His Hands, *Link* 26(10) October 16, p 11.

Anon, 1983, India Hails Canada's Stand on Khalistan, *Times of India* July 5, p 1, col 7-8+

Anon, 1983, A Machiavellian Design to Divide and Rule, *Link* 25(50) July 24, p 12-14.

Anon, 1983, Meeting Ends in Confusion: Akalis Divided on Centre's Proposal, *Times of India*, May 13, p 1, col 2-4+.

Anon, 1983, Militants 'Kidnap' Jail Official in Amritsar, *Times of India*, October 9, p 1, col 2-4+.

Anon, 1983, More Punjab Villages Raided: 13 Akalis Held: Police Spread Dragnet, *Times of India*, October 23, p 1, col 2-4+.

Anon, 1983, Move to Fight Akalis at Political Level, *Times of India*, July 12, p 1, col 7-8+.

Anon, 1983, Movement of Trains in Punjab Suspended, *Times of India*, June 16, p 1, col 2-4+.

Anon, 1983, Naxalite Influence on Akali Extremists, *Times of India*, May 18, p 5, col 2-5.

Anon, 1983, No Deal with Akalis on Darbara's Status, *Times of India*, April 23, p 1, col 2-4+.

Anon, 1983, Non Plan to Send Police into Gurdwaras: PM, *Times of India*, October 14, p 1, col 5-6+.

Anon, 1983, On the Punjab Situation, *People's Democracy* 7(15) April 10, p 1.

Anon, 1983, Operation Destabilisation, *Link* 25(39) May 8, p 9.

Anon, 1983, Opposition Exploiting Punjab Crisis: PM, *Times of India*, June 20, p 1, col 2-4+.

Anon, 1983, Opposition Fanning Punjab Trouble: PM, *Times of India*, July 25, p 1, col 7-8+.

Anon, 1983, Parliament Approves 3 Bills on Punjab, *Times of India*, November 22, p 1, col 2-4+.

Anon, 1983, People's Help Sought to Nab Extremists, *Times of India*, November 21, p 1, col 4-5+.

Anon, 1983, PM May have Talks with Longowal Soon, *Times of India*, April 20, p 1, col 2-4+.

Anon, 1983, PM Raps Opposition, Akalis: Alarming Increase in Anti—national Moves, *Times of India*, June 21, p 1, col 2-4+.

Anon, 1983, PM Rules Out Change in Punjab Leadership, *Times of India*, May 14, p 1, col 3-4+.

Anon, 1983, Police Firing in Many Punjab Areas: 20 Killed as Akali Stir Turns Violent, *Times of India*, April 5, p 1, col 2-4.

Anon, 1983, Politbureau Statement on Punjab, *People's Democracy* 7(25) June 19, p 1-2.

Anon, 1983, Punjab Alert to Meet Akali Threat, *Times of India* August 29, p 1, col 4-5.

Anon, 1983, Punjab and Chandigarh Declared Disturbed Areas, *Times of India*, October 8, p 1, col 1-4+.

Anon, 1983, Punjab Brought Under President's Rule, *Times of India* October 7, p 1, col 2-5.

Anon, 1983, Punjab on the Precipice, *Link* 25(36) April 17, p 8-12.

Anon, 1983, Raids Cover Most of Punjab, *Times of India*, October 24, p 1, col 6-8+.

Anon, 1983, Return of Ahmed Shah Abdali's Days in Punjab, *Organiser* 35(22) October 16, p 4.

Anon, 1983, Sethi Hopeful of Solution: New Proposal Sent to Akali Leaders, *Times of India* May 10, p 1, col 6-8+.

Anon, 1983, Settlement on Punjab Should be Final: PM, *Times of India*, May 11, p 1, col 4-5+.

Anon, 1983, Sikhs a 'nation' Cashing on an Erroneous Concept, *Link* 25(50) July 24, p 7-9.

Anon, 1983, Sikh Demands, *Times of India*, June 16, p 8, col 6.

Anon, 1983, Sikhs Urged to Shun Path of Violence, *Times of India*, December 5, p 1, col 2-5+.

Anon, 1983, Six Extremists Killed in Punjab Village, *Times of India*, October 15, p 1, col 1-3+.

Anon, 1983, Solution to Punjab Tangle: Cabinet Panel Finds Forum Acceptable, *Times of India*, April 22, p 1, col 2-3.

Anon, 1983, Sweeping Powers for Armed Forces, *Times of India*, October 16, p 1, col 1-2+.

Anon, 1983, Talks with Akalis when Peace Returns, *Times of India*, October 27, p 1, col 7-8.

Anon, 1983, The Luring Dangers, *Link* 25(25) January 30, p 9-10.

Anon, 1983, The Sikh Power Syndrome *Secular Democracy* (Independence Day Number) 16(7-8), p 67-70.

Anon, 1983, The Tragic Talks of Two Windows, *Link* 26(6) September 18, p 7-8.

Anon, 1983, Through a Critical Phase, *Link* 26(11) October 23, p 14-15.

Anon, 1983, Troubled Punjab: Surface Calm Hides Turbulence, *Times of India*, July 23, p 1, col 2-3+; July 24, p 1, col 2-4+; July 25, p 1, col 2-4, July 26, p 1, col 2-4+.

Anon, 1983, Violence in Punjab, *Link* 26(10) October 16, p 15-16.

Anon, 1983, Violent Stir by Akalis Deplored: Government Always Willing for Talks Says Sethi, *Times of India*, April 16, p 1, col 2-4+.

Anon, 1983, White Paper Demand on Punjab Rejected, *Times of India* July 15, p 1, col 1-2.

Anon, 1984, Akali Demands X-Rayed, *Manthan* 5(3) August, p 4-9.

Anon, 1984, Akalis Are on the Norms of Many Dilemmas, *Manthan* 5(3) August, p 79-81.

Anon, 1984, The Akalis Inexorable March to Khalistan, *Organiser* 36(19)s September 23, p 5-6.

Anon, 1984, Akalis Plan Agitation from July 16, *Times of India* July 9, p 1, col 7-8+.

Anon, 1984, All-Party Meet for Tripartite Talks, *Times of India*, February 8, p 1, col 2-4.

Anon, 1984, The Anandpur Saheb Resolutions, *Manthan* 5(3) August, p 84-85.

Anon, 1984, Another Swoop on Terrorists Soon, *Times of India* March 26, p 1, col 2-4.

Anon, 1984, Arson at Five Railway Stations: 3 Killed in Cinema Blast in Punjab, *Times of India*, January 29, p 1, col 2-4+.

Anon, 1984, Baba Fears Confrontation; Kharak Singh to do Kar Seva, *Times of India*, July 29, p 1, col 1-3+.

Anon, 1984, Bomb Attack on CRPF Post Near Amritsar, *Times of India* May 7, p 1, col 7-8+.

Anon, 1984, (Book Review) *Economic and Political Weekly* 19(10) March 10, p 421.

Review of the Book: Harbans Singh, 1982, *Khalistan*, Punjāb Writers Cooperative Industrial Society, New Delhi, 112p.

Anon, 1984, (Book Review) *Economic Times* May 13, p 4, col 3-7; *Indian Express* (Magazine), June 24, p 5, col 4-8.

Review of the Book: **Pramod Kumar**, et al, 1984, *Punjab Crisis: Context and Trends*, Centre for Research in Rural and Industrial Development, Chandigarh, 172p.

Anon, 1984, (Book Review) *India Quarterly* 40(1) January-March, p 151-152.

Review of the Book: **Wallace, Paul and Chopra, Surendra**, eds., 1981, *Political Dynamics of Punjab*, Guru Nanak Dev University, Amritsar, x, 381p.

Anon, 1984, (Book Review), *Indian Express* (Magazine) November 18, p 5, col 1-5.

Review of the Book: **Joshi, Chand**, 1984, *Bhindranwale: Myth and Reality*, Vikas Publications, New Delhi.

Anon, 1984, (Book Review), *Link* 27(12) October 28, p 45; *Patriot* November 18, p 4, col 4-8.

Review of the Book: **Chopra, V.D.**, et al, 1984, *Agony of Punjab*, Patriot Publications, New Delhi, 224p.

Anon, 1984, (Book Review) *Mysore Economic Review* 69(5) May, p 27.

Review of the Book: **Satvinder Singh**, 1984, *Khalistan: An Academic Analysis*, Amar Prakashan, New Delhi.

Anon, 1984, (Book Review), *National Herald* December 9, p 7, col 1-4.

Review of the Book: **Shitish**, 1984, *Toofan Ke Daur Se Punjab*, World Publications (H), New Delhi, 20p.

Anon, 1984, Brutal Murder of IAF Officer: 4 Terrorists, Two Others Killed, *Times of India*, April 24, p 1, col 1-3+.

Anon, 1984, CRPF Jawan Killed in Ambush: Curfew Extended in Punjab Towns, *Times of India* February 17, p 1, col 1-3+.

Anon, 1984, CRPF Man and Priest Shot, *Times of India*, April 25, p 1, col 7-8+.

Anon, 1984, Call for Punjab Bandh on February 8, *Times of India*, January 28, p 1, col 2-4+.

Anon, 1984, Early Return to Popular Rule in Punjab Ruled Out, *Times of India*, October 4, p 1, col 1-3.

Anon, 1984, Ill Conceived Terrorism, *Radical Humanist* 49(4) 71, p 5-7.

Anon, 1984, Pitfalls, *Janata* 39(22) 7-14 October, p 2-3+.

Anon, 1984, Popular Government in Punjab Ruled Out, *Times of India*, August, p 1, col 4-5+.

Anon, 1984, The Problem, *Seminar*, February 294, p 12-13.

Anon, 1984, Punjab: CPI Council Assesses Situation, *New Age*, 32(370 July 1, p 10.

Anon, 1984, Roots of Terrorism: *Link* 26(44) June 10, p 20-22.

Anon, 1984, Satarawala Replaces Pande as Governor, *Times of India*, June 30, p 1, col 1-4+.

Anon, 1984, Situation in Punjab, *Secular Democracy* May, p 10-27.

Anon, 1984, Terrorists Must be Curbed, Says PM, *Times of India*, February 23, p 1, col 5-7+.

Anon, 1984, Why Zia Blows Hot and Cold, *Link* 27(15) November 18, p 19.

Anon, 1985, 5 Parties Boycott Cabinet Panel, *Times of India*, April 8; p 1, col 1-3+.

Anon, 1985, 7 Lok Sabha Seats to Dal, 6 to Cong., *Times of India*, September 28, p 1, col 6-7.

Anon, 1985, 15 Member Akali Minister to be Sworn in Today, *Times of India* September 29, p 1, col 1-3.

Anon, 1985, 60 Percent Voting in Punjab, *Times of India*, September 26, p 1, col 5-8.

Anon, 1985, Action Plan on Punjab Likely, *Times of India*, March 31, p 1, col 1-3.

Anon, 1985, Agreement with Akalis Signed at Last, Punjab Gets Chandigarh, PM Tells Cheering MPs Confrontation Over, *Times of India*, July 25, p 1, col 1-4.

Anon, 1985, Akali Dal Endorses Ultimatum to Government, *Times of India*, March 20, p 1, col 5-6+.

Anon, 1985, Akali Dal Ratifies Settlement, *Times of India*, July 27, p 1, col 1-3+.

Anon, 1985, Akali Dal Secures 73 Seats, *Times of India*, September 28, p 1, col 1-3.

Anon, 1985, Akali Leader's Call for Panthic Unity, *Times of India*, August 21, p 9, col 3-6.

Anon, 1985, Akali Leadership Crisis Resolved, *Times of India* August 26, p 1, col 1-3.

Anon, 1985, Akali Meet Cancelled, *Times of India*, May 10, p 1, col 7-8.

Anon, 1985, Akali Optimism on 'Longowal Wave', *Times of India*, September 5, p 9, col 1-2.

Anon, 1985, Akali Panel for Selection of Candidates Set Up *Times of India*, August 27, p 1, col 1-3.

Anon, 1985, Akali Stakes in Widened Base, *Times of India*, September 14, p 5, col 3-5.

Anon, 1985, Akali Sweep in Punjab, *Times of India*, September 27, p 1, col 1-4.

Anon, 1985, The Akali Victory in Punjab: Rajiv Gandhi's Role, *Times of India*, October 2, p 8, col 3-5.

Anon, 1985, Akalis Boycott Cabinet Panel, *Times of India*, April 4, p 1, col 1-3.

Anon, 1985, Akalis on Loose Ground, *Link* 27(30) March 3, p 21-22.

Anon, 1985, Akalis Should Remove Confusion about Anandpur Sahib Resolution, *Organiser* 36(49) April 21+.

Anon, 1985, Akalis Split Over Succession Issue, *Times of India*, August 23, p 1, col 7-8.

Anon, 1985, Akalis Urged Not to Stand on Prestige, *Times of India*, April 14, p 1, col 1-2+.

Anon, 1985, The Anandpur Sahib Resolution, *Commerce* 151(3871) August 3, p 202+.

Anon, 1985, Anandpur Sahib Resolution, *Sikh Review* (Supplement) 33(382) October, p 1-19.

Anon, 1985, Assam and Punjab Accords, *Call* 1(2) September-December, p 3-4.

Anon, 1985, Assembly Results in Detail, *Times of India*, September 28, p 9,col 4-6.

Anon, 1985, BJP-Cong. Contest in Jalandhar, *Times of India*, December 7, p 5, col 3-5.

Anon, 1985, BJP Emerges as Third Force, *Organiser* 37(23) October 20, p 5.

Anon, 1985, Barnala's Election as Dal Chief Likely, *Times of India*, December 1, p 9, col 6-7.

Anon, 1985, Barnala's Election as Party Chief Almost Certain, *Times of India* December 15, p 1, col 4-6.

Anon, 1985, Barnala is Dal Chief, *Times of India*, December 16, p 1, col 3-5+.

Anon, 1985, Barnala to be CM, Choice is Unanimous: Swearing in on Sunday *Times of India*, September 28, p 1, col 1-4.

Anon, 1985, Between the Gun and the Ballot, *Commerce* 151(3880) October 5, p 652-655.

Anon, 1985, Black Laws in Punjab *Economic and Political Weekly* 20(19) May 11, p 826-830.

Anon, 1985, (Book Review) *Economic Times*, June 2, p 6, col 2-3; *Tribune* December 15, p 4, col 3-4.
Review of the Book: **Gaur, Madan**, 1984, *Pointers in Punjab (Power Pelf and Personality-Cult)*, Press and P.R Services, Bombay, 196p.

Anon, 1985, (Book Review) *Financial Express*, January 6, p 5, col 1-3; *Seminar*, 308, April, p 45-47; *Times of India*, January 19, p 4, col 5-8.
Review of the BooK: **Amarjit Kaur**, et al, 1984, *The Punjab Story*, Rolibooks International, New Delhi, 199p.

Anon, 1985, (Book Review) *Indian Express Magazine* March 3, p 4, col 1-4.
Review of the Book: **Akbar, M.J.**, 1985, *The Siege Within*, Penguin Book Ltd., Middlesex.

Anon, 1985, (Book Review) *Indian Express Magazine* December 8, p 5, col 1-5.
Review of the Book: **Tully, Mark and Jacob, Satish**, 1985, *Amritsar: Mrs, Gandhi's Last Battle*, Rupa and Co., Calcutta.

Anon, 1985, (Book Review) *Indian Political Science Review* 19(1-2) January-December, p 1901-91.
Review of the Book: **Narang, A.S.**, 1983, *Storm Over the Sutlej: The Akali Politics*, Gitanjali Prakashan, New Delhi, 161p.

Anon, 1985, (Book Review) *International Studies* 22(3) July-September, p 277-278.
Review of the Book: **Tandon, Prakash**, 1980, *Return to Punjab, 1961-1975*, Vikas Publications, New Delhi, xvi, 227p.

Anon, 1985, (Book Review) *Seminar* 306 February, p 38-41.
Review of the Book: **Wallace, Paul and Chopra, Surendra**, eds., 11981, *Political Dynamics of Punjab*, Guru Nanak Dev University, Amritsar, x, 381p.

Anon, 1985, (Book Review) *Seminar* 306 February, p 41-42; *Times of India*, June 9, p 8, col 1-8.
Review of the Book: **Pramod Kumar**, et al, 1984, *Punjab Crises Context and Trends*, Centre for Research in Rural and Industrial Development, Chandigarh.

Anon, 1985, (Book Review), *Seminar*, 30, April, p 45-47.
Review of the Book: **Nayar, Kuldip and Khushwant Singh**, 1984, *Tragedy of Punjab: Operation Bluestar and After*, Vision Books, New Delhi.

Anon, 1985, (BooK Review) *Tribune*, May 4, p 4, col 6-7.
Review of the Book: **Jagmohan Singh**, ed., 1985, *The Agony of Punjab*, Shaheed Bhagat Singh Research Committee, Ludhiana, 42p.

Anon, 1985, CPI Leaders Meet Prime Minister: Call for Early Solution to Punjab Tangle, *New Age* 33(13) March 31, p 1.

Anon, 1985, Can Akalis Become a Regional Secular Party, *Link* 27(52) August 4, p 9-11.

Anon, 1985, Central Executive on Assam and Punjab, *New Age* 33(35) September 1, p 1+.

Anon, 1985, Centre Reviews Situation, *Times of India*, May 4, p 1, col 5-6+.

Anon, 1985, Centre Wants Early Poll in Punjab, *Times of India*, January 5, p 1, col 1-3+.

Anon, 1985, Cheema and Five Others quit 'United' Akali Dal, *Times of India*, November 12, p 1, col 4-6.

Anon, The Coming Punjab Election: An Assessment, *Monthly Commentary on India Economic Conditions*, 27(1) August, p 19-26.

Anon, 1985, Concern Over 'Hate Longowal' Drive, *Times of India*, June 13, p 1, col 2-5.

Anon, 1985, A Congress Akali Alliance Way Out, *Times of India*, August 23, p 8, col 7-8.

Anon, 1985, Cong, Akali Flags Flying Equally High, *Times of India*, September 23, p 5, col 1-4.

Anon, 1985, Cong Confident of Win in Punjab, *Times of India*, September 3, p 1, col 1-3.

Anon, 1985, Congress Doesn't Gain by Understanding Indira's Martyrdom, *Link*, 28(6) September 15, p 7-9.

Anon, 1985, Congress Leading, Akalis just Behind, *Times of India*, September 23, p 1, col 2-5.

Anon, 1985, A Controversial Report *Illustrated Weekly of India* 105(35) January 6, p 28-33.

Anon, 1985, Crucial Akali Dal Meeting Today, *Times of India*, August 25, p 1, col 1-3.

Anon, 1985, Dal is Opposed to Khalistan: Minister, *Times of India*, November 3, p 1, col 1-2.

Anon, 1985, A Droll Tug of War, *Link* 27(34) April 7, p 21-22.

Anon, 1985, Elections in Punjab on September 22, *Times of India*, August 18, p 1, col 1-4.

Anon, 1985, Eyewitness Account of Operation Bluestar, *Sikh Review* 33(376) April, p 31-34.

Anon, 1985, Government Preparing Package Plan for Punjab Solution, *Times of India*, March 28, p 1, col 1-3.

Anon, 1985, Government Should Accept Anandpur Sahib Resolution, *Organiser* 36(50) April 28, p 7+.

Anon, 1985, Inflitrators from Pak behind Terrorism: PM, *Times of India*, September 17, p 1, col 1-3.

Anon, 1985, Janata Call to Government and Akalis for Early Talks, *Times of India*, April 1, p 1, col 5-6+.

Anon, 1985, Joginder Singh Adds to the Confusion, *Times of India*, May 16, p 1, col 2-5.

Anon, 1985, Judicial Probe into Delhi Riots Ordered: Ban on AISSF Lifted, *Times of India*, April 12, p 1, col 1-5.

Anon, 1985, Longowal Disowns Separatists, *Times of India*, April 3, p 1, col 1-2+.

Anon, 1985, Longowal Resignation: Surrender or Resistance to Terrorists, *Link*, 27(41) May 19, p 12-13.

Anon, 1985, Longowal Supporters Beat up AISSF Men at 'Samagam', *Times of India*, June 10, p 1, col 4-6.

Anon, 1985, Looking at New Alternatives, *Indian Express* (Magazine) April 28, p 1, col 1-3+.

Anon, 1985, Militants Disrupt SGPC Function, *Times of India*, April 14, p 1, col 1-3+.

Anon, 1985, Militants Regroups under Bhindranwale's Father to Oust Akali Moderates, *Organiser* 37(1) May 19, p 16+.

Anon, 1985, Minorities Voted for Akali Dal, *Times of India*, October 1, p 1, col 4-5.

Anon, 1985, The Most Debated Questions *Link* 27(24) January 20, p 17-22.

Anon, 1985, Need for an Ideological Struggle, *Link* 28(1) August 15, p 26-28.

Anon, 1985, No Consolation from Stir Postponement, *Times of India*, April 13, p 1, col 6-7+.

Anon, 1985, No Early Initiative on Punjab Likely, *Times of India*, April 18, p 1, col 1-2.

Anon, 1985, Normalcy, Fresh Controversies, *Link* 27(29) February 24, p 17-18.

Anon, 1985, P.B. Statement on Punjab Election Results, *People's Democracy* 9(40) October 6, p 1.

Anon, 1985, P.M. Assails BJP-Dal tie up, *Times of India*, September 23, p 1, col 5-7+.

Anon, 1985, PM, Opposition Discuss Punjab, *Times of India*, January 12, p 1, col 7-8+.

Anon, 1985, PM President Differences Over Punjab, *Organiser* 36(48) April 14, p 1+.

Anon, 1985, PM's Concern at Punjab Violence, *Times of India* April 7, p 1, col 2-3+.

Anon, 1985, Panel on Punjab Urged to Take Unilateral Decision, *Times of India*, April 9, p 1, col 1-3.

Anon, 1985, 'Panthic' Government for Punjab, *Organiser* 37(17) September 8, p 1-2.

Anon, 1985, Plea for Release of Akalis, Probe into November Riots, *Times of India* March 30, p 1, col 1-3+.

Anon, 1985, Promises to State will be Kept, PM., *Times of India*, March 24m p 1, col 1-3+.

Anon, 1985, Punjab: A Blow for Federal India, *Commerce* 151(3871) August 3, p 197.

Anon, 1985, Punjab: CPI Releases Ten Point Manifesto, *New Age* 33(38) September 22, p 11.

Anon, 1985, The Punjab Election, *Monthly Commentary on India Economic Conditions* 27(2) September, p 8-10, tables.

Anon, 1985, Punjab Poll: People's Answer to 'Brute Force' PM, *Times of India*, August 24, p 1, col 1-3.

Anon, 1985, Punjab Poll in Unprecedented Circumstances, *Times of India*, September 24, p 7, col 1-4.

Anon, 1985, Punjab State Committee Appeals to Voters, *People's Democracy* 9(36) September 8, p 12.

Anon, 1985, Punjab State Conference, *People's Democracy* 9(51) December 22, p 12.

Anon, 1985, Requisition Move Ill-timed: CM, *Times of India*, November 26, p 9, col 7-8.

Anon, 1985, A Resolution That will Not Go Away, *Times of India*, (Sunday Review) August 18, p 1, col 1-8.

Anon 1985, Sant's Stance Evokes Hope, *Times of India*, April 20, p 1, col 7-8.

Anon, 1985, Series of Blasts in Punjab: 3 Dead, *Times of India*, September 24, p 1, col 1-3.

Anon, 1985, Shadow Boxing in Punjab, *Organiser* 36(49) April 21, p 1+.

Anon, 1985, Sikh, J and K Extremists Plan Joint Action, *Times of India*, February 6, p 1, col 5-6+.

Anon, 1985, Sikh Leaders for Tough Posture, *Times of India*, April 16, p 1, col 7-8+.

Anon, 1985, Sikhism is a Mystical Correlative and Not a Substitute of Hinduism, *Organiser* 36(39) February 10, p 5.

Anon, 1985, The Sikhs Can't Do What Has Been Done to Them, *Indian Express* (Magazine) January 20, p 4, col 4-8.

Anon, 1985, A Sinister Phase, *Times of India*, May 12, p 1, col 1-2.

Anon, 1985, Stalemate Continues, *Link* 28(20) December 22, p 22-23.

Anon, 1985, Talwandi Group to Contest Poll, *Times of India*, September 2, p 1, col 1-3.

Anon, 1985, Text of Punjab Agreement, *Commerce* 151(3871) August 3, p 202.

Anon, 1985, Three Arrested in Raids on Temple 'Sarais', *Times of India*, April 21, p 1, col 1-4+.

Anon, 1985, Top Akali Leaders Quit Posts, *Times of India*, May 12, p 1, col 3-5+.

Anon, 1985, Tohra's Challenge Upstages Longowal: Punjab on the Brink, *Link* 27(37) April 28, p 4-10.

Anon, 1985, Tohra Insists on Remaining Demands, *Times of India*, April 22, p 1, col 4-5.

Anon, 1985, Toll in Bomb Blasts in New India Rises to 74, *Times of India*, May 12, p 1, col 3-5+.

Anon, 1985, Top Priority for Accord Implementation CM, *Times of India*, September 30, p 1, col 1-4.

Anon, 1985, Two Akali Factions Dissolved, *Times of India*, May 2, p 1, col 4-6+.

Anon, 1985, The Ugly Face of Terrorism, *Link* 28(18) December 8, p 12-13.

Anon, 1985, Uncertainty Hangs Over Transfer of Chandigarh, *Times of India*, December 24, p 1, col 1-3+.

Anon, 1985, We Must Look for Deeper Reasons, *Hindustan Times*, (Magazine) October 27, p 8, col 1-8.

Anon, 1986, 2 More Shot, Rail Station Burnt, *Times of India*, September 10, p 1, col 1-3.

Anon, 1986, 2 More Terrorists Shot in Punjab, *Times of India*, April 2, p 1, col 1-3.

Anon, 1986, 2 Terrorists Killed by Villagers, *Times of India*, April 24, p 1, col 1-3.

Anon, 1986, 3 Nakodar Killers Held: 2 Terrorists Shot in Encounter, *Times of India*, March 31, p 1, col 1-3.

Anon, 1986, 3 Terrorists and 3 Cops among Eight Killed, *Times of India*, April 11, p 1, col 1-4.

Anon, 1986, 5 More Ministers in Punjab Cabinet, *Times of India*, March 3, p 1, col 1-2+.

Anon, 1986, 21 New Ministers in Barnala Cabinet, *Times of India*, May 7, p 1, col 1-3.

Anon, 1986, 29 MLAs Flay Temple Operation: Barnala to Expand Cabinet Soon, *Times of India*, May 5, p 1, col 1-3.

Anon, 1986, Accord is Dead, *Times of India*, June 22, p 1, col 1-2.

Anon, 1986, Akali Antics, *Times of India*, May 19, p 8, col 6.

Anon, 1986, Akali Leader's Son Shot Dead, *Times of India*, February 9, p 1, col 1-3+.

Anon, 1986, Akali Legislature Party Splits: *Times of India*, May 9, p 1, col 1-4.

Anon, 1986, Akalis Mobilise Support for Sarbat Khalsa, *Times of India*, February 14, p 1, col 7-8.

Anon, 1986, The Akalis Must Give Up the Illusion of Raj Karega Khalsa, *Organiser* 37(52) May 11, p 13+.

Anon, 1986, Akali Resolve to Crush Terrorism, *Times of India*, January 7, p 1, col 1-3.

Anon, 1986, All-out Effort to Meet Deadline on Chandigarh, *Times of India*, June 20, p 1, col 1-3+.

Anon, 1986, Badal, BJP Make Common Cause, *Link* 28(41) May 18, p 8-10.

Anon, 1986, Barnala Government Paralysed by Terrorist Onslaught, *Organiser* 37(46) March 30, p 16.

Anon, 1986, Barnala to Call Party Meet to Finalise Strategy, *Times of India*, February 18, p 1, col 1-3.

Anon, 1986, Barnala Unaware of Any New Move, *Times of India*, July 9, p 1, col 5-6+.

Anon, 1986, Barnala Warns Terrorists of Harsh Steps, *Times of India*, February 16, p 1, col 1-3.

Anon, 1986, (Book Review) *Economic and Political Weekly* 21(24) June 14, p 1056-1057; *India Express* (Magazine) February 9, p 5, col 4-5, *Patriot* January 19, p 4, col 3-7.
Review of the Book: **Amrik Singh**, ed., 1985, *Punjab in Indian Politics: Issues and Trends* Ajanta Publications, Delhi, 479p.

Anon, 1986, (Book Review) *Economic and Political Weekly* 21(24) June 14, p 1056-1057; *Link* 28(33) March 23, p 39; *Tribune* (Magazine) July 6, p 11, col 5-8.
Review of the BooK: **Samiuddin, Abida**, ed., 1985, *The Punjab Crisis: Challenges and Response*, Mittal Publication, New Delhi, xxi, 714p.

Anon, 1986, (Book Review) *Economic Times* October 5, p 6, col 5-8, *Indian Express* (Magazine), p 5, col 1-8.
Review of the Book: **Kapur, Rajiv A.**, 1986, *Sikh Separatism: The Politics of Faith*, George Allen and Unwin, London, 272p.

Anon, 1986, (Book REview) *India Express* (Magazine) August 31, p 5, col 1-8.
Review of the Book: **Jefrey, Robin**, 1986, *What's Happening to India*, Macmillan C., Publishers, London.

Anon, 1986, (Book Review) *India Express* (Magazine) August 31, p 5, col 1-8.
Review of the Book: **Bhutani, D.H.**, 1986, *The Third Sikh War*, Promilla and Company Publishers, New Delhi.

Anon, 1986, (Book Review), *Mainstream* 24(45) July 12, p 23-24; *Tribune* (Magazine) September 28, p 11, col 3-4.
Review of the Book: **Rai, Satya M.**, 1986, *Punjab Since Partition*, Durga Publications, Delhi, xii, 446p.

Anon, 1986, (Book Review) *Tribune* (Sunday Magazine) August 31, p 11, col 6-8.
Review of the Book: **Gobinder Singh**, 1986, *Religion and Politics in Punjab*, Deep and Deep Publications, New Delhi, 342p.

Anon, 1986, Buta Bid to Persuade Barnala Fails, *Times of India*, June 23, p 1, col 1-8.

Anon, 1986, CM's Assurance to Rajiv on Stemming Exodus, *Times of India*, July 3, p 1, col 1-3.

Anon, 1986, CM Blames Centre for Akali Split, *Times of India*, June 15, p 1, col 5-6+.

Anon, 1986, Centre's Bid for Compromise Fails, *Times of India*, January 25, p 1, col 1-3.

Anon, 1986, Centre's Bid to Avert Crisis: Buta Singh, Arjun Fly to Chandigarh, *Times of India*, June 19, p 1, col 1-3.

Anon, 1986, Commission Fails to Break the Deadlock, *Link* 28(47) June 29, p 18.

Anon, 1986, Commission for Transfer of 70,000 Acres to Haryana, *Times of India*, June 13, p 1, col 1-5.

Anon, 1986, Compromise Bid Fails: Venkataramiah Panel Submits Report, *Times of India*, June 11, p 1, col 1-3.

Anon, 1986, Contiguity Criterion Stumps Mathew Commission: Chandigarh Transfer Put Off, *Economic Times*, January 26, p 1, col 1-5+.

Anon, 1986, Dal Splits: Badal Heads New Party, *Times of India*, July 6, p 1, col 5-6+.

Anon, 1986, Decks Cleared for Transfer of Chandigarh, *Times of India*, June 15, p 1, col 1-3.

Anon, 1986, Elders Concern at Punjab Situation, *Times of India* July 23, p 1, col col 1-3+.

Anon, 1986, Give Barnala Time: On Akali Gul Shahs, *Link* 28(41) May 25, p 9-11.

Anon, 1986, Haryana May Seek 2,500 Crore for Capital: Punjab Agrees to Give 6,000 Hectares, *Times of India*, May 28, p 1, col 1-3+.

Anon, 1986, Is Akali Congress Honeymoon Over, *Link* 28(33) March 23, p 22-23.

Anon, 1986, Mathew Panel Orders Fazilka, Muktsar Census, *Times of India*, January 15, p 1, col 1-4.

Anon, 1986, New Enumerators for Kandu: Census Runs into Serious Problems in 25 Villages, *Times of India*, January 18, p 1, col 1-4+.

Anon, 1986, Nine Killed in Punjab: Batala under Curfew, *Times of India*, March 17, p 1, col 7-8.

Anon, 1986, One More Punjab Minister Quits, *Times of India*, May 4, p 1, col 1-3.

Anon, 1986, Opposition Backs PM on Punjab, *Times of India*, April 1, p 1, col 1-3.

Anon, 1986, Panel for 70,000 Acres to Haryana, *Economic Times* June 13, p 1, col 1-4+.

Anon, 1986, PM Asks Barnala to Curb Violence, *Times of India*, June 24, p 1, col 1-3.

Anon, 1986, PM, Barnala Agree to Review of Desai Panel Issue, *Times of India*, July 17, p 1, col 7-8.

Anon, 1986, PM for Non-Violent Movement in Punjab, *Times of India*, April 8, p 9, col 1-3.

Anon, 1986, Policemen in Punjab Demoralised, *Times of India*, February 2, p 8, col 1-4.

Anon, 1986, Political Status for Terrorists under the Guise of Political Solution in Punjab, *Organiser* 35(32) December 25, p 6.

Anon, 1986, Presidential Order on Chandigarh being Finalised, *Times of India*, June 17, p 1, col 1-3.

Anon, 1986, Punjab: A Battle Not Joined, *Link* 28(24) March 30, p 22-23.

Anon, 1986, Punjab: The Fire Within, *New Age* 34(33) August 17, p 1-2.

Anon, 1986, Punjab Government Not Party to Accord: Barnala, *Times of India* March 12, p 7, col 3-4.

Anon, 1986, Punjab Government Seeks Re-enumeration in 26 Villages, *Times of India*, January 19, p 1, col 1-3.

Anon, 1986, Ravi Inder Quits Vidhan Sabha, *Link* 28(45) June 15, p 16-17.

Anon, 1986, Ribeiro's Fight to Finish against Terrorists, *Link* 29(16) November 23, p 22-24.

Anon, 1986, Sikhs Unhappy at Tussle, *Times of India*, February 3, p 1, col 4-6.

Anon, 1986, Six Cops Shot Dead, 3 Terrorists Freed, *Times of India*, April 6, p 1, col 1-4.

Anon, 1986, Six Shot in Kapurthala, *Times of India*, March 7, p 1, col 7-8.

Anon, 1986, Temple Complex in Taksal: AISSF Control, *Link* 28(32) March 16, p 22-23.

Anon, 1986, Terms of Reference Changed: Punjab Cabinet Rejects Desai Panel, *Times of India*, June 22, p 1, col 3-5.

Anon, 1986, Terror Turns Green Revolution Red, *Link* 28(37) April 20, p 14-16.

Anon, 1986, Terrorism in Punjab: Low-Level Pak Involvement, *Times of India* August 16, p 1, col 2-5+.

Anon, 1986, Terrorism Still Rides High in Punjab, *Organiser* 38(19) September 21, p 1+.

Anon, 1986, Terrorists Base Smashed in Raid, *Times of India*, July 20, p 1, col 1-3.

Anon, 1986, Terrorist Gun Down two in Punjab, *Times of India*, April 10, p 1, col 1-3.

Anon, 1986, Text of the Post Script to the Report of the Commission, *Times of India* June 13, p 5, col 1-8.

Anon, 1986, Text of the Venkataramiah Award on Territory Transfer, *Times of India*, June 13, p 5, col 1-7.

Anon, 1986, Three More Shot in Punjab, *Times of India*, March 20, p 1, col 1-2.

Anon, 1986, Tide Turning in Punjab, but Dangers Lurk in Depths, *Link* 28(50) July 20, p 4-8.

Anon, 1986, Transfer of Chandigarh by January 26 Certain, *Economic Times*, January 25, p 1, col 5-7+.

Anon, 1986, Transfer of Chandigarh Deferred Till July 15, *Times of India*, June 21, p 1, col 1-4.

Anon, 1986, Transfer Plan in Crisis as Punjab Rejects Panel, *Economic Times*, June 21, p 1, col 6-8+.

Anon, 1986, Two Barnala Government Minister Quit: Tohra, Badal and Thekedar Resign Party Posts, *Times of India*, may 3, p 1, col 1-4.

Anon, 1986, Whither Punjab: A Symposium, *Parlance* 10(1) October, p 8- 29.

Anon, 1986, Why CPI Backs General Aurora, Not Congress?, *Link* 28(48) July 6, p 11-13.

Anon, 1989, *General Elections 1989*, Press Information Bureau, Ministry of Information and Broadcasting, Government of India.

Anon, 1991, *General Elections 1991: Reference Handbook* , vol.-I, Press Information Bureau, Ministry of Information and Broadcasting, Government of India, New Delhi.

Argyll (8th Duke of), 1865, *India Under Dalhousie and Canning*, Longmans Green and Co., London.

Arnold, Edwin, 1862-1865, *The Marquis of Dalhousie's Administration of British India*, Saunders, Otley and Co., London, 2 vols.

Arora, F.C., 1930, *Commerce by River in the Punjab*, P.G.R.O., Lahore.

Arora, S.C., 1990, *Terrorism in Punjab Politics*, Mittal Publication, New Delhi.

Arora, Subhash C., 1982, Punjab in Turmoil, *Journal of State Politics and Administration* 5(1-2) January-December, p 26-32, bibliography.

Ashraf, M., 1946, *Cabinet Mission and After*, Islamic Literature Publishing House, Lahore.

Ashraf, M., 1942, *Speeches and Writings of Mr. Jinnah*, Ashraf, Lahore.

Attar Singh, 1961, *Basic Fact regarding Punjabi Language*, Author, Ambala.

Attar Singh, 1984, What Went Wrong, *Seminar* 294 February, p 24-28.

Aurora, J.S., 1984, Even if Khalistan Comes about the Sikhs will be the Losers, *Illustrated Weekly of India*, 105(30) July 22, p 50-53.

Ayer, S.A., 1951, *Unto Him a Witness*, Thacker and Co., Bombay.

Azad, Abul Kalam, 1959, *India Wins Freedom*, Orient Longmans, Calcutta.

Bajpai, K.D., 1984, MP State Government Publication Lauds Khalistan and Jharkhand Movements, *Organiser* 36(30) December 9, p 7.

Baldev Parkash, 1982, Why Punjab is Resounding with Separatist Slogans, *Organiser* 34(21) October 10, p 2+.

Bamzai, P.N.K., 1962, *A History of Kashmir*, Metropolitan Book Co., Delhi.

Banerjee, Sumanta, 1984, The Best Lack all Conviction, while the Worst are Full of Passionate Intensity, *Economic and Political Weekly* 19(27) July 7, p 1019-1021.

Barkat Ram (Kalia), 1929, *A History of the Development of the Police in the Punjab 1849-1905*, P.G.R.O., Lahore.

Barkley, D.G., 1875, *Directions for Revenue Officers in the Punjab*, Superintendent of Government Press, Lahore.

Barnala, Surjit Singh, 1983, Punjab: No Time to Lose, *Illustrated Weekly of India* 104(14) April 10, p 10-11.

Barnala, Surjit Singh, 1986, Special Status for Chandigarh after Transfer: *Times of India*, January 4, p 1, col 1-3.

Barstow, A.E., 1928, *Sikhs*, Government of India, Publications Branch, Calcutta.

Bell, Evans, 1882, *Annexation of the Punjab and the Maharajah Duleep Singh*, Trubner, London.

Bell, Evans, 1868, *Retrospects and Prospects of Indian Policy*, Turbner, London.

Benson, A.C. and Esher, V., eds., 1908, *The Letters of Queen Victoria*, vol ii, 1844-1953, London.

Bhagwant Singh, S., 1985, Sikh Separatist Theory Blasted: The Mahabharata and the Gita are the Main Source of Sikhism, *Sindhu Organiser* 36(41) February 24, p 8-9.

Bhajan Lal, 1983, The Writing on the Wall is Clear, *Link* 26(10) October 16, p 15.

Bharadwaj, A.K., 1985, Of Firm Stand and Obstinacy, *Link* 27(26) February 3, p 18-22.

Bhasin, Prem, 1984, Margindpuri's Letter to Rashtrapati, *Janata* 39(20) September 23, p 4-5.

Bhasin, Prem, 1986, Akalis in a Blind, *Janata* 41(2) March 16, p 6-8+.

Bhatnagar, S. and Verma, P.S., 1981, Coalition Governments, 1867-80, *Indian Journal of Politics* 5(1) January-June, p 125-140.

Bhullar, Jaswant Singh, 1983, Akali Agitation and the Services, *Illustrated Weekly of India* 104(14) April 10, p 13.

Bhutani, D.H., 1986, *The Third Sikh War*, Promilla and Co., Publishers, New Delhi.

Bingley, A.H. (Capt), 1899, *Handbook for the Indian Army*, Government Printing Press, Calcutta.

Bingley, A.H. (Capt), 1899, *Handbook on the Sikhs*, Government Central Printing Office, Simla.

Birdwood, C., 1947, *A Continent Experiments*, Skeffington & Co., London.

Birdwood, F.T. (Col), *The Sikh Regiment in the Second World War*, Jarrod and Sons Ltd., Norwich.

Bolitho, H., 1954, *Jinnah, Creator of Pakistan*, Murray, London.

Bombwall, K.R., 1981, Akali Demand for State Antonomy: Nature Rationale and Motivation, *Political Science Review* 20(2) April-June, p 151-162.

Bombwall, K.R., 1983, The Nation, State and Ethno-nationalism: A Note on the Akali Demand for a Self Determined Political Status for Sikhs, *Punjab Journal of Politics* 7(2) July-December, p 166-183, footnotes.

Bombwall, K.R., 1984, Ethno-nationalism, *Seminar* 294 February, p 44-54, footnotes.

Bombwall, K.R., 1986, Sikh Identity, Akali Dal and Federal Policy, *Economic and Political Weekly* 21(20) May 17, p 888-890, footnotes.

Bondurant, Joan V., 1958, *Regionalism Versus Provincialism: A Study in Problems of Indian National Unity*, University of California Press, Berkeley.

Bosworth Smith R., 1883, *Life of Lord Lawrence* , Smith Elder & Co., London, 2 vols.

Brayne, F.L., 1929, *Socrates in an Indian Village*, Oxford University Press, Bombay.

Brayne, F.L., 1929, *Remaking of Village India*, Oxford University Press, Bombay.

Brayne, F.L., 1932, *Socrates Persists in India*, Oxford University Press, Bombay.

Briggs, (Major General), 1849, *What are We to do with the Punjab?* James Madden, London.

Brodfoot, W., 1888, *Career of Major George Broadfoot*, John Murray, London.

Buist, G., 1849, *Annals of the Year 1848 to the End of the Sikh War in March, 1949,* Times Press, Bombay.

Burton, R.G., 1911, *The First and the Second Sikh Wars*, Government Central Branch Press, Simla.

Butler, David et al, 1991, *India Decides: 1952-1991 Elections*. Media Books, New Delhi.

Call (Periodical), 1983, The Punjab Situation, *Call* 33(6-7) July-August, p 3-4, editorial.

Callard, Keith, 1957, *Pakistan*, Allen and Unwin, London.

Calvert, H., 1927, *The Wealth and Welfare of the Punjab*, Civil & Military Gazette Press, Lahore.

Campbell, Colin (Sir), 1951, *Memorandum on the Part Taken by the Third Division of the Army of the Punjab at the Battle of Jallianwala*, James Ridgway, London.

Campbell, George, 1893, *Memoirs of my Indian Career*, Macmillan, London.

Campbell-Johnosn, A., 1951, *Mission with Mountbatten*, Robert Hale, London.

Carmichael Smyth, G. (Major), 1847, *History of the Reigning Family of Lahore*, W. Thacker and Co., London.

Caulfield, (General), 1846, *The Punjab and the Indian Army*, London.

Cave-Browne, J., 1861, *The Punjab and Delhi in 1857*, , William Blackwood & Sons, London, 2 vols.

Chaddha, T.R., 1954, *A Study of the Communist Movement in the Punjab*, Jyoti Prakashan, Ghaziabad.

Chakravarty, Nikhil, 1986, A Tale of Three Judges, *Times of India (Sunday Review)* July 20, p 1, col 1-8.

Chakravartty, Nikhil, 1986, The Crisis in Punjab is the Crisis of India Today, *Times of India (Sunday Review)*, April 6, p iv, col 5-8.

Chakravartty, Nikhil, 1986, The Killing Goes on, *Times of India (Sunday Review)* November 3, p 1, col 1-8.

Chalapathi Rau, M., 1981, Separatism, again, *Link* 24(9) October 11, p 7.

Chandrashekhar, S., 1944, Indian Immigration in America, *Far Eastern Survey*, July 26.

Charan Singh (Maharaj), 1960, *Light on Sant Mat*, Radha Soami Satsang, Beas.

Chaudhury, Prem, 1980, The Congress Triumph in South East Punjab: Elections of 19843, *Studies in History* 2(2) July-December, p 81-110, footnotes, tables.

Chavan, 1985, Rigid Akali Stance won't Discourage Government says Chavan, *Times of India*, March 27, p 1, col 1-3+.

Chawla, G.S., 1981, Khalistan: A Conspiracy Hatched in America, *Illustrated Weekly of India*, October 25, p 26-29.

Chawla, G.S., 1981, Zail-Darbara Feud while Punjab Bleeds, *Illustrated Weekly of India*, 102(38) December 27, p 24-25.

Chawla, G.S,, 1982, Punjab: Another Assam?, *Illustrated Weekly of India* 103(36) September 26, p 30-31.

Chhabra, G.S., 1960, *Advanced Study in History of the Punjab*, Sharanjit, Ludhiana, 2 vols.

Chitta Ranjan, C.N., 1983, Times for Statesmanship, *Mainstream* 21(37) May 14, p 1-3, editorial.

Chopra, Pran, 1986, Punjab Needs a Broader Unity, *Economic Times*, October 5, p 3, col 1-8+.

Chopra, V.D., 1983, Smearing a Heroic Past, *Link* 25(47) July 3, p 7-9.

Chopra, V.D., 1984, The Dilemma of a 'Healing Touch', *Link* 27(9) October 7, p 15-16.

Chopra, V.D., et al., 1984, *Agony of Punjab*, Patriot Publications, New Delhi, 224p.

Chowdhry, Prem, 1982, Jat Domination in South East Punjab: Socio-economic Basis of Jat Politics in a Punjab District, *Indian Economic and Social History Review* 19(3-4) July-December, p 325-346, footnotes.

Chowla, N.L., 1985, Electronic Media in Punjab Poll, *Times of India*, September 24, p 8, col 7-8.

Chum, B.K, 1983, Punjab: A Powderkeg Explodes, *Indian Express* (Magazine) November 6, p 1, col 1-8+.

Chum, B.K., 1983, A War of Nerves, *Indian Express (Magazine)* May 8, p 1, col 1-8.

Chum, B.K., 1984, Breaking the Punjab Deadlock, *Indian Express* (Magazine) May 6, p 1, col 1-8.

Chum, B.K, 1984, Will the Hour Produce the Man, *Indian Express* (Magazine) October 21, p 3, col 1-8.

Colchester (Lord), 1874, *History of the Indian Administration of Lord Ettenborough*, Richard Bentley and Sons, London.

Cole, J.J., 1849, *A Sketch of the Siege of Multan*, P.S. Rozario & Co., Calcutta.

Coley, James, 1856, *A Journal of the Sutlej Campaign, 1845-1946*, Smith Elder and Co., London.

Commerce (Periodical), 1981, Mirage of Khalistan, *Commerce* 143(3669) October 10, p 652, editorial.

Commerce (Periodical), 1983, Punjab: What Next, *Commerce* 147(3777) October 22, p 624, editorial.

Commerce (Periodical), 1984, Punjab; Sikhs Saved from Themselves, *Commerce* 148(3811) June 16, p 813, editorial.

Commerce (Periodical), 1985, Election: The Only Answer to Terrorism, *Commerce* 151(3875) August 31, p 403, editorial.

Commerce (Periodical), 1985, Punjab: An Akali Healing Touch, *Commerce* 151(3880) October 5, p 645, editorial.

Conlvin, Ian, 1931, *The Life of General Dyer*, William Blackwood & Sons, Edinburgh.

Cooper, Fredieric, 1858, *The Crisis in the Punjab*, Smith Elder & Co., London 1858.

Corbett, D.C., 1947, *Canada's Immigration Policy; A Critique*, University of Toronto Press, Toronto.

Cork, Barry Joynson, 1958, *Rider on a Grey Horse*, Cassell, London.

Coupland, R., 1944, *The Constitutional Problem in India*, Oxford University Press, Bombay.

Cunningham, Alexander, 1882, *Report of a Tour in the Punjab, 1878-1979*, Superintendent of Government Printing, Calcutta.

Cunningham, J.D., 1955, *History of the Sikhs,* ed. by H.L.O. Garrett, S. Chand & Co., Delhi, Ist edn., 1849, .

Cust, R.N., 1904, *Memories of Past Years of a Septuagenarian*, London, Printed for Private Circulation.

Cust, R.N., 1906, *Linguistic and Oriental Essays*, Trubner & Co., London.

Dadabhoy, Yusuf, 1954, Circuitous Assimilation among Rural Hindustanis in California, *Social Forces, 33*, 138-141.

Dalip Singh, 1981, *Dynamics of Punjab Politics*, Macmillan Co., Publishers, New Delhi, vii, 295p.

Dang, Satyapal, 1981, Anti-national Mischief in Punjab, *Mainstream* 19(39) May 30, p 19-20.

Dang, Satyapal, 1981, Foreign Inspiration behind Demand of Khalistan, *New Age* 29(16) April 19, p 8-6.

Dang, Satyapal, 1981, Punjab: Dealing with Mischief, *Mainstream* 20(7) October 17, p 12-14.

Dang, Satyapal, 1981, The Wrong Foot Forward, *Link* 24(14) November 15, p 30.

Dang, Satyapal, 1982, Autonomy, Akalis and the Left, *Mainstream* 21(14) December 4, p 11-12+.

Dang, Satyapal, 1982, Both RSS and Dal Khalsa Behind Punjab Mischief, *New Age* 30(22) May 30, p 6.

Dang, Satyapal, 1982, CPI(M) Breaks with Akali Dal but Not Fully, *New Age*, 30(34) August 22, p 11.

Dang, Satyapal, 1982, Report from Amritsar: Good Sense Prevails Over Extremist Plot, *New Age*, 30(19) May 8, p 1+.

Dang, Satyapal, 1983, Atwal Murder and the Aftermath, *Link* 25(39) May 8, p 7-8.

Dang, Satyapal, 1983, Class Basis of Akali Demands, *Mainstream*, 21(30) March 26, p 15-18.

Dang, Satyapal, 1983, How Akalis Misinterpret Article 25, *Link* 26(7) September 25, p 14-15.

Dang, Satyapal, 1983, Place National Interests above Electoral Interests for Punjab, *Student Action* 2(7) December, p 12-13.

Dang, Satyapal, 1984, Police and Terrorist, *Mainstream* 22945) July 7, p 6+.

Dang, Satyapal, 1983, The Problem of Isolating Extremists Separatists, *Link* 25(51) July 31, p 12-13+.

Dang, Satyapal, 1983, Punjab: Issues and Complication, *Mainstream* 21(20) January 15, p 11-14.

Dang, Satyapal, 1983, Punjab: Religion against Politics, *Mainstream* 22(17) December 24, p 15-16.

Dang, Satyapal, 1983, Punjab: Way Out of Mess, *Mainstream* 22(12) November 19, p 7-8+.

Dang, Satyapal, 1983, The Punjab Scenario, *Mainstream* 21(45) July 9, p 7-8+.

Dang, Satyapal, 1983, The Punjab: Suba Movement, *Punjab Journal of Politics* 7(2) July-December, p 151-164.

Dang, Satyapal, 1985, The Akali Who's Who, *Mainstream* 23(27) March 2, p 4-5.

Dang, Satyapal, 1985, Sikh Problems: Looking Back, *Mainstream* 23(37) May 11, p 5-6+.

Dang, Satyapal, 1985, Some Aspects of Punjab Situation, *Mainstream* 23(42) June 15, p 5-6.

Dang. Satyapal , 1985, Some Features of Punjab Elections, *New Age* 33(43) October 27, p 5.

Dang, Satyapal, 1985, Time for Akalis to Talk, *Mainstream* 23(31) March 30, p 5-6+.

Dang, Satyapal, 1986, If Barnala Can Dispel People's Doubts, *New Age*, 34(38) July 13, p 8.

Dang, Satyapal, 1986, Pak's Red Face Vis-a-Vis Sikhs, *New Age*, 34(36) September 7, p 5.

Dang, Satyapal, 1986, Punjab: Grim but Not Hopeless, *Mainstream* 24(44) July 5, p 4-5+.

Dang, Satyapal, 1986, Punjab: Onset of Turmoil, *Mainstream* 24(29) March 22, p 4+.

Dang, Satyapal, 1986, Punjab Police: Why Ineffective? *Mainstream* 24(48) August 2, p 5+.

Dang, Satyapal, 1986, Such was Ajit Ram, *New Age*, 34(28) July 13, p 1-2.

Darbara Singh, 1949, *The Punjab Tragedy*, Steno Press, Amritsar.

Darbara Singh, 1981, Punjab Boldly Faces Challenge, *Mainstream* (Annual number) 20(1-5) p 19-20+.

Darbara Singh, 1982, Darbara for Early Political Solution, *Times of India*, November 12, p 1, col 7-8+.

Darbara Singh, 1982, Darbara Singh Urges Longowal to meet PM, *Times of India* December 11, p 1, col 1-2.

Darling, M.L., 1925, *The Punjab Peasant in Prosperity and Debt*, Oxford University Press, Bombay.

Darling, M.L., 1934, *Wisdom and Waste in the Punjab Village*, Oxford University Press, Bombay.

Das, R.K., 1923, *Hindustani Workers on the Pacific Coast*, Walter De Gruyter & Co., Berlin.

Das, S.R., Chairman, 1962, *Commission Report on Grievances of the Sikhs*, Government of India Press, Delhi.

Das, Sitansu, 1982, What the Sikhs Really Want, *Illustrated Weekly of India*, 103(44) December 12, p 12-13.

Dayal, John, 1985, Akali Response; Blow Hot Again, *Link* 27(33) March 24, p 12-13.

Dayal, John, 1985, Punjab Scenarios of Hope and Nightmare, *Link* 28(7) September 22, p 9-10.

Desai, M.V., 1984, Amritsar and all That, *Commerce* 148(3812) June 23, p 851-852.

Deva Singh, 1929, *Colonisation in the Rechna Doab*, P.G.R.O., Lahore.

Dhagamwar, Vasudha, 1985, Anandpur Resolution: In Whose Interest?, *Mainstream* 23(32) April 6, p 5-8.

Dhami, Sadhu Singh, 1943, *The Sikhs and Their Religion: A Struggle for Democracy*, K.D. Society, Vancouver.

Dhami, M.S., 1985, Punjab and Communalism, *Seminar* 314 October, p 25-38.

Dhami, M.S., 1986, Ethnic Politics in Punjab: A Review Article, *Indian Quarterly* 42(2) April-June, p 193-199.

Dharam Pal, 1952, *Administration of Sir John Lawrence 1864-1869*, Minerva, Simla.

Dharam Yash Dev, 1940, *Our Countrymen Abroad*, All India Congress Committee, Delhi.

Dhawan, Deepak, 1982, What Punjab Bye Election Results Show, *People's Democracy* 6(25) June 20, p 7-8.

Dhillon, D.S., 1984, A Juristic View on Operation: Bluestar, *Sikh Review* 32(371) November, p 25-28.

Dhillon, G.S., 1979, Sikh Politics in the Later Half of the 19th Century, *Journal of Sikh Studies* 6(2) August, p 93-107, bibliography, footnotes.

Dhillon, Ganga Singh, 1983, Towards a Sikh Revolution, *Illustrated Weekly of India* 104(14) April 10, p 11.

Dikshit, Sandip, 1985, CPI Poll Campaign in Support of Accord, *New Age* 33(38) September 22, p 1+.

Diver, Maud, 1936, *Honoria Lawrence*, John Murray, London.

Dodwell, H., 1925, *A Sketch of the History of India 1858-1918*, Longmans, Green & Co., London.

Douie J.M. (Sir), 1916, *The Punjab, North West Frontier Province and Kashmir*, Cambridge University Press, Cambridge.

Druhe, D.N., 1959, *Soviet Russia and India*, Communist Bookman Associates.

Dubasbi, Jay, 1984, A Khalistani Scenario, *Organiser* 36(22) October 14, p 2.

Duggal, K.S., 1981, Tryst with an Award, *Mainstream* 20(13) November 28, p 14+.

Duggal, K.S., 1982, Sikhs in Secular India, *Mainstream* 20(31) April 3, p 21-22.

Duggal, K.S., 1983, The Crisis of Identity, *Link* 25(39) May 8, p 11-12+.

Duggal, K.S., 1983, Polarization in Punjab, *Link* 26(6) September 18, p 11.

Dunbar, George (Sir), 1951, *India and the Passing of the Empire*, Nicholson & Watson, London.

Dunlop, J., 1849, *Multan during and after the Siege*, W.S. Orr & Co., London.

Dunn, H.H., The Stranglers, *World Wide Magazine*, vol 25, p 338-351.

Durlabh Singh, 1942, *The Valiant Fighter*, Hero Publications, Lahore.

Eastern Economist (Periodical), 1981, Who Rules Punjab, *Eastern Economist* 77(13) September 25, p 578-579, editorial.

Economic and Political Weekly (Periodical) 1981, Playing with Fire, *Economic and Political Weekly* 16(40) October 3, p 1585, editorial.

Economic and Political Weekly (Periodical) 1983, No Respite, *Economic and Political Weekly* 18(44) October 29, p 1858, editorial.

Economic and Political Weekly, (Periodical), 1983, Presidents Rule in Punjab, *Economic and Political Weekly*, 18(41) October 8, p 1725-1726, editorial.

Economic and Political Weekly (Periodical), 1984, The Legal and the extra-legal, *Economic and Political Weekly* 19(26) June 30, p 965-966, editorial.

Economic and Political Weekly (Periodical), 1984, Nothing Learnt, *Economic and Political Weekly* 29(19) July 21, p 1117-1118, editorial.

Economic and Political Weekly (Periodical), 1984, Rising Tension in Punjab, *Economic and Political Weekly* 19(7) February 18, p 265, editorial.

Economic and Political Weekly (Periodical), 1985, Beyond the Elections in Punjab, *Economic and Political Weekly* 20(39) September 28, p 16-17, editorial.

Economic and Political Weekly (Periodical), 1985, Congress (I) and Punjab, *Economic and Political Weekly* 20(2) January 12, p 41, editorial.

Economic and Political Weekly (Periodical), 1986, Setback in Punjab, *Economic and Political Weekly* 21(25-26) June 21-28, p 1088-1086, editorial.

Economic Times (Periodical), 1983, Punjab in Turmoil, *Economic Times* April 14, p 5, col 1-2, editorial.

Economic Times (Periodical), 1984, Crisis of Leadership, *Economic Times* February 22, p 5, col 1-2, editorial.

Economic Times (Periodical), 1984, The Healing Touch, *Economic Times*, June 11, p 5, col 1-2, editorial.

Economic Times (Periodical) 1984, Return to Sanity, *Economic Times*, June 7, p 5, col 1-2, editorial.

Economic Times (Periodical), 1985, Akali Dal Victory, *Economic Times*, September 28, p 5, col 1-2. editorial.

Economic Times (Periodical), 1985, Black Friday, *Economic Times*, May 13, p 5, col 1-2, editorial.

Economic Times (Periodical), 1985, Punjab Agreement, *Economic Times*, July 26, p 5, col 1-2, editorial.

Economic Times (Periodical), 1986, Accord and Disquiet, *Economic Times*, January 4, p 5, col 1-2, editorial.

Economic Times (Periodical) 1986, Punjab Polarisation, *Economic Times*, May 10, p 5, col 1-2, editorial.

Edwardes, Emma (Lady), 1886, *Memorials of the Life and Letters of Major General Sir Herbert B. Edwardes*, Kegan Paul, Trench & Co., London, 2 vols.

Edwardes, H.B. and Merivale, H., 1873, *Life of Sir Henry Lawrence*, Smith Elder & Co., London.

Edwardes, Herbert, 1851, *A Year on the Punjab Frontier in 1848-1949*, Richard Bentley, London, 2 vols.

Edwards, W., 1866, *Reminiscences of a Bengal Civilian*, Smith Elder and Co., London.

Edwards, M., 1958, *The Necessary Hell: John and Henry Lawrence and the Indian Empire*, Cassell, London.

Elsmie, G.R., 1908, *Thirty Five Years in the Punjab, 1858-1893*, David Douglas, Edinburgh.

Falcon, R.W., 1896, *Handbook on the Sikhs for Regimental Officers*, Government Printing Press, Allahabad.

Farquhar, J.N., 1929, *Modern Religious Movements in India*, Macmillan, London.

Fauja Singh, *Eminent Freedom Fighter of Punjab* (1972), Punjabi University, Patiala.

Fauja Singh , 1964, *Military System of the Sikhs*, Moti Lal Banarsi Das, Delhi.

Fera, Ivan, 1986, Battlecry, *Illustrated Weekly of India* 107(7) February 16, p 32-35.

Fera, Ivan, 1986, The Blitzkrieg, *Illustrated Weekly of India* 107(7) February 16, p 26-29.

Fitchett, W.H., 1939, *The Tale of the Great Mutiny*, John Murray, London.

Forbes, A., 1892, *The Afghan Wars*, Macmillan, London.

Forbes, A., 1916, *Sir Colin Campbell, Lord Clyde*, Macmillan, London.

Forbes, A., 1924, *Havelock: Englishmen of Action*, Macmillan, London.

Forbes, Angus, 1947, East Indian in Canada, *International Journal*, p 47-50.

Forbes–Mitchell, W., 1910, *Reminiscences of the Great Mutiny*, Macmillan, London.

Forsyth, Douglas, 1887, *Autobiography and Reminiscences*, Richard Bentley, London.

Francis, R.A., 1952, B.C.'s Turbaned Tribe, *Canadian Business*, February 25, 44-45.

Furneaux, R., 1963, *Massacre at Amritsar*, Allen & Unwin, London.

Ganda Singh, n.d., Some Correspondence of Maharaja Duleep Singh, *Journal of Indian History*, vol xxvii, part 1, no. 79.

Ganda Singh, 1935, *History of Gurdwara Shahid-Ganj, Lahore, From its Origin to November*, the author, Amritsar.

Ganda Singh, 1949, *A History of the Khalsa College*, Khalsa College, Amritsar.

Ganda Singh, 1952, *The Punjab in 1839-1840*, Sikh History Society, Amritsar 1952.

Gandhi Singh, 1955, *Private Correspondence relating to the Anglo–Sikh Wars*, Sikh History Society, Amritsar.

Gandhi, J.S., 1981, System, Process and Popular Ethos: A Study in Contemporary Politics in Punjab, *Indian Journal of Politics* 5(1) January-June, p 52-66, footnotes.

Gandhi Marg (Periodical), 1983, The Akali Agitation, *Gandhi Marg* 15(4) July, p 187-190, editorial.

Gandhi Marg (Periodical), 1985, The Punjab Agreement, *Gandhi Marg* 7(5) August, p 259-262, editorial.

Gandhi, Rajiv, 1985, Rajiv Decries Remarks by Akali Leaders, *Times of India*, April 23, p 1, col 6-8+.

Gandhi, Surjeet Singh, 1980, *Struggle of the Sikhs for Sovereignty*, Gurdas Kapur and Sons (P) Ltd., Delhi, xxii, 552p.

Gardner, Ray, 1958, When Vancouver Turned Back the Sikhs, *Macleans Magazine*, November 8, p 65.

Garmit, Singh, 1984, *History of Sikh Struggle* (1984), New Delhi, Atlantic Publisher.

Gaur, Madan, 1984, *Pointers in Punjab: Power, Pelf and Personality Culcutta*, Press and P.R. Services, Bombay, 196p.

Ghosh, K.C., 1965, *The role of Honour*, Vidya Bharati, Calcutta.

Gibbon, F.P., 1908, *The Lawrences of the Punjab*, J.M. Dent, London.

Gill, Y.S., 1984, AITUC Delegation in Punjab: Working Class Solidly Against Communal Division Forces, *New Age*, 32(160 April 15, p 3+.

Glegg, J.A. (Lieutenant Colonel), 1940, *Notes on the History of the Samana*, Fort Lockhart.

Gobinder Singh, 1986, *Religion and Politics in Punjab*, Deep and Deep Publications, New Delhi, 342p.

Goldsmid, F.J., 1880, *James Outram: A Biography*, Smith Elder & Co., London, 2 vols.

Gopal, S. 1953, *Viceroyalty of Lord Ripon, 1880-1884* Oxford University Press, Oxford.

Gopal, S., 1957, *Viceroyalty of Lord Irwin, 1926-1931*, Oxford University Press, Oxford.

Gopal Singh, 1986, Misinterpretation of Sikhism, *Seminar* 326, October, p 14-16.

Gore, M., 1949, *Remarks on the Present State of the Punjab*, James Ridgway, London.

Gough, C. and Innes, A.S., 1897, *The Sikhs and the Sikh Wars*, A.D. Innes & Co., London.

Gough (Lord), 1946, *War in India: Dispatches*, Ackermann & Co., London.

Graham–Bailey, T., 1938, *Studies in North India Languages*, Lund Humphries & Co., London.

Grant, I.F., 1921, Sikh Wars: Everyday letters written during the 1st and 2nd wars, *Army Quarterly*.

Grant, K. J. (Rev), 1915, Among the Hindus of British Columbia, *Missionary Messenger*.

Greenwood, J., 1844, *Narrative of the Late Victorious Campaigns in Afghanistan under General Pollock with Recollections of Seven Years' Service in India*, Henry Colburn, London .

Grey, C., 1932, Panchayat Rule of the Khalsa Army 1841-1845, *Journal of the United Services Institution of India*.

Griffin, Lepel, 1869, *Law of Inheritance to Chiefship as observed by the Sikhs previous to the Annexation of the Punjab*, Superintendent of Government Printing, Lahore 1869.

Griffin, Lepel, 1873, *Rajas of the Punjab*, Trubner & Co., London.

Griffiths, C.J., 1910, *A Narrative of the Siege of Delhi with an Account of the Mutiny at Ferozepore in 1957*, ed. H.J. Yonge, John Murry, London.

Gubbins, M.R., 1858, *An Account of the Mutinies in Oudh and of the Siege of Lucknow Residency*, Richard Bentley, London.

Gujral, I.K., 1982, The Politics of Punjab Economics, *Sikh Review* 30(346) October, p 61-65.

Gujral, I.K., 1982, Punjab's Anguish *Mainstream* 20(50) August 14, p 12-14+.

Gujral, I.K., 1984, The Sequence, *Seminar* 294 February, p 14-17.

Gujral, I.K., 1985, Unravelling the Punjabi Knot, *Mainstream* (Republic Day Number) 23(22) p 17-18.

Gulab Singh, 1948, *Thorns Thistles: Autobiography of a Revolutionary*, National Information Publications, Bombay.

Gupta, H.R., 1956, *Punjab on the Eve of the First Sikh War*, University of Punjab, Hoshiarpur.

Gupte, Pranay, 1985, Cul-De Sac, *Illustrated Weekly of India* 196(18) September 8, p 14-17.

Gurbachan Singh and Gyani Lal Singh, 1946, *The Idea of a Sikh State*, Lahore Book Shop, Lahore.

Gurbachan Singh Talib, 1950, *Muslim League Attack on Sikhs and Hindus in the Punjab*, S.G.P.C., Amritsar.

Gurbhagat Singh, 1985, Towards a New Paradigm, *Mainstream* 23(37) May 11, p 7-8+.

Gurcharan Singh, 1983, The Sikh homeland and the myth and Reality, *Sikh Review* 31(352) April, 48-67.

Gurdit Singh, n.d., *The Voyage of the Komagatamary*, Compiler, 32, Ashutosh Mukherjee Road, Calcutta.

Gurmit Singh, 1984, *History of Sikh Struggle*, Atlantic Publishers, New Delhi.

Gurnam Singh, 1960, *A Unilingual Punjabi State and the Sikh Unrest*, Super Press, New Delhi.

Gurtej Singh, 1983, What Bhindranwale Stands for, *Illustrated Weekly of India* 104(14) April 10, p 12-13.

Gyan Singh Naqqash, 1956, *Giun Chitravali*, G.S. Sohan Singh, Amritsar.

Handa, R.L., 1927, *A History of the Development of the Judiciary in the Punjab, 1846*, P.G.R.O, Lahore.

Hans, Surjit, 1982, An Alternative View of Akali Politics, *New Quest* January-February 31, p 13-16.

Harbans Singh, n.d., *Sikh Political Parties*, Sikh Publishing House, Delhi.

Harbans Singh, 1964, *The Heritage of the Sikhs*, Asia Publishing House, Bombay.

Harbans Singh, 1982, *Khalistan*, Punjab Writers Cooperative Industrial Society, New Delhi, 112p.

Hardinge, Charles, 1964, *Dispatches of Lord Hardinge*, Parliamentary Papers, London.

Hardinge, Charles, 1947, *My Indian Years, 1910-1916*, John Murray, London.

Harnam Singh, 1945, *Punjab: The Homeland of the Sikhs*, Civil & Military Gazette Press, Lahore.

Harris (Mrs.), 1858, *A Lady's Diary of the Siege of Lucknow*, London.

Hilton , Richard (Major General), 1957, *The Indian Mutiny*, Hollis and Carter, London.

Hodson, W.S.R., 1859, *Hodson of Hodson's Horse or Twelve Years of a Soldier's Life in India*, J.W. Parker & Son, London .

Holland, Robert (Sir), 1943, Indian Immigration into Canada: The Question of Franchise, *Asiatic Review* April 1943, p 167.

Hollingsworth, L.W., 1960, *The Asians of East Africa*, Macmillan, London.

Holmes, T.R.E., 1888, *A History of the Indian Mutiny*, W.H. Allen & Co., London.

Honigberger, J.M., 1852, *Thirty Five Years in the East*, H. Bailliere, London.

Horniman, B.G., 1920, *Amritsar and Our Duty to India*, Fisher Unwin, London.

Hough, W., 1953, *Political and Military Events in British India From the Years 1756 to 1849*,, William Allen.& Co., London, 2 vols.

Hukam Singh, 1951, *The Sikh Problem and Its Solution*, Shiromani Akali Dal, Amritsar.

Hukam Singh, 1983, The Other Side, *Sikh Review* 31(354) June, p 45-46.

Humbley, W.W., 1854, *Journal of a Cavalry Officer including the Sikh Campaign of 1854-46*, Longmans, Green & Co.

Hunter, W.W., 1895, *The Marques of Dalhousie*, Clarendon Press, Oxford.

Hunter, W.W., 1920, *Disorders Inquiry Committee Report, 1919-1920*, Government Printing Press, Calcutta .

Husain, Azim, 1946, *Fazl-i-Husain: A political biography*, Orient Longmans, Green & Co., Calcutta.

Hutchison, L., 1935, *Conspiracy in Meerut*, Allen & Unwin, London.

Hutton, Martin, 1951, The Sikhs in Malaya, *Straits Times Annual*, Singapore 1951 p 96.

Ibbetson, D.C., 1883, *Punjab Census, 1881,* , Central Goal Press, Lahore, 3 vols.

Inderjit, 1983, Stamping Out Terrorism, *Economic Times*, October 25, p 5, col 7-8.

Inderjit. 1985, The Punjab Poll and Beyond, *Economic Times*, September 24, p 5, col 7-8.

Inderjit, 1986, New Strategy for Punjab Terrorism, *Economic Times*, August 5, p 5, col 7-8.

Inderjit Singh, 1982, The Punjab Situation, *Mainstream* 21(11) November 13, p 13-16; 21(2) November 22, p 25-29.

Inderjit Singh, 1983, Clouded Perception *Mainstream* 21(30) March 26, p 11-15.

Inderjit Singh, 1983, Punjab Situation: The Realities, *Mainstream* 21(18) January 1, p 18-19+.

Inderjit Singh, 1985, Attack on Akal Takht Recalled, *Sikh Review* 33(378) June, p 29-37.

Inder Pal Singh, 1958, A Sikh Village, *Journal of American Folklore*, vol 71, July-September.

Innes, J.J. M., 1898, *Sir Henry Lawrence: The Pacificator*, Oxford University Press, Oxford.

Isemonger, F.C., and Slattery, J., 1921, *An Account of the Ghadr Conspiracy*, Superintendent of Printing, Punjab, Lahore.

Jacoby, Harold S., 1956, *A Half Century Appraisal of Indians in the United States*, College of the Pacific, Stockton,

Jacoby, Harold S., 1958, More Thing against than Sinning, *Pacific Historian*, Stockton.

Jafa, Jyoti, 1986, Keep the Army Out, *Seminar* 326, October, p 29-31.

Jagat Singh (Maharaj), 1961, *The Science of the Soul*, Radha Soami Satsang, Beas.

Jagmohan Singh, ed., 1985, *The Agony of Punjab*, Saheed Bhagat Singh Research Committee, Ludhiana, 42p.

Jagtar Singh, 1986, Why the Left is Under Attack in Punjab, *Indian Express*, (Magazine) November 16, p 3, col 1-7.

Jain, Girilal, 1983, The Akali Psychology: Problem of Insecure Identity, *Times of India*, May 18, p 8, col 3-5.

Jain, Girilal, 1983, Resistance to Integration: Akalis Fight Last Battle, *Times of India*, May 11, p 6, col 3-5.

Jain, Girilal, 1984, Article 25 is Not the Issue: Akali Search for Political Community, *Times of India*, April 3, p 8, col 3-5.

Jain, Girilal, 1984, Failure of Sikhs Intellectuals to Recognise the Bhindranwale Menace, *Times of India* July 4, p 6, col 3-5.

Jain, Girilal, 1984, Identity is Not the Issue: Akalis' Search for Power is, *Times of India*, October 17, p 8, col 3-5.

Jain, Girilal, 1984, Insurgency, Not Terrorism: Nature of Challenge India Faces, *Times of India* June 12, p 6, col 3-5.

Jain, Girilal, 1984, Panth before the Nation: But not Necessarily in Conflict, *Times of India* October 10, p 6, col 3-5.

Jain, Girilal, 1985, After the Assassination: Fresh Complications in Punjab, *Times of India* August 24, p 8, col 3-5.

Jain, Girilal, 1985, The Akali Victory in Punjab: Rajiv Gandhi's Role, *Times of India* October 2, p 8, col 3-5.

Jain, Girilal, 1985, Roots of Punjab Problem: The Jat Sikh's Dilemma, *Times of India*, May 1, p 8, col 3-5.

Jain, Girilal, 1985, What If the Akalis lose: Some Basic Problems in Punjab, *Times of India* August 31, p 8, col 3-5.

Jain, Girilal, 1986, Barnala on a Crucifix: No More Nails into Him, Please, *Times of India*, March 25, p 8, col 3-5.

Jain, Girilal, 1986, The Exodus has Begun: Towards a National Disaster, *Times of India*, May 28, p 8, col 3-5; May 29, p 8, col 7-8.

Jain, Girilal, 1986, Importance Akali Split; No Cause for Panic or Concessions, *Times of India*, July 8, p 8, col 3-5.

Jain, Girilal, 1986, Scrap Rajiv Longowal Accord: Chandigarh not for Killing, *Times of India*, June 24, p 8, col 3-5.

Jain, Girilal, 1986, Why the Accord has Failed: Question Rajiv Gandhi should have asked, *Times of India*, August 18, p 6, col 3-5.

James, Hugo, 1954, *A Volunteer's Scramble through Sind, the Punjab, Hindustan and the Himalayan Mountains*, W. Thacker & Co., London, 2 vols.

Janata (Periodical) 1981, Desh Punjab, *Janata* 36(12) May 10, p 2-4, editorial.

Janata (Periodical) 1982, Curiouser and Curiouser, *Janata* 37(3) February 21, p 2-3, editorial.

Janata (Periodical), 1982, National Issues, Partisan Interests, *Janata* 37(40) December 12, p 1-2, editorial.

Janata (Periodical), 1982, Punjab: This Way Lies Disaster, *Janata* 37(14) May 16, p 1-3, editorial.

Janata (Periodical), 1982, The Punjab Tangle, *Janata* 37(36) October 31, p 1-3, editorial.

Janata (Periodical), 1983, Bhindranwale, *Janata* 38(35) December 11, p 3-4, editorial.

Janata (Periodical), 1983, A Dangerous Prescription, *Janata* 38(15) June 5, p 1-3, editorial.

Janata (Periodical), 1983, Is the Punjab Next, *Janata* 38(5) March 13, p 1, editorial.

Janata (Periodical) 1983, Punjabis Must Save Punjab, *Janata* 38(33) November 27, p 1-2, editorial.

Janata (Periodical), 1983, Smt Gandhi's Concern, *Janata*, 38(10) April 17, p 1-2, editorial.

Janata (Periodical), 1983, Worse Times for Punjab, *Janata* 38(29) October 16, p 1-3. editorial.

Janata (Periodical), 1984, A Great Pity, *Janata* 39(5) April 8, p 1-3, editorial.

Janata (Periodical), 1985, Initiatives on Punjab, *Janata* 40(7) March 24, p 1-2, editorial.

Janata (Periodical), 1985, Torture in Punjab, *Janata* 40(5) March 10, p 2-3, editorial.

Janata (Periodical), 1984, A very Dangerous Situation, *Janata* 39(3) March 4, p 2-4, editorial.

Jeffrrey, Robin, 1986, *What's Happening to India*, Macmillan Co., Publishers, London.

Jesmail Singh, 1981, Socio-economic Background of CPI Leadership in the Punjab, *Punjab Journal of Politics*, 5(2) July-December, p 135-145, tables.

Jha, Padmanand, 1984, Poll Explodes the Myth, *Link* 26(49) July 8, p 21-23.

Jha, Prem Shankar, 1984, Beyond the Immediate Crisis: How can Punjab Return to Normal, *Times of India*, November 12, p 8, col 3-5.

Jha, Prem Shankar, 1984, Punjab and Kashmir: Relevance of Opposition Stand, *Times of India* August 6, p 8, col 3-5.

Jha, Prem Shankar, 1984, Terrorism in Punjab: A Surgical Use of Force, *Times of India*, April 23, p 8, col 3-5; April 24, p 8, col 7-8.

Joginder Singh, 1985, Joginder Assails Longowal, *Times of India*, June 7, p 1, col 4-6.

Johnson, Julian, 1939, *The Path of the Masters*, Radha Soami Satsang, Beas.

Joshi, Chand, 1984, *Bhindranwale: Myth and Reality*, Vikas Publications New Delhi.

Kakar, Sudhir, 1985, Cause of Sikh Misperception, *Mainstream* 23(37) May 11, p 9-10.

Kakar, Sudhir, 1985, Legends as History: Cause of Sikh Misperception, *Times of India*, April 30, p 8, col 3-5.

Kamath, M.V, 1984, Myth and Reality, *Hindustan Times* (Magazine) April 26, p 1, col 1-8.

Kamlesh, Mohan, 1980, The Babbar Akalis: An Experiment in Terrorism, *Journal of Regional History*, 1, p 142-174, bibliography, footnotes.

Kapoor, L.C., 1986, Lord Dalhousie Laid the Roots of Sikh Separatism, *Organiser* (Independence Day Number) 38(14), p 31-33+.

Kapur, Rajiv A., 1986, *Sikh Separatism: The Politics of Faith*, George Allen and Unwin, London, 272p.

Karlekar, Hirammay, 1985, The Anatomy of Terrorism, *India Express* (Magazine) June 2, p 1, col 1-8+.

Kartar Singh Campbellpuri, 1944, *The Light of the Sikhs*, Servants of Sikhs Society, Lahore.

Katre, D.P., *Sant Harchand Singh Longowal: A Martyr For Peace* (1985) New Age Publication, Inllendary.

Kaye, Cecil (Sir), 1926, *Communism in India*, Govt., Press, Delhi.

Kaye, J.W., 1851, *History of the War in Afghanistan,* , Richard Bently, London, 2 vols.

Kaye, J. and Holmes, T.R.E., 1888-1889, *LIves of Indian Officers*, W.H. Allen & Co., London, 3 vols.

Kaye, J. and G.B. Malleson, 1897, *Indian Mutiny of 1857-1958* , Longmans, Green, London.

Kennedy, R.H., 1840, *Narrative of the Campaign of the Army of the Indus in Sindh and Kabul in 1838-1939*, London .

Khaliquzzaman, Choudhry, 1961, *Pathway to Pakistan*, Longmans, Lahore.

Khanna, H.R., 1986, The Killings in Punjab: How Long Must They Go on, *Times of India*, August 8, p 8, col 3-5.

Khanna, H.R., 1986, The Tragedy of Punjab: Wages of Inaction, *Times of India*, August 7, p 8, col 3-5.

Khanna, K.C., 1983, Whither Punjab?, *Illustrated Weekly of India* 104(14) April 10, p 8-9.

Khanna, K.C., 1985, Terrorism and Punjab Poll: A Gamble on Sikh Psyche, *Times of India* August 27, p 8, col 3-5.

Khanna, K.C., 1986, Mr. Barnala in Bind: Test of Leadership and Courage, *Times of India*, April 22, p 8, col 3-5.

Khanna, K.C., 1986, Protecting Precious Lives: A "Soft" State Cannot Endure, *Times of India*, October 7, p 8, col 3-5.

Khanna, K.C., 1986, Security Belt on Border: Many Imaginary Fears, *Times of India*, August 19, p 8, col 3-5.

Khilnani, N.B., 1951, *The Punjab under the Lawrences*, P.G.R.O., Simla.

Khosla, G.D., 1949, *Stern Reckoning*, Bhawnani and Sons, New Delhi.

Khosla, K.S., 1982, Akali Dal(L) Divided Over Bhindranwale Issue, *Times of India*, July 26, p 5, col 1-5.

Khosla, K.S., 1982, Akali Extremists and Moderates Come Closer, *Times of India*, August 26, p 1, col 2-3 +.

Khosla, K.S., 1982, Akalis are Caught in a Cleft-Stick, *Times of India* July 22, p 6, col 7-8.

Khosla, K.S, 1982, Bold Initiative Needed to End Punjab Crisis, *Times of India*, October 18, p 9, col 1-2.

Khushwant Singh, 1962, *Fall of the Kingdom of the Punjab*, Orient Longmans, Calcutta.

Khushwant Singh, 1966, *A History of the Sikhs*, Oxford University Press, Delhi.

Khushwant Singh, 1983, Defaulter Who: Khushwant Singh's Speech on the Punjab Situation in the Rajya Sabha, *Sikh Review* 31(357) September, p 32-34.

Khushwant Singh, 1985, Give Peace a Chance, *Illustrated Weekly of India* 105(12) July 28, p 8-15.

Kirpiekar, Subhash, 1985, Cong Nominee on Firm Wicket, *Times of India* September 15, p 7, col 6-8.

Kirpal Singh, 1991, *Partition of Punjab, 1947*, National Bookshop, New Delhi

Kirpekar, Subhash, 1985, Cong Vote Bank that Failed, *Times of India*, October 23, pp 8, col 7-8.

Kirpekar, Subhash, 1985, Rebuff to Poll Boycott Call, *Times of India*, September 18, p 5, col 1-3.

Kirpekar, Subhash, 1985, Son Rides on Sympathy Wave, *Times of India*, September 22, p 5, col 4-6.

Kirpekar, Subhash, 1985, Tough Fight in 'Terrorist Territory, *Times of India*, September 17, p 5, col 4-6.

Kirpekar, Subhash, 1986, Conspiracy in Punjab, *Times of India* (Sunday Review) February 16, p 1, col 1-8.

Kishwar, Madhu, 1986, Journey into Despair, *Illustrated Weekly of India*, 107(6) February 9, p 20-23.

Kothari, Rajni and Deshingkar, Giri, 1984, Punjab: The Longer View, *Illustrated Weekly of India* 105(29) July 15, p 20-23.

Knollys, H. (Col), 1894, *Life of General Sir Hope Grant* , William Blackwood & Sons, London .

Kohli, S.R., 1932 *Trial of Dewan Mulraj*, P.G.R.O., Lahore.

Kohli, S.R., 1919 *Catalogue of Khalsa Durbar Records*, Government Printing Press, Lahore.

Krishan, Indra 1952, *An Historical Interpretation of the Correspondence of Sir George Russel clerk, Political Agent at Ambala and Ludhiana, 1831-1843*, the author, Simla.

Krishan Kant, 1985, Premonitions on Punjab, *Mainstream* 23(37) May 11, p 2-4+.

Krishan Kant, 1986, Perceptions of Sikh Extremists, *Mainstream* 24(35) May 3, p 5-9.

Krishan Kant, 1986, Punjab, Pakistan and United States, *Mainstream* 24(29) March 22, p 3.

Krishnan, G.V., 1985, Akali Favourites in Sant's Land, *Times of India*, September 28, p 4, col 3-5.

Krishnan, G.V., 1985, Baba Factor Worries Akalis, *Times of India*, September 17, p 5, col 1-3.

Krishan, N.K., 1983, Situation in Punjab Crosses Danger Mark, *New Age* 31(19) May 8, p 1.

Kular, Kulvinder, 1986, Knitting the Tie that Binds, *India Express* (Magazine) September 21, p 111, col 1-8.

Lajpat Rai, 1908, *Story of My Deportaion*, Jaswantrai, Lahore.

Lajpat Rai, 1915, *Arya India: An Interpretation and a History of the Nationalist Movement from Within*, B.W. Huebsch, New York.

Lajpat Rai, 1917, *Reflection on the Political Situation in India*, Olto Wingand, Leipzing.

Lajpat Rai, 1921, *India's Will to Freedom: Writings and Speeches on the Present Situation*, Ganesh & Co., Madras.

Lajpat Rai, 1920, *The Agony of the Punjab*, Tagore & Co., Madras.

Lajpat Rai, 1965, *Autobiographical Writings*, ed. V.C. Joshi, University Publishers, Delhi.

Lake, Edward, 1874, *Sir Donald McLeod*, Religious Tract Society, London.

Lakshman, Nikhil, 1985, Back to Square One, *Illustrated Weekly of India*, 106(2) May 19, p 26-27.

Lakshman Singh (Bhagat), 1965, *Autobiography*, ed., Ganda Singh, Sikh Cultural Centre, Calcutta.

Lakshman Singh (Bhagat), 1918, *The Sikh and his New Critics*, Published by the author.

Landau, Henry, 1937, *The Enemy Within*, Putnam, London.

Latif, Syed M., 1891, *History of the Punjab*, Calcutta Central Press, Calcutta.

Latif. Syed M., 1957, *Lahore, Its History, Architectural Remains and Antiquities*, Mohammed Minhajuddin, Lahore.

Law, Sir A., 1926, *India under Lord Ellenborough*, London.

Lawrence, George, 1874, *Reminiscences of Forty-Three Years in India*, London.

Lawrence, Henry M., 1859, *Essays: Military and Political, Written in India*, Henry Colburn, London.

Lawrence, Henry M., 1846, *Some Passages in the Life of an Adventurer in the Punjab*, Henry Colburn, London.

Lawrence, R., 1952, *Charles Napier*, John Murray, London.

Lawrence, W.R., 1895, *The Valley of Kashmir*, Henry Frowde, London.

Lawrence-Archer, J.H., 1878, *Commentaries on the Punjab Campaign of 1848-1849*, W.H. Allen, London.

Lee Warner, Wm., 1904, *The Life of Marques of Dalhousie*, Macmillan, London.

Leigh, M.S., 1922, *The Punjab and the War*, Government Printing Press, Lahore.

Lockley, F., 1907, The Hindu Invasion: A New Immigration Problem, *Pacific Monthly*, 17, 584.

Login, (Lady), 1890, *Sir John Login and Duleep Singh*, W.H. Allem & Unwin, London .

Login, E.D., 1916, *Lady Login's Recollections*, Smith Elder & Co., London.

Longowal (Sant), 1982, Longowal Rules out Talks with Swaran, *Times of India*, November 9, p 1, col 1-2+.

Longowal (Sant), 1982, Morcha Not to Disrupt Games, *Times of India* November 6, p 1, col 4-5.

Longowal (Sant), 1982, Morcha to Continue, Akali Detenus Resist Eviction From Jails, *Times of India*, October 17, p 1, col 2-4+.

Longowal (Sant), 1982, No Question of Further Talks, Says Longowal, *Times of India*, December 10, p 1, col 2-3+.

Longowal (Sant), 1985, Talks Still Possible Says Longowal, *Times of India*, April 28, p 1, col 2-3+.

Lumby, E. E.R., 1956, *The Transfer of Power in India*, Allen & Unwin, London.

Lumsden, P.S. and Elsmie, G.R., 1899, *General Sir Harry Lumsden of the Guides*, John Murray, London.

MacKinnon, D.H., 1945, *Military Services and Adventurers in the Far East*, London.

MacLagan, M., 1962, *Clemency Canning: Charles John, 1st Earl Canning, Governor General and Viceroy of India 1856-1962*, Macmillan, London.

MacLeod, Hew, 1968, *Guru Nanak and the Sikh Religion*, Princeton & Oxford.

MacMunn, G., 1931, *The Indian Mutiny in Perspective*, G. Bell & Sons, London.

MacMunn, G., 1936, *The History of the Sikh Pioneers*, Sampson Low & Co., London.

MacMunn, G., 1936, *Romance of the Indian Frontier*, Jonathan Cape, London.

MacMunn, G., 1932, *Vignettes from Indian Wars*, Sampson Low & Co., London.

MacMunn, G., 1935, *Turmoil and Tragedy in India in 1914 and after*, Jarrolds, London.

Maconachie, R., 1917, *Rowland Bateman*, London Church Missionary Society, London.

Mahajan, J.M., 1949, *Circumstances leading to the Annexation of the Punjab 1846-1849*, Kitabistan, Allahabad.

Mahajan, J.M., 1947, *Private Correspondence of Sir Fredrick Currie 1846-1948*, Saraswati Publications, New Delhi.

Mahajani, Usha, 1960, *The Role of Indian Minorities in Burma and Malaya*, Vera & Co., Bombay.

Mahendra Pratap, 1947, *My Life Story of Fifty Five Years*, World Federation Centre, Dehra Dun.

Maini, Darshan Singh, 1983, Darbara Singh Speaks, *Illustrated Weekly of India* 104(14) April 10, p 18-19.

Maini, Darshan Singh, 1983, The Punjab Imbroglio, *Illustrated Weekly of India* 104(2) January 9, p 15.

Mainstream (Periodical) 1981, No Times for Finding, *Mainstream* 20(7) October 17, p 1-2, editorial.

Mainstream (Periodical), 1982, Eyeless in Punjab, *Mainstream* 20(35) May 1, p 1-3, editorial.

Mainstream (Periodical), 1982, Punjab, *Mainstream* 21(8) October 23, p 1-2, editorial.

Mainstream (Periodical), 1983, Akali Brinkmanship, *Mainstream* 21(32) April 9, p 1-2, editorial.

Mainstream (Periodical), 1983, Impasse in Punjab, *Mainstream* 22(10) November 5, p 1-2, editorial.

Mainstream (Periodical), 1983, Punjab Portents, *Mainstream* 21(46) July 16, p 1-2+, editorial.

Mainstream (Periodical), 1984, Crisis Mismanagement, *Mainstream* 22(45) July 7, p 1-3, editorial.

Mainstream (Periodical), 1984, Haryana and Punjab, *Mainstream* 22(26) February 25, p 1-2, editorial.

Mainstream (Periodical), 1984, Offering Solace to Sikhs, *Mainstream* 22(43) June 23, p 1-2, editorial.

Mainstream (Periodical), 1984, Punjab: What Next, *Mainstream* 22(41) June 9, p 1-3, editorial.

Mainstream (Periodical), 1984, Punjab in Agony, *Mainstream* 22(25) February 18, p 1-3, editorial.

Mainstream (Periodical), 1985, The Akali Accord, *Mainstream* 23(48) July 27, p 1-2, editorial.

Majumdar, R.C., 1963, *History of the Freedom Movement in India*, Mukhopadhyay, Calcutta.

Makkan Singh, 1986, Untenable Positions of Haryana Sangharsh Samiti, *New Age* 34(15) August 13, p 3+.

Malhotra, Avtar Singh, 1981, Punjab: Danger Persists, *New Age* 29(49) December 6, p 1+.

Malhotra, Avtar Singh, 1981, Punjab: Defend Communal Harmony and Peace, *New Age* 29(45) November 8, p 3.

Malhotra, Avtar Singh, 1982, Sikh Revivalism and Khalistan Movement *Link* (Republic Day Number) 24(24) January 26, p 35-37.

Malhotra, Avtar Singh, 1983, CPI Action Programme Begins in Punjab, *New Age* 31(37) September 11, p 1+.

Malhotra, Avtar Singh, 1983, Economic Changes and Emerging Politics, *Link* 26(4) September 4, p 14-16.

Malhotra, Avtar Singh, 1983, Punjab; Expectant Mood as Talks Begin, *New Age* 31(3) January 16, p 5.

Malhotra, Autar Singh, 1983, Who are Behind the Khalistan Movement, *Student Action* 2(4) August, p 4-9.

Malhotra, Avtar Singh, 1985, Relief and Expectancy in Punjab, *New Age* 33(16) April 21, p 1+.

Malhotra, Avtar Singh, 1985, Some Positive Aspects in Punjab Situation, *New Age* 33(40) October, p 1+.

Malhotra, Avtar Singh, 1986, Barnala Ministry Caught on Tenter-Hooks, *New Age* 34(44) November 2, p 7.

Malhotra, Avtar Singh, 1986, Punjab: Terrorists Desperate as Mass Campaign Picks up, *New Age* 34(18) May 4, p 15.

Malhotra, Inder, 1981, Real Problem in Punjab: Rolling Back Bigotry's Tide, *Time of India*, October 9, p 6, col 3-5.

Malhotra, Inder, 1985, Terror Crime and State Infra-Structure Remains Rusted, *Times of India*, August 29, p 6, col 3-5.

Malhotra, S.L., 1983, A Study of Non-Cooperation Movement in the Punjab and Its Impact on Punjab Politics, *Punjab Journal of Politics* 7(2) July-December, p 126-150, footnotes.

Malik, Harji, 1984, Amritsar Revisited, *Mainstream* 22(52) August 25, p 10+.

Malik, Harji, 1986, Punjab: An Uneasy Twilight, *Mainstream* 24(42) June 21, p 5-6.

Malik, Yogendra K., 1982, Politics and Power in an Urban Community of Punjab, *Indian Journal of Public Administration*, p 20-44, bibliography, tables.

Malkani, K.R., 1983, Sikh Fears are Groundless, *Illustrated Weekly of India* 104(14) April 10, p 14.

Malleson, G.B., 1914, *Decisive Battles of India, 1746-1849*, Peeves & Turner, London.

Malleson, G.B., 1906, *Indian Mutiny of 1857*, 9th edn., Seeley & Co., London.

Manchanda, Rita, 1986, Nothing More Can be Expected from the Chandra Sekhars and the Vajpapyees, *Hindustan Times* (Magazine) August 31, p 6, col 5-6+.

Manda, Y.A., 1985, Unity Integrity and Harmony, *U.S.I Journal* 115(482) October-December, p 293-307.

Manjit Singh, 1984, Election and School Children, *Punjab Journal of Politics* 8(1) January-June, p 134-143, bibliography, tables.

Mankekar, D.R., 1983, High Stakes in Punjab, *Mainstream* 21(40) June 4, p 6-8+.

Marshman, J.C., 1960, *Memoirs of Major General Sir Henry Havelock*, Longmans, Green & Co., London.

Masain, M.R., 1954, *The Communist Party of India*, Derek Verschoyle, London.

Masud, Iqbal, 1986, An Eye to Punjab, *Indian Express* (Magazine) August 10, p 111, col 1-8.

Mathur, B.K, 1986, Punjab-Haryana Dispute: Two Decades of Controversy, *Economic Times*, January 26, p 3, col 1-5+.

Mathur, Girish, 1985, All—right it's Akali Ministry: But Don't Forget Dangers, *Link* 28(8) September 29, p 4-6.

Mathur, Girish, 1985, Barnala's Bid for Power: Akalis Also Want Hindu Seats, *Link* 28(5) September 8, p 4-7.

Mathur, Girish, 1985, CFD Report is What Pirpur Report was for League Demanding Partition, *Link* 28(7) September 22, p 6-8.

Mathur, Girish, 1986, Akalis and Extremists, *Link* 28(260 February 2, p 13-14.

Mathur, Girish, 1986, Barnala's Panthic Rhetoric and Surrender to Terror, *Link* 28(35) April 6, p 7-9.

May, C.W., *History of the 2nd Sikhs, 12th Frontier Force Regiment 1846-1933*, Mission Press, Jubbulpore.

Maynard, John, 1923, The Sikh Problem in the Punjab, 1920-1923, *Contemporary Review*, September.

Mead, Henry, 1857, *The Sepoy Revolt: Its Causes and Its Consequences*, John Murray, London.

Medley, J.G., 1858, *A Years' Campaign in India: March 1857-1858*, Thacker & Co., London.

Mehta, H.R., 1929, *A History of the Growth and Development of Western Education in the Punjab, 1846-1884*, P.G.R.O., Lahore.

Menon, V.R., 1956, *The Story of the Integration of the Indian States*, Orient Longmans, Bombay.

Menon, V.P., 1957, *Transfer of Power in India*, Orient Longmans, Bombay.

Merewether, J.W.B. and Smith, Fredrick, 1917, *The Indian Corps in France*, John Murray, London.

Mishra, Girish, 1986, Some Aspects of Political Economy of Punjab Agitation, *Commerce* 153(3938) November 8, p 892-895.

Mitra, Chandan, 1986, Emotional Masochism, *Seminar*, 32, October, p 32-34.

Mitra, Nripendra Nath, *Indian Annual Register, 1919* onward, Annual Register Office, Calcutta.

Mittal, S.C., 1977, *Freedom Movement in Punjab, 1909-1929*, Concept Publishing Co., New Delhi, 256p.

Mohan, O.P., 1983, Lull Before a Fresh Storm, *Link* 26(7) September 25, p 16-17.

Mohinder Singh, 1978, *The Akali Movement*, Macmillan Co., Publishers, New Delhi, xiv, 245p.

Mohinder Singh, 1980, Akali Agitation over the Key's Affair, *Punjab Past and Present* 14(1) April, p 199-209.

Montagu-Chelmsford , 1918, *Indian Constitutional Reforms Report*, Government Printing Press, Calcutta.

Moon, Penderel, 1961, *Divide and Quit*, Chatto & Windus, London.

Morrison, J.L., 1936, *S Survey of Imperial Frontier Policy from Alexander Burnes to Fredrick Roberts*, Oxford University Press.

Morrison, J.L., 1934, *Lawrence of Lucknow, 1806-1837*, G. Bell, London.

Mores, Eric W., 1936, Some Aspects of the Komagatamaru Affair, 1914, *Canadian Historical Association Journal*, p 100-108.

Mosley, Leonard, 1961, *The Last Days of the British Raj*, Weidenfeld and Nicholson, London.

Mukarji, Nirmal, 1984, Before and after in Punjab, *Monthly Commentary on India Economic Conditions* 25(11) June, p 9-10.

Mukherjee, Kalyan, 1985, Punjab: The Wounded Falcon, *Hindustan Times* (Magazine) June 2, p 1, col 1-8.

Mukherji, Partha N., 1984, Gandhi, Akalis and Nonviolence: An Analysis in Retrospect, *Man and Development* 6(3) September, p 58-77, bibliography.

Muthamma, C.B., 1986, Political Arithmetic, *Mainstream* 24(46) July 19, p 6+.

Muthuswamy, M., 1983, Khalistan: The Politics of Religions in Punjab, *Administrator* 28(1) January-March, p 129-138, bibliography.

Nada Singh Sehra, 1913, Indians in Canada, *Modern Review*, Vol 14 (2), p 140.

Nagi, Saroj, 1985, To This Night, a Dawn, *Illustrated Weekly of India* 106(14) April 11, p 20-23.

Nahar Singh 1965, *Gooroo Ram Singh and the Kuka Sikhs: Documents 1863-1871*, Amrit Book Co., New Delhi.

Naidis, M., 1951, Propaganda of the Gadar Party, *Pacific Historical Review*, 20.

Nair, Kusum, 1946, *The Story of the INA*, Padma Publications, Bombay.

Nanda, J., 1948, *Punjab Uprooted*, Hind Kitabs Ltd., Bombay.

Napier, W., 1857, *Life and Opinions General Sir Charles James Napier*, John Murray, London.

Narang, A.S., 1983, *Storm Over the Sutlej: The Akali Politics*, Gitanjali Prakashan, New Delhi, 261p.

Narang, Surjeet Singh, 1981, Election and the Shiromani Akali Dal: A Socio—Psychological Approach, *Punjab Journal of Politics* 5(2) July-December, p 19-31, footnotes, tables.

Narendra Nath, 1928, *Memorandum on the Rights Claimed by the Hindu Community of North West India*, Civil and Military Gazette Press, Lahore.

Narula, R.S., 1985, Anandpur Sahid Resolution, *Sikh Review* (Supplement) 33(382) October, p 1-19.

Nayar, Kuldip and Khushwant Singh, 1984, *Tragedy of Punjab: Operation Bluestar and after*, Vision Books, New Delhi.

Nehru, J.L., 1961, *Synopsis of the Nehru-Fateh Singh Talks (on the Issue of the Formation of Punjabi Speaking State)*, Secretary, Shiromani Akali Dal, Amritsar.

Nehru, Moti Lal, 1928, *Nehru Report of the All Parties Conference*, Secretary, Indian National Congress Committee, Allahabad.

New Age (Periodical), 1984, Impasse in Punjab, *New Age* 32(15) April 8, p 2, editorial.

New Age (Periodical), 1984, Next Step of Punjab, *New Age* 32(25) June 17, p 2, editorial.

New Age (Periodical), 1984, Perilous Path, *New Age* 32(9) February 26, p 2, editorial.

New Age (Periodical), 1985, Mixing Politics and Religion, *New Age* 33(14) April 7, p 2, editorial.

New Age (Periodical), 1986, Danger in Punjab, *New Age* 34(5) February 2, p 2, editorial.

New Age (Periodical), 1986, Punjab Calls, *New Age* 34(22) June 8, p 2, editorial.

Nihal Singh, S., 1982, Why Sikhs are Angry, *Sikhs Review* 30(345) September, p 35-37.

Nijhawan, P.K., 1982, The Genesis of the Punjab Problem: The Language Question, *Man and Development* 4(1) March, p 144-166; *Mainstream* 20(39) May 29, p 23-25.

Nijhawan, P.K., 1982, The Story of Punjab, *Times of India* (Sunday Review), November 21, p 1, col 1-8.

Nijhawan, P.K., 1983, The Importance of Darbara Singh, *Times of India*, May 19, p 8, col 7-8.

Nijhawan, P.K., 1983, The Story of Punjab, *Sikh Review* 31(350) February, p 23-27.

Nijhawan, P.K., 1985, No End of Terrorism in Punjab, *Times of India*, August 22, p 8, col 7-8.

Nijhawan, P.K., 1985, The Disaster in Punjab, *Time of India* (Sunday Review), July 21, p 1, col 1-8+.

Noorani, A.G., 1984, Rule of Law and Terrorism in Punjab and Northern Ireland, *Economic and Political Weekly* 19(42-43) 20-27 October, p 1821.

Noorani, A.G., 1985, The Punjab Accord: A Balance Sheet, *Illustrated Weekly of India* 106(14) April 11, p 24-25.

Noorani, A.G., 1986, Who Maimed the Accord, *Seminar*, 326, October, p 20-25.

Norgate, T.R. and Phillott, 1911, *From Sepoy to Subedar*, Calcutta.

Oberoi, Harjot Singh, 1983, Two Poles of Akali Politics: Moderate Extremist Distinction False, *Times of India*, June 1, p 6, col 3-5.

O'Donnell, C.J., 1908, *The Causes of Present Discontent in India*, Fisher Unwin, London.

O'Dwyer, M., 1925, *India as I knew It: 1885-1925*, Constable, London.

Onkar Singh and Behl, Vinod, 1986, Punjab: On the Precipice, *Illustrated Weekly of India* 107(21) May 18, p 20-23.

Onkar Singh and Behl, Vinod, 1986, Vortex of Violence, *Illustrated Weekly of India* 107(28) July 13, p 18-21.

Onn, Chin Kee, 1946, *Malaya Upside Down*, Jitts and Co., Singapore.

Organiser (Periodical), 1982, The Agony of Punjab, *Organiser* 33(52) May 16, p 3, editorial.

Organiser (Periodical), 1984, End or the Beginning, *Organiser* 36(5) June 17, p 3, editorial.

Organiser (Periodical), 1984, Khushwant Deserves Attention, *Organiser* 36(6) June 24, p 3, editorial.

Organiser (Periodical), 1984, The Task in Punjab, *Organiser* 36(7) July 1, p 3, editorial.

Organiser (Periodical), 1984, A Varnished Version, *Organiser* 36(10) July 22, P 3, editorial.

Organiser (Periodical), 1985, Akali Victory, *Organiser* 37(21) October 6, p 3, editorial.

Organiser (Periodical) 1986, Unending Discord, *Organiser* 38(6) June 22, p 3, editorial.

Overtreet, G. and Windmiller, M., 1959, *Communism in India*, University of California Press, Berkeley and Los Angeles.

Panikkar, K.M., 1930, *Founding of the Kashmir State: 1792-1858*. Allen & Unwin, .

Pardaman Singh, 1922, *Ethnological Epitome of the Hindustanees of the Pacific Coast*, Khalsa Diwan Society, Stockton.

Parker, A., 1962, *Sadhu Sundar Singh*, Christian Literature Society.

Parker, C.S., 1899, *Sir Robert Peel*, John Murray, London.

Parmanand, Bhai, *The Story of My Life*.

Parminder, 1981, Punjab: The Struggle Against Divisive Forces, People's *Democracy* 5(339) September 27, p 8+.

Parminder, 1982, CPI(M) Campaign for Communal Harmony, *People's Democracy* 6(28) July 11, p 1+.

Parminder, 1983, Campaign for Communal Harmony, *People's Democracy* 7(23) June 5, p 3+.

Parminder, 1983, Militant Protest Rally, *People's Democracy* 7(38) September 18, pp 1+.

Parry, R.E., 1921, *The Sikhs of the Punjab*, Dranes, London.

Pearse, Hugh, *The Memories of Alexander Gardner*, William Blackwood & Sons.

People's Democracy (Periodical) 1981, PM Akali Dal (L) Talks, *People's Democracy* 5(43) October 25, p 1-2, editorial.

People's Democracy (Periodical), 1982, Defuse the Situation, *People's Democracy* 6(43) October 24, p 1-2, editorial.

People's Democracy (Periodical), 1983, For a Solution in Punjab, *People's Democracy* 7(44) October 30, p 1-2, editorial.

People's Democracy (Periodical) 1984, Extremist Killings in Punjab, *People's Democracy* 8(39) September 23, p 1, editorial.

People's Democracy (Periodical), 1984, The Punjab Tangle and Its Perils, *People's Democracy* 8(16) April 15, p 1-2, editorial.

Pettigrew, Joyce, 1978, Robber Nobleman, Ambika Publication, New Delhi.

Pitamber Singh, 1986, My Dear Follow Sikhs . . ., *Times of India* (Sunday Review), March 30, p 1, col 1-8.

Prabha K., 1979, A Structural Analysis: A Case Study of Punjab, Inter-India Publication, New Delhi 214p.

Pradeep Kumar and Garg, Nisha, 1981, Assembly Elections 1980: A Case Study of Candidates in a Punjab Constituency, *Indian Journal of Politics* 5(1) January-June, p 141-156.

Pramod Kumar, et al, 1984, Punjab Crisis: Context and Trends, *Mainstream* 22(48) July 28, p 33-34.

Pramod Kumar, at al, 1984, *Punjab Crisis: Context and Trends*, Centre for Research in Rural and Industrial Development Chandigarh, 172p.

Pramod Kumar, et al, 1984, Punjab Crisis: Why? Whither?, *Mainstream* 22(39) May, p 35-40.

Prem Singh, 1982, Sikhs and Freedom Struggle, *Secular Democracy* 15(6) June, p 13-15.

Prem Singh, 1983, Roads Blocks in Punjab, *Secular Democracy* April, p 10-12.

Prem Singh, 1983, Urgency of Settlement, *Secular Democracy* June, p 18-21.

Prem Singh, 1984, Akali Leader Must Repent, *Times of India*, August 1, p 6, col 7-8.

Pritam Singh, 1982, Current Akali Politics: Some Trends, *Secular Democracy* October, p 46-48.

Pritam Singh, 1983, Lessons of Panchayat Elections, *Economic and Political Weekly* 18(43) October 22, p 1822-1823.

Pritam Singh, 1984, AIR and Doordarshan Coverage of Punjab after Army Action, *Economic and Political Weekly* 19(36) September 8, p 1569-1571.

Puri, Balraj, 1982, The Akali Tragedy: Failure to Rise above Religion, *Times of India*, December 15, p 8, col 3-5.

Puri, Balraj, 1983, Crux of Punjab Problem, *Janata* 38(32) November 20, p 6-7.

Puri, Balraj, 1984, Another Approach to Punjab Tangle, *Janata* 39(12) June 24, p 5-6.

Puri, Harish K., 1981, Akali Politics: Emerging Compulsions, *Indian Journal of Politics* 5(1) January-June, p 33-51, footnotes.

Puri, Harish K., 1983, The Akali Agitation: An Analysis of Socio-economic Bases of Protest, *Economic and Political Weekly* 18(4) January 22, p 113-118.

Puri, Harish K., 1983, Anandpur Sahib Resolution: What Do the Akalis Really Want, *Interdiscipline* 15(2) October, p 47-63, bibliography.

Puri, Harish K., 1983, Green Revolution and Its Impact on Punjab Politics, *Indian Political Science Review* 17(1) January, p 98-111, footnotes.

Puri, Harish K., 1985, Elections and after, *Economic and Political Weekly* 20(40) October 5, p 1681-1683.

Puri, Rajinder, 1983, Indira Gandhi's Created Crisis in the Punjab, *Sikh Review* 31(357) September, p 45-48.

Puri, Rajinder, 1984, The Road to Khalistan, *Sikh Review* 32(367), July, p 59-62.

Puri, Rajinder, 1984, Russian Hand in Punjab, *Sikh Review* 32(369) September, p 56-58.

Puri, Rajinder, 1985, Punjab Elections: The Aftermath, *Illustrated Weekly of India* 106(25) October 27, p 51.

Quresh, Major Mohammed Ibrahim, 1958, *The First Punjabis: (History of the First Punjab Regiment, 1759-1956)*, Gale and Polden, Alershot.

Radical Humanist (Periodical) 1981, Demand for Khalistan, *Radical Humanist* 46(8) November, p 8-9, editorial.

Radical Humanist (Periodical), 1983, The Punjab Issue, *Radical Humanist* 48(3) June, p 1-4, editorial.

Radical Humanist (Periodical) 1985, The Punjab Report and Its Suppression, *Radical Humanist* 49(7) October, p 1-4, editorial.

Radical Humanist (Periodical), 1985, What Has Happened in Punjab, *Radical Humanist* 49(6) September, p 1-3, editorial.

Rahul Singh, 1985, The Contentious Resolution, *Mainstream* 23(25) April 27, p 7-8.

Rahul Singh, 1986, Punjab: Once again at Flashpoint, *Indian Express* (Magazine) February 9, p 1, col 1-8.

Rahmat Ali, 1940, *Pakistan: The Fatherland of the Pak Nation*, the author, Cambridge.

Rahmat Ali, 1946, *The Mallet and Its Mission*, 3rd edn., published by the author, Lahore.

Rait, R.S., 1903, *The Life and Campaigns of Viscount Gough*, Archibald Constable and Co., London.

Rai, Satya M., 1981, the Structure of Regional Politics in the Punjab, *Indian Journal of Politics* 5(1) January-June, p 95-113, footnotes.

Rai, Satya M., 1986, *Punjab Since Partition*, Durga Publications, Delhi, xii, 446p.

Raina, Aoska, 1984, Khalistan: A House Divided, *Illustrated Weekly of India* 105(32) August 5, p 22-23.

Raj Narayan, 1983, Akali Agitation in Punjab, *Arya Call* 33(6-7) July-August, p 9-11.

Rajput, R.B., 1948, *The Muslim League: Yesterday and Today*, Ashraf, Lahore.

Rajeswara Rao, C., 1982, CPI Concern over Akali Agitation, *New Age* 30(16) April 18, p 3.

Rajeswara Rao, C., 1982, Rajeswara Rao Calls for Left and Democratic Unity in Punjab State Conference, *New Age* 30(13) March 28, p 8.

Rajeswara Rao, C., 1985, Our Message: Implementation of Punjab Accord, *Link* 28(6) September 15, p 10.

Rallia Ram, K.L., 1930, *Report on the Firing into the Gurdwara Sis Ganj, Delhi*, S.G.P.C., Amritsar.

Ram Chandra, 1916, *Indian against Britain*, Hindustan Ghadr, San Francisco.

Ram Chandra, 1916, *Exclusion of Hindus from America due to British Influence*, Hindustan Ghadr, San Francisco.

Ram Narayan Kumar and Sieberer, Grory, 1991, *The Sikh Struggle Origin, Evolution and Present Phase* (1991), Delhi Chandige.

Ram Swarup, 1984, Akali Politics and Terrorism, *Times of India*, July 30, p 8, col 7-8.

Ram Swarup, 1986, Sikh Separatism: Its Genesis and Development, *Times of India*, August 20, p 8, col 3-5; August 21, p 8, col 7-8.

Randhawa, M.S., 1954, *Out of the Ashes*, News Jack Printing Works, Bombay.

:andhir Singh, 1945, *The Ghadr Heroes*, People's Publishing House, Bombay .

Rattigan, W.H., 1909, *Digest of Civil Law for the Punjab*.

Reid, Robie L., 1941, The Inside Story of the 'Komagatamaru', *British Columbia Historical Quarterly*, vol 5.

Riberio, J.F., 1986, A Pyrrhic War: An Interview, *Illustrated Weekly of India* 107(28) July 13, p 22-23.

Roberts, (Field Murshal), 1898, *Forty One Years in India*, Macmillan, London.

Ross, D., 1883, *The Land of the Five Rivers*, Chapman & Hall, London.

Rowlatt Committee , 1918, *Sedition Committee Report, 1918*, Bengal Secretariat Press, Calcutta.

Roy, M.N., 1964, *Memoirs*, Allied Press, Bombay.

Roy, P.C., 1958, *Gurcharan Singh's Mission in Central Asia*, Indian Historical Records Commission, Trivandrum.

Rustomji, K.F., 1986, Belts and Security, *Seminar* 326 October, p 26-28.

Saberwal, Satish, 1986, On Certain Habits of Mind, *Seminar* 326 October, p 39-42.

Sabharwal, O.P., 1981, Spectre of Dal Khalsa, *Mainstream* 20(6) October 10, pp 3-4.

Sabharwal, O.P., 1982, Punjab: Changing Contours, *Mainstream* 20(33) April 17, p 4.

Sabharwal, O.P., 1983, Flashpoint in Punjab, *Mainstream* 21(43) June 25, p 6.

Sabharwal, O.P., 1983, Punjab Today; Many-sided Challenge, *Mainstream* 21(49) August 6, p 10-11+.

Sabharwal, O.P., 1985, Winds of Change in Punjab, *Mainstream* 23945) July 6, p 4+.

Sabharwal, O.P., 1986, Options in Punjab, *Mainstream* 24(30) March 29, p 2-3.

Sahay, Anand K., 1985, Temple in Punjab, *Mainstream* 23(35) April 27, p 5-7.

Sahay, Anand K., 1985, Watching Punjab Poll Campaign, *Mainstream* 24(3) September 21, p 3-5.

Sahni, Ruchi Ram, 1922, *The Gurdwara Reform Movement and the Sikh Awakening*, Desh Sewak Book Agency, Jalandhar.

Sahni, Ruchi Ram, 1924, *Guru Ka Bagh Congress Inquiry Committee*, Hindi Press, Lahore.

Sahni, Ruchi Ram, 1965, *Struggle for Reform in Sikh Shrines*, ed. by Ganda Singh, Sikh Itihas, Amritsar.

Saksena, N.S., 1983, Roots of Terrorism in Punjab, *Times of India*, December 6, p 8, col 7-8.

Sandford, D.A., 1849, *Leaves from the Journal during the Campaign in the Punjab, September 1848-March 1849*, William Blackwood & Sons, London.

Sant Singh, 1955, *Akali Problem*.

Samber, Bhupinder, 1983, Punjab: CPI Improves Position in Local Polls, *New Age* 31(43) October 23, p 29.

Samber, Bhupinder, 1986, Punjab Working Class against Terrorism, *New Age* 34(28) July 13, p 9.

Samber, Bhupinder, 1986, Rajeswara Rao Lists Five Tasks in Punjab, *New Age* 34(48) November 30, p 3.

Samiuddin, Abida, ed., 1985, *The Punjab Crisis; Challenges and Response*, Mittal Publications, New Delhi, xxi, 714p.

Sandhu, Kanwar, 1985, The Baba and the Sant, *Indian Express*, May 12, p 5, col 1-8.

Sandhu, Kanwar, 1985, Punjab: The First Test, *Indian Express* (Magazine), January 20, p 1, col 1-8.

Sandhu, Kanwar, 1985, Punjab: A Spirit of Defiance, *Indian Express* (Magazine), April 28, p 1, col 1-8+.

Sandhu, Kanwar, 1985, Unravelling the Punjab Tangle, *Indian Express*, July 21, p 6, col 1-6.

Sangwan, R.S., 1982-1983, Role of Akali's during the Emergency *Kurukshetra University Research Journal* 16-17, p 186-194.

Sapru, A.N., 1931, *The Building of the Jammu and Kashmir State*, P.G.R.O., Lahore.

Sapru, T.B., 1946, *Constitutional Proposals of the Sapru Committee*, Padma, Bombay.

Saran Singh, 1985, Sikh Demands Not Secessionist, *Sikh Review* 33(374) February, p 19-22.

Sarasfield, Landen, 1946, *Betrayal of the Sikhs*, Lahore Bookshop, Lahore.

Sardul Singh Caveeshar, 1950, *Sikh Politics*, National Publications, Delhi.

Sareen, Rajendra, 1984, Sources of Trouble, *Seminar*, 294, February, p 18-23.

Sarkar, Jadunath, 1907, Bibliography of Sikh History, *Modern Review*, Calcutta.

Sathyamurthy, T.V., 1984, Crisis with in the Crisis, *Seminar*, 294, February, p 29-34.

Satinder Singh, 1982, *Khalistan: An Academic Analysis*, Amar Prakashan, New Delhi, 184p.

Saund, D.S., 1960, *Congressman from India*, Dutton & Co., New York.

Seaton, Thomas, 1866, *From Cadet to Colonel*, London.

Seetaram, 1880, *From Sepoy to Soobadar*, James Tomes Norgate, Lahore.

Sen, N.B., 1953, *History of Koh-i-Noor*, New Book Society, New Delhi.

Sen, S.N., 1957, *Eighteen Fifty Seven*, Government of India Publications Division, Delhi.

Sen Sunil, 1985, Major Shard, Akali Dal and Punjab Politics, 1940-1947, *Mainstream* 23(37) May 11, p 13-14+.

Sethi, G.R., 1927, *Sikh Struggle for Gurdwara Reform*, Union Press, Amritsar.

Sethi, J.D., 1985, Punjab: Towards a Durable Coalition, *Gandhi Marg* 7(7) October, p 387-391, editorial.

Sethi, R.R., 1930, *John Lawrence as Commissioner of the Jullundur Doab, 1846-1849*, P.G.R.O., Lahore.

Sethi, R.R, 1933, *Trial of Raja Lal Singh*, P.G.R.O., Lahore.

Sewa Ram Singh, 1920, *Reforms and the Sikhs*, Mufid-i-Am Press, Lahore.

Shadwell (Lt. Gen.), 1881, *Life of Colin Campbell, Lord Clyde*, London.

Shah Nawaz Khan, 1946, *My Memories of the I.N.A. and Its Netaji*, Raj Kamal Publication, Bombay.

Shahabuddin, Syed, 1983, The Punjab Situation, *Janata* 38(14) May 29, inside coverpage 2+.

Sham Lal, 1984, The National Scene: Deep Are the Roots, *Times of India*, August 4, p 8, col 3-5.

Sharma, S.R., 1941, *Mahatma Hans Raj*, Arya Pradeshik Pratinidhi Sabha, Lohore.

Sharma, Brahm Dev, 1983, When Zail Singh and Buta Singh Touched the Feet of Bhindranwale, *Organiser* 35(4) June 12, p 14.

Sharma, J.M., 1982, Akali Politics; A Rejoinder, *Mainstream* 21(15) December 11, p 8.

Sharma, Narendra, 1981, Ominous Trends in Punjab, *Mainstream* 29(9) October 31, p 5-6.

Sharma, Narendra, 1982, Punjab: Fighting the Fire, *Mainstream* 20(52) August 28, p 4.

Sharma, Narendra, 1982, Punjab: Promising Signs, *Mainstream* 21(1) September 4, p 5-6.

Sharma, Narendra, 1982, Punjab's Guilty Men, *Mainstream* 20(380 May 22, p 5-6.

Sharma, Narendra, 1983, Opposition Meet: Futility over Punjab, *Mainstream* 21(45) July 9, p 3-4.

Sharma, Narendra, 1986, Punjab: Balance of Forces, *Mainstream* 24(44) July 5, p 6+.

Shaukin, Rita, 1986, Punjab: Moves and Countermoves, *Illustrated Weekly of India* 107(24) June 8, p 16-17.

Shaukin Singh, 1984, The Bloodiest Week, *Link* 26(30) March 4, p 22-23.

Shaukin Singh, 1984, The Dreaded Terrorists of Punjab, *Link* 26(28) February 19, p 17-20.

Shaukin Singh, 1984, Punjab: Behind the Hush Hash in Holy Complex, *Link* 26(26) February 5, p 12-15.

Shaukin Singh, 1985, The Akalis Dilemma, *Link* 27(33) March 24, p 14.

Shaukin Singh, 1985, A Mind-Boggling Exercise, *Link* 27(35) April 14, p 11-12.

Shaukin Singh, 1985, A Tangle and a Widening Horizon, *Link* 27(23) January 13, p 10-11.

Shaukin Singh, 1985, Inside the Akali Camp: Who Outwits Who?, *Link* 27(42) May 26, p 25-26.

Shaukin Singh, 1985, Punjab: Towards Reconciliation, *Link* 27(25) January 26, p 26-28.

Shaukin Singh, 1985, The Two-horse Ride of Badal, Tohra, *Link* 28(5) September 8, p 8-9.

Shaukin Singh, 1985, Without its Traditional Adherents Congress Can't Win Punjab, *Link* 28(6) September 15, p 4-6.

Shaukin Singh, 1986, Akali Dal Prepares for Show of Strength, *Link* 28(27) February 9, p 14-15.

Shourie, Arun, 1985, New Tasks for a New Situation, *Illustrated Weekly of India* 106(22) October 6, p 20-23.

Simon Commission, 1930, *Indian Statutory Commission Report*, Government of India Central Publication Branch, Calcutta.

Singh, B., 1985, Terrorist's Mind, *Patriot* (Magazine) October 20, p 1, col 1-6.

Singh, B.D., 1984, Punjab: Lessons and Prospects, *Mainstream* 22(43) June 23, p 6-8+.

Singh, J.D., 1983, Troubled Punjab: A Postscript: Where Punjab Leads Other States, *Times of India* July 28, p 7, col 3-6.

Singh, S., 1981, Khalistan: The Politics of Passion, *Hindustan Times* (Magazine), October 4, p 1, col 1-5+.

Singhal, M.M., 1983, Akali Politics, *Mainstream* 21(34) April 23, p 32.

Sinha, B.M., 1982, Sant Jarnail Singh Bhindranwale: The Man Who Set Punjab Aflame, *Illustrated Weekly of India* 103(38) October 24, p 22-23.

Sinha, S.K., 1986, The Greatest Threat to National Security Since Independence: The Punjab Imbroglio, *Organiser* (Independence Day Number) 38(14) p 35-37+.

Smillie, Emmaline E., 1923, An Historical Survey of Indian Migration within the Empire, *Canadian Historical Review*, 4, 1923, 217-257.

Smith. Harry, 1902, *Autobiography*, ed., by G.C. Moor, John Murray, London.

Smith, Marian, 1948, Synthesis and Other Processes in Sikhism, *American Anthropologist*, 50, July-September, p 457-462.

Smith, Marian, 1952, Social Structural Village Group of India and Pakistan, *American Anthropologist*, 54, January-March, p 41-56.

Smith, Marian, 1953, Social Structure in the Punjab, *Economic Weekly*, 5, November 21.

Smith, Marian, 1944, Sikh Settlers in Canada, *Asia and the Americas*, 44, August, p 359-364.

Smith, R.B., 1849, *Agricultural Resources of the Punjab*, Stewart & Murray, London.

Smith, V.W., comp., 1922, *Akali Dal and Shiromani Gurduwara Prabandhak Committee: CID Report*, compiled by V.W. Smith, (Superin- tendent of Police), Superintendent of Government Printing, Simla.

Sosanjh, Ujjal Singh, 1984, A Call for Sanity, *Link* 27(10) October 14, p 32-33.

Southern Economics (Periodical), 1983, Challenges to Nation's Integrity, *Southern Economic* (Annual Number) 22(1) May 1, p 1-7, editorial.

Speary, E., and West, Willis M., *German plots and Intrigues in the United States During the Period of Our Neutrality*, No. 10. Committee of Public Information.

Spellman, John W., 1959, The International Extensions of Political Conspiracy as Illustrated by the Ghadr Party, *Journal of Indian History*, 31, 23-45.

Steinbach (Lt. Col.), 1845, *The Punjab: Being a Brief Account of the Country of the Sikhs*, Smith, Elder & Co., London.

Stephens, Ian, 1963, *Pakistan*, Ernest Benn Ltd., London.

Stephens, William, D., 1922, *California and the Oriental: Japanese, Chinese and Hindus*, State Board of Control of California, Sacramento (Report of Governor William D. Stephens of California to the Secretary of State).

Stevens, G.R., *History of the 4th Indian Division*.

Sufi, G.M.D., 1949, *Kashmir*, University of Punjab, Lahore.

Sullivan, John 1850, *the Koh-i-Noor or Mountain of Light: To Whom does It Belong?* Effingham Wilson, London.

Sullivan, John, 1853, *Are We Bound by Our Treaties*? Effingham Wilson, London.

Sundram, G.A., 1923, *Guru-Ka-Bagh Satyagrah*, Madras.

Suri, Dona, 1985, Where Do They Go from Here, *Tribune*, October 27, p 1, col 1-8.

Suri, P.C., 1985, The Punjab Crisis, *Mainstream* 23(43) June 22, p 10-15; 23(45) July 6, p 21-26; 23(46) July 13, p 24-26.

Suri, Surinder, 1985, Humanism and Nationalism: Answer to Irrational Hatred, *Times of India* May 25, p 8, col 3-5.

Suri, Surinder, 1985, Implications of Punjab Accord, *Times of India*, August 28, p 6, col 7-8.

Surjeet, Harkrishan Singh, 1981, On the Slogans of Sikh Nationhood and Khalistan, *People's Democracy* 5(20) May 17, p 5+.

Surjeet, Harkrishan Singh, 1981, Recent Development in Punjab, *People's Democracy* 5(42) October 18, p 7+.

Surjeet, Harkrishan Singh, 1982, Harkishan Singh Surjeet's Open Letter to Sant Longowal, *People's Democracy* 6(33) August 5, p 6-7; 6(34) August 22, p 6-7+.

Surjeet, Harkrishan Singh, 1982, Surjeet on Disturbing Punjab Situation, *People's Democracy* 6(19) May 9, p 1+.

Surjeet, Harkrishan Singh, 1982, Surjeet's Letter to Prime Minister; Appeal for Bold Initiative in Punjab, *People's Democracy* 6(42) October 17, p 10-11.

Surjeet, Harkrishan Singh, 1983, Harkrishan Singh Surjeet in Rajya Sabha: Stop Drifting, Settle Punjab Issue, *People's Democracy* 7(31) July 31, p 1+.

Surjeet, Harkrishan Singh, 1983, Surjeet on Punjab Situation, *People's Democracy* 7(45) November 6, p 2.

Surjeet, Harkrishan Singh, 1983, What is the Deadlock in the Punjab Talks, *People's Democracy* 7(8) February 20, p 1+.

Surjeet, Harkrishan Singh, 1983, Why the Deadlock in Punjab, *People's Democracy* 792) January 9, p 1+.

Surjeet, Harkrishan Singh, 1984, Campaign to Fight Sikh Extremist Abroad, *People's Democracy* 8(22) May 27, p 3+.

Surjeet, Harkrishan Singh, 1984, Has Punjab Question been Solved *People's Democracy* 8(41) October 7, p 1-2.

Surjeet, Harkrishan Singh, 1984, Khalistan Has Now Become a Reality, *Illustrated Weekly of India*, 105(31) July 29, p 28-31.

Surjeet, Harkrishan Singh, 1984, Superficial Healing Touches Cannot Restore Normalcy, *People's Democracy* 8(43) October 21, p 7.

Surjeet, Harkrishan Singh, 1985, Accord and After, *People's Democracy* 9(31) August 4, p 1-2.

Surjeet, Harkrishan Singh, 1985, Can Solution to Punjab Problem be Delayed? *People's Democracy* 9(6) February 10, p 1+.

Surjeet, Harkrishan Singh, 1985, Electoral Verdict in Punjab Will Create Surprises, *People's Democracy* 9(39) September 29, p 5.

Surjeet, Harkrishan Singh, 1985, Failure to Confront Basic Issues, *People's Democracy* 9(38) September 22, p 1-2.

Surjeet, Harkrishan Singh, 1985, The Perplexing Question, *Sikh Review* 33(374) February, p 23-26.

Surjeet, Harkrishan Singh, 1985, Punjab Elections and after, *People's Democracy* 9(41) October 13, p 1+.

Surjeet, Harkrishan Singh, 1985, Punjab Solution Demands Top Priority, *People's Democracy* 9(14) April 7, p 1-2.

Surjeet, Harkrishan Singh, 1986, Punjab Accord in Danger, *People's Democracy* 10(6) February 9, p +.

Surjeet, Harkrishan Singh, 1986, Rise above Partition Interests and Solve Punjabi Problem, *People's Democracy* 10(26) June 29, p 1+.

Surjeet, Harkrishan Singh 1986, Save Punjab Save India, *People's Democracy* 10(14) April 6, p 1+.

Surjeet, Harkrishan Singh, 1986, Situation in Punjab: Is There Any Way Out? *People's Democracy* 10(40) October 5, p 1-2.

Surjeet, Harkrishan Singh, 1986, Unitedly Fight Extremist Menec, *People's Democracy* 10(19) May 11, p 6.

Susam Ram, 1986, Confused Indian Response, *Mainstream* 24(20) January 18, p 5-6.

Swarup Singh (Sadhu), 1946, *The Sikhs Demand Their Homeland*, Lahore Bookshop, Lahore.

Swaran Singh, 1982, Swaran's Talk with Longowal, Bhindranwale, *Times of India*, October 25, p 1, col 2-3+.

Talib, Gurbachan Singh, 1982, The Khalistan Issue: A Study, *New Quest* January-February 31, p 5-11.

Tandon, P., 1960, *Punjabi Century*, Harcourt Brace, New York.

Tandon, Prakash, 1980, *Return to Punjab, 1961-1975*, Vikas Publications, New Delhi, xvi, 227p.

Tandon, Prakash,1984, Another Angle, *Seminar*, 294, February, p 35-37.

Tarkunde, V.M., 1985, The Black Laws, *Sikh Review* 33(375) March, p 35-39.

Taylor, A.C., 1913, *General Sir Alexander Taylor*, William & Norgate London.

Teja Singh, 1921, *Growth of Responsibility in Sikhism*, 2nd edn., Sikh Tract Society, Lahore.

Teja Singh, 1922, *Gurdwara Reform Movement and the Sikh Awakening*, Desh Sewak, Jalandhar.

Teja Singh, 1948, *Sikhs as Liberators*, Sikhs Sammelan, Simla.

Temple, R.C., 1882, *Men and Events of My Times in India*, John Murray, London.

Temple, R.C., 1883, *Names and Name Places*, Bombay Education Society, Bombay.

Temple, R.C., 1884, *The Legends of the Punjab*, Bombay Education Society, Bombay.

Temple, R.C., 1890, *Lord Lawrence*, Macmillan, London.

Tewari, V.N., 1983, Punjabiat in Peril, *Illustrated Weekly of India*, 104(14) April 10, p 19, editorial.

Thackwell, E.J., 1851, *Narrative of Second Sikh War, 1848-1849*, Richard Bentley, London.

Thakur, Janardan, 1985, Behind the Akali Victory, *Times of India* (Sunday Review), October 13, p 1, col 1-8.

Thakur, Janardan, 1986, Its a No-Win Situation, *Times of India* (Sunday Review), January 19, p 1, col 1-4+.

Thapar, K.S., 1976, All Parties Conference (1928) and the Sikhs, *Journal of Sikh Studies* 3(1) February, p 96-108, bibliography.

Thapar, K.S., 1983, Akali Communalism: Genesis and Implications, *Mainstream* 21(24) February 12, p 15-19.

Thapar, K.S., 1986, Elements of Crisis in Punjab, *Mainstream* 24(40) June 7, p 9-12.

Thapar, Romesh, 1983, Fear Stalks the Punjab, *Economic and Political Weekly* 18(23) June 4, p 989

Thapar, Romesh, 1985, The Awesome Costs of Correction, *Economic and Political Weekly* 20(35) August 31, p 1461.

Thapar, Romesh, 1985, The Messy Punjab, *Economic and Political Weekly* 20(15) April 13, p 623.

Thomas, Wendell, 1930, *Hinduism Invades America*, Beacon Press, New York.

Thorburn, S.S, 1886, *Mussalmans and Money Lenders in the Punjab*, William Blackwood & Sons, London.

Thorburn, S.S., 1986, *Report on Peasant Indebtedness and Land Alienations to Money-Lenders in Parts of the Rawalpindi Division*, Civil and Military Gazette Press.

Thorburn, S.S., 1904, *The Punjab in Peace and War*, William Blackwood & Sons, London.

Tilak Raj, 1954, *A Study of the Communist Movement in the Punjab*, Jyoti Prakashan, Ghaziabad.

Times of India (Periodical), 1981, Irresponsibility Plus, *Times of India*, January 23, p 8, col 1-2, editorial.

Times of India (Periodical), 1981, Mischief in Punjab, *Times of India*, April 15, p 8, col 1-2, editorial.

Times of India (Periodical), 1981, Saving Punjab, *Times of India*, October 19, p 6, col 1-2, editorial.

Times of India (Periodical), 1981, The Task in Punjab, *Times of India*, October 14, p 6, col 1-2, editorial.

Times of India (Periodical), 1982, An Avoidable Tragedy, *Times of India*, October 13, p 8, col 1-2, editorial.

Times of India (Periodical), 1982, Crackdown in Punjab, *Times of India*, September 1, p 6, col 1-2, editorial.

Times of India (Periodical), 1982, Distressing Discord, *Times of India* April 9, p 6, col 1-2, editorial.

Times of India (Periodical) 1982, Khalistan in United States, *Times of India*, February 17, p 8, col 1-2, editorial.

Times of India (Periodical), 1982, Mischief in Punjab, *Times of India* April 28, p 8, col 1-2, editorial.

Times of India (Periodical), 1982, Not the Right Remedy, *Times of India*, June 5, p 8, col 1-2, editorial.

Times of India (Periodical), 1982, Punjab and the Ban, *Times of India*, May 4, p 6, col 1-2, editorial.

Times of India (Periodical), 1982, The Punjab See-saw, *Times of India*, November 24, p 8, col 1-2, editorial.

Times of India (Periodical), 1982, Times for Hard Decision, *Times of India*, May 11, p 6, col 1-2, editorial.

Times of India (Periodical), 1982, Times to Think again, *Times of India*, November 6, p 8, col 1-2, editorial.

Times of India (Periodical), 1983, After 'Kam Roko' What, *Times of India*, August 31, p 6, col 1-2, editorial.

Times of India (Periodical), 1983, Aggravating the Agony, *Times of India*, June 22, p 6, col 1-2, editorial.

Times of India (Periodical), 1983, Akali Brinkmanship, *Times of India*, July 12, p 6, col 1-2, editorial.

Times of India (Periodical), 1983, Back Darbara Singh, *Times of India*, April 27, p 8, col 1-2, editorial.

Times of India (Periodical), 1983, Butchery in Punjab, *Times of India*, November 22, col 1-2, editorial.

Times of India (Periodical), 1983, Communications Gap, *Times of India*, July 16, p 6, col 1-2, editorial.

Times of India (Periodical), 1983, A Fair Offer, *Times of India* June 24, p 6, col 1-2, editorial.

Times of India (Periodical), 1983, From Strife to Talks, *Times of India*, November 15, p 8, col 1-2, editorial.

Times of India (Periodical), 1983, Highw to Disaster, *Times of India*, April 6, p 6, col 1-2, editorial.

Times of India (Periodical), 1983, It's a National Task, *Times of India*, April 22, p 8, col 1-2, editorial.

Times of India (Periodical), 1983, Mess in Punjab, *Times of India*, September 10, p 8, col 1-2, editorial.

Times of India (Periodical), 1983, Murder in the Temple, *Times of India*, April 26, p 8, col 1-2. editorial.

Times of India (Periodical), 1983, No Place for Sophistry, *Times of India*, June 29, p 6, col 1-2, editorial.

Times of India (Periodical), 1983, No President's Rule, *Times of India*, May 3, p 8, col 1-2, editorial.

Times of India (Periodical), 1983, Punjab: What Next, *Times of India*, October 8, p 5, col 1-2, editorial.

Times of India (Periodical), 1983, Stalemate in Punjab, *Times of India* December 23, p 6, col 1-2, editorial.

Times of India (Periodical) 1983, Stop this Desecration, *Times of India*, May 18, p 8, col 1-2, editorial.

Times of India (Periodical), 1983, Temporary Respite, *Times of India*, June 18, p 8, col 1-2, editorial.

Times of India (Periodical), 1983, Terror's Beastly Tail, *Times of India*, November 11, p 8, col 1-2, editorial.

Times of India (Periodical), 1983, The Timely Offer, *Times of India*, October 26, col 1-2, editorial.

Times of India (Periodical), 1983, Tragic Failure, *Times of India*, February 22, p 6, col 1-2, editorial.

Times of India (Periodical), 1983, Training for Terror, *Times of India*, December 21, p 6, col 1-2, editorial.

Times of India (Periodical), 1983, Under President's Rule, *Times of India*, October 8, p 8, col 1-2, editorial.

Times of India (Periodical), 1983, Vandalism in Punjab, *Times of India*, December 6, p 8, col 1-2, editorial.

Times of India (Periodical), 1983, Worst Sacrilege, *Times of India*, April 29, p 8, col 1-2, editorial.

Times of India (Periodical), 1984, An Act of Courage, *Times of India*, July 18, p 8, col 1-2, editorial.

Times of India (Periodical), 1984, Alarming Backlash, *Times of India*, February 16, p 8, col 1-2, editorial.

Times of India (Periodical), 1984, Baffling Ineptitude, *Times of India*, April 5, p 8, col 1-2, editorial.

Times of India (Periodical), 1984, Confusion in Amritsar, *Times of India*, September 28, p 6, col 1-2, editorial.

Times of India (Periodical), 1984, Coping with Akalis, *Times of India*, March 22, p 8, col 1-2, editorial .

Times of India (Periodical), 1984, A Crying Shame, *Times of India*, January 7, p 8, col 1-2, editorial.

Times of India (Periodical), 1984, Danger is Not Over, *Times of India*, June 16, p 8, col 1-2, editorial.

Times of India (Periodical), 1984, A Dangerous Agitation, *Times of India*, April 16, p 8, col 1-2, editorial.

Times of India (Periodical), 1984, A Day Before the Action, *Times of India*, June 16, p 1, col 2-4+.

Times of India (Periodical), 1984, Disturbing Exposure, *Times of India*, November 17, p 8, col 1-2, editorial.

Times of India (Periodical), 1984, Grave Implications, *Times of India*, February 29, p 8, col 1-2, editorial.

Times of India (Periodical), 1984, Gravity of It All, *Times of India*, June 15, p 6, col 1-2, editorial.

Times of India (Periodical), 1984, Heart of the Matter, *Times of India*, July 11, p 6, col 1-2, editorial.

Times of India (Periodical), 1984, In a Dark Tunnel, *Times of India*, September 27, p 8, col 1-2, editorial.

Times of India (Periodical), 1984, Keep the Army Out, *Times of India*, May 18, p 6, col 1-2, editorial.

Times of India (Periodical), 1984, Laying the Spectre, *Times of India*, June 4, p 8, col 1-2, editorial.

Times of India (Periodical), 1984, Leave the Army Alone, *Times of India*, November 28, p 8, col 1-2, editorial.

Times of India (Periodical), 1984, Mischief Still Afoot, *Times of India*, June 30, p 8, col 1-2, editorial.

Times of India, (Periodical), 1984, Murders in the Temple, *Times of India*, April 18, p 8, col 1-2, editorial.

Times of India (Periodical), 1984, Next Step in Punjab, *Times of India*, February 10, p 8, col 1-2, editorial.

Times of India (Periodical), 1984, No One is Blameless, *Times of India*, July 27, p 8, col 1-2, editorial.

Times of India (Periodical), 1984, No Room for Illusion, *Times of India*, October 6, p 6, col 1-2, editorial.

Times of India (Periodical), 1984, No Soft Options, *Times of India*, June 21, p 6, col 1-2, editorial.

Times of India (Periodical), 1984, Not by Mollycoddling, *Times of India*, May 1, p 8, col 1-2, editorial.

Times of India (Periodical), 1984, Not by Power Alone, *Times of India*, April 7, p 8, col 1-2, editorial.

Times of India (Periodical), 1984, On Brink of Disaster, *Times of India*, February 21, p 6, col 1-2, editorial.

Times of India (Periodical), 1984, Overdue Ordinance, *Times of India*, July 17, p 8, col 1-2, editorial.

Times of India (Periodical), 1984, The Right Note, *Times of India*, June 19, p 6, col 1-2, editorial.

Times of India (Periodical), 1984, The Score in Moga, *Times of India*, May 5, p 8, col 1-2, editorial.

Times of India (Periodical), 1984, A Second Violation, *Times of India*, October 2, p 8, col 1-2, editorial.

Times of India (Periodical), 1984, Sense from Amritsar, *Times of India*, August 14, p 8, col 1-2, editorial.

Times of India (Periodical), 1984, Tragic but Unavoidable, *Times of India*, June 7, p 6, col 1-2, editorial.

Times of India (Periodical), 1984, Valid Criticism, *Times of India*, July 26, p 8, col 1-2, editorial.

Times of India (Periodical), 1984, Violence in Punjab, *Times of India*, January 31, p 8, col 1-2, editorial.

Times of India (Periodical), 1985, Bhindranwale's Ghost, *Times of India*, May 4, p 8, col 1-2, editorial.

Times of India (Periodical), 1985, The Cloud Lifts, *Times of India*, July 26, p 8, col 1-2, editorial.

Times of India (Periodical), 1985, Dilemma in Punjab, *Times of India*, August 9, p 8, col 1-2, editorial.

Times of India (Periodical), 1985, Distressing Downturn, *Times of India*, April 23, p 8, col 1-2, editorial.

Times of India (Periodical), 1985, An Expected Turn, *Times of India*, May 11, p 8, col 1-2, editorial.

Times of India (Periodical), 1985, In Clear Terms, *Times of India*, January 26, p 8, col 1-2, editorial.

Times of India (Periodical) 1985, In a State of Flux, *Times of India*, August 27, p 8, col 1-2, editorial.

Times of India (Periodical), 1985, Intransigence Again, *Times of India*, March 21, p 6, col 1-2, editorial.

Times of India (Periodical), 1985, A Long Haul Ahead, *Times of India*, May 16, p 8, col 1-2, editorial.

Times of India (Periodical), 1985, Need for Caution, *Times of India*, September 28, p 8, col 1-2, editorial.

Times of India (Periodical), 1985, New Akali Leadership, *Times of India*, October 1, p 8, col 1-2, editorial.

Times of India (Periodical), 1985, No Magic Wand, *Times of India*, April 10, p 8, col 1-2, editorial.

Times of India (Periodical), 1985, Of Doubtful Legality, *Times of India*, September 10, p 8, col 1-2, editorial.

Times of India (Periodical), 1985, Old Danger Again, *Times of India*, March 27, p 6, col 1-2, editorial.

Times of India (Periodical), 1985, Old Talk, Old Memories, *Times of India*, August 1, p 8, col 1-2, editorial.

Times of India (Periodical), 1985, Playing with Fire, *Times of India*, October 26, p 8, col 1-2, editorial.

Times of India (Periodical), 1985, Poll Logic for Akalis, *Times of India*, August 20, p 8, col 1-2, editorial.

Times of India (Periodical), 1985, Premature Concessions, *Times of India*, April 12, p 8, col 1-2, editorial.

Times of India (Periodical), 1985, The Right to Know, *Times of India*, June 20, p 6, col 1-2, editorial.

Times of India (Periodical), 1985, Signs of Hope, *Times of India*, April 6, col 1-2, editorial.

Times of India (Periodical), 1985, A Strange Election, *Times of India*, September 13, p 8, col 1-2, editorial.

Times of India (Periodical), 1985, A Win in the Heats, *Times of India*, December 17, p 8, col 1-2, editorial.

Times of India (Periodical), 1986, The Akali Split, *Times of India*, May 10, p 6, col 1-2, editorial.

Times of India (Periodical), 1986, Akali Unity Moves, *Times of India*, October 31, p 8, col 1-2, editorial.

Times of India (Periodical), 1986, A Brave Policeman, *Times of India*, September 17, p 8, col 1-2, editorial.

Times of India (Periodical) 1986, Cause for Alarm, *Times of India*, February 26, p 8, col 1-2, editorial.

Times of India (Periodical), 1986, The Connection, Please, *Times of India*, April 5, p 8, col 1-2, editorial.

Times of India (Periodical), 1986, Delhi Stands up, *Times of India*, June 28, p 8, col 1-2, editorial.

Times of India (Periodical), 1986, Deploy the Army, *Times of India*, May 11, p 8, col 1-2, editorial.

Times of India (Periodical), 1986, Discipline Them, *Times of India*, August 2, p 8, col 1-2, editorial .

Times of India (Periodical), 1986, Discord in Accord, *Times of India*, January 4, p 8, col 1-2, editorial.

Times of India (Periodical) 1986, The Enemy Within, *Times of India*, April 17, p 8, col 1-2, editorial.

Times of India (Periodical), 1986, Extremists Challenge, *Times of India*, January, p 8, col 1-2, editorial.

Times of India (Periodical), 1986, The Fourth Attempt, *Times of India*, July 12, p 8, col 1-2, editorial.

Times of India (Periodical), 1986, If Akalis Unite, *Times of India*, June 26, p 8, col 1-2, editorial.

Times of India (Periodical), 1986, Little of Show, *Times of India*, September 30, p 8, col 1-2, editorial.

Times of India (Periodical), 1986, Loss of Nerve, *Times of India*, March 29, p 8, col 1-2, editorial.

Times of India (Periodical), 1986, Pak Involvement, *Times of India*, August 16, p 8, col 1-2, editorial.

Times of India (Periodical), 1986, A Poser to Akalis, *Times of India*, June 7, p 8, col 1-2, editorial.

Times of India (Periodical), 1986, The Punjab Logjam, *Times of India*, October 21, p 8, col 1-2, editorial.

Times of India (Periodical), 1986, A Redundant Demand, *Times of India*, November 13, p 8, col 1-2, editorial.

Times of India (Periodical), 1986, A Responsible Move, *Times of India*, October 25, p 8, col 1-2, editorial.

Times of India (Periodical), 1986, Security Too Lax, *Times of India*, October 4, p 8, col 1-2, editorial.

Times of India (Periodical), 1986, Signs of Appeasement, *Times of India*, March 12, p 8, col 1-2, editorial.

Times of India (Periodical), 1986, Sikhs Speak up, *Times of India*, April 1, p 8, col 1-2, editorial.

Times of India (Periodical), 1986, Spurt in Killings, *Times of India*, October 29, p 8, col 1-2, editorial.

Times of India (Periodical), 1986, A Sensible Move, *Times of India*, June 13, p 8, col 1-2, editorial.

Times of India (Periodical), 1986, The Task Ahead, *Times of India*, May 8, p 6, col 1-2, editorial.

Times of India (Periodical), 1986, The Trap in Punjab, *Times of India*, February 20, p 8, col 1-2, editorial.

Times of India (Periodical), 1986, Towards Clarity, *Times of India*, July 21, p 8, col 1-2.

Times of India (Periodical), 1986, A Welcome Decision, *Times of India*, September 23, p 8, col 1-2, editorial.

Times of India (Periodical), 1986, Who Speaks for Sikhs, *Times of India*, May 5, p 8, col 1-2, editorial.

Tinker, Hugh, 1962, *India and Pakistan*, Praeger, New York.

Tiwari, B.K., 1983, I Want Peace in Punjab, *Indian Express* (Magazine) July 31, p 5, col 1-8.

Tompson, Edward, 1930, *The Other Side of the Medal*, Hogarth Press, London.

Toye, Hugh, 1959, *The Springing Tiger*, Cassell, London.

Trevaskis, H.K., 1928, *The Land of Five Rivers*, Oxford University Press, Bombay.

Trevaskis, H.K., 1931, *The Punjab of Today*, Civil & Military Gazette Press, London.

Tribune, (Periodical), 1983, New Order in Punjab, *Tribune*, October 8, p 4, col 1-2, editorial.

Tribune, (Periodical), 1983, Peace between Battles, *Tribune*, September 17, p 4, col 1-2, editorial.

Tribune, (Periodical), 1983, Who Rules in Punjab, *Tribune*, October 1, p 4, col 1-2, editorial.

Trilok Nath, 1986, Punjab Scene: Identity of Terrorism, *Patriot* (Magazine), June 22, p 1, col 5-6+.

Trotter, L.J., 1880, *Life of Lord Lawrence*, Oxford University Press, Oxford.

Trotter, L.J.,1886, *History of India under Queen Victoria from 1836-1880*, W.H. Allen and Co., London.

Trotter, L.J., 1889, *Life of Marquess of Dalhousie*, Oxford University Press, Oxford.

Trotter, L.J., 1901, *A Leader of Light Horse: The Life of Hodson of Hodson's Horse*, J.M. Dent, London.

Trotter, L.J., 1904, *Life of John Nicholson*, John Murray, London.

Tuker, Francis, 1950, *While Memory Serves*, Cassell, London.

Tully, Mark and Jacob, Satish, 1985, *Amritsar: Mrs. Gandhi's Last Battle*, Rupa & Co., Calcutta.

Tupper, C.L., 1883-1908, ed., *Punjab Customary Law*, Government Printing Press, Calcutta.

Uprety, Prem Raman, 1980, *Religion and Politics in Punjab in the 1920s*, Sterling Publishers Pvt. Ltd., New Delhi, vii, 222p.

Varma, Kewal, 1985, The Options on Punjab, *Mainstream* 23(20) January 12, p 5+.

Vajpayee, Atal Bihari 1983, Roots of Khalistan in Delhi: Vajpayee, *Times of India* November 14, p 1, col 4-5+.

Veera, Dayabir Singh, 1981, Khalsa or the Humility Raj. *Sikh Review* 31(329) May, p 21-24.

Wade, C.M., 1846, *History of the Campaign on the Sutlej and the War in the Punjab*, G.Butler, London.

Wade, C.M., 1847, *A Narrative of the Services: Military and Political*, G. Butler, London.

Wade, C.M., 1848, *On the State of our Relations with the Punjab and the Best Mode of their Settlement*, Ryde, Isle of Wight.

Wade, C.M., 1849, *War in the Punjab*, G. Butler, London.

Waiz, S.A., 1927, *Indians Abroad*, 2nd edn., Imperial Indian Citizenship Association, Bombay.

Wallace, Paul and Chopra, Surendra, eds., 1981, *Political Dynamics of Punjab*, Guru Nanak Dev University, Amritsar, 381p.

Wallace, Paul, 1981, Religions and Secular Politics in Punjab: The Sikh Dilemma in Competing Political Systems, *Indian Journal of Politics* 5(1) January-June, p 1-32, footnotes.

Wilkins, Charles, 1940, *The Sikhs and Their College at Patna*, ed., by Ganda Sing, Khalsa College, Amritsar.

Williams, D. Elwyn, 1947-1948, Makers of the Sikh Army, *Army Quarterly*, vol 55-56.

Woodruff, P., 1954, *The Men Who Ruled India*, Jonathan Cape, London.

Wylly, H.C., ed., 1908, *Military Memories of Lieutenant General Sir Joseph Thackwell*, John Murray, London.

Younghusband, G.J., 1908, *Story of the Guides*, Macmillan, London.

Zail Singh, 1981, No Talks on Khalistan Asserts Zail Singh, *Times of India*, December 2, p 1, col 2-5+.

CICIL LIST

CONCEPTS IN COMMUNICATION, INFORMATICS & LIBRARIANSHIP

(CICIL)

General Editor: **S.P. AGRAWAL**

CICIL-1 Development of Library Services in India: Social Science Information
S.P. Agrawal Rs. 150

CICIL-2 Development of Documentation in India: Social Science Information
S.P. Agrawal Rs. 250

CICIL-3 UNESCO and Social Sciences: Retrospect and Prospect
S.P. Agrawal and **J.C. Aggarwal** Rs. 250

CICIL-4 INDIANA : A Bibliography of Bibliographical Sources
M.K. Jain Rs. 200

CICIL-5 Dimensions of Library and Information Science: Kaula Festschrift
V. Venkatappaiah (Eds.) Rs. 600

CICIL-6 Book Numbers: Some Indian Methods
M.P. Satija and **S.P. Agrawal** Rs. 100

CICIL-7 National Policy for University Libraries in India: Problems and Perspectives
N.B. Inamdar and **L.S. Ramaiah** (Ed.) Rs. 250

CICIL-8 Media Utilisation for the Development of Women and Children
B.S. Thakur and **Binod C. Agrawal** Rs. 150

CICIL-9 Terrorism: An Annotated Bibliography
Susheela Bhan (Ed.) Rs. 275

CICIL-10 Transnational Library Relations: The Indo-American Experience
M.B. Konnur Rs. 175

CICIL-11 Geography of Marketing and Commercial Activities in India (Documentation on Research Information)
R.S. Dixit Rs. 130

CICIL-12 Information India 1988: Global View
S.P. Agrawal and J.C. Aggarwal Rs. 200

CICIL-13 Women's Education in India: Historical Review, Present Status and Perspective Plan
S.P. Agrawal and J.C. Aggarwal Rs. 360

CICIL-14 Cultural Communication in India: Role and Impact of Phonograms
J.M. Ojha (in press)

CICIL-15 Second Historical Survey of Educational Development in India: Select Documents 1985-1989
S.P. Agrawal and J.C. Aggarwal Rs. 490

CICIL-16 Documentation Encyclopaedia of UNESCO and Education
J.C. Aggarwal and S.P. Agrawal Rs. 800 (set of 2 parts)

CICIL-17 Attitude Towards Information: A Study of Post-Graduate Teachers and Researchers in Social Sciences
N.G. Satish (in press)

CICIL-18 Librarianship and Bureaucratic Organisation: A Study in the Sociology of Library Profession in India
P.K. Jayaswal Rs. 175

CICIL-19 Literature Search
K.A. Isaac Rs. 150

CICIL-20 Child Education in India: Index to Scholarly Writings in Indian Educational Journals and Newspapers since independence
S.P. Agrawal and Naresh Kanta Rs. 100

CICIL-21 Lok Sabha and Vidhan Sabha Elections in India 1989 & 1990: Process and Results with Comparative Study of Manifestos
S.P. Agrawal and **J.C. Aggarwal** Rs. 250

CICIL-22 Islamic Studies in India: A Survey of Human, Institutional and Documentary Sources
Mohamed Taher Rs. 180

CICIL-23 Panchayati Raj: An Annotated Bibliography
N.B. Inamdar, N.G. Satish and Anil Takalkar 290

CICIL-24 Information India 1989-90: Global View
S.P. Agrawal and J.C. Aggarwal Rs. 500